THE POLITICAL ECONOMY OF THE PERSIAN GULF

MEHRAN KAMRAVA

Editor

The Political Economy
of the Persian Gulf

CIRS
CENTER FOR
INTERNATIONAL
AND REGIONAL
STUDIES

GEORGETOWN UNIVERSITY
SCHOOL OF FOREIGN SERVICE IN QATAR

Published in Collaboration with
Center for International and Regional Studies
School of Foreign Service in Qatar
Georgetown University

HURST & COMPANY, LONDON

Published in Collaboration with
Georgetown University's
Center for International and Regional Studies,
School of Foreign Service in Qatar

First published in the United Kingdom in 2012 by
C. Hurst & Co. (Publishers) Ltd.,
41 Great Russell Street, London, WC1B 3PL
© Mehran Kamrava and the Contributors, 2012
All rights reserved.
Printed in the United Kingdom

A Cataloguing-in-Publication data record for this book
is available from the British Library.

ISBNs: 1-84904-209-3 *paperback*

This book is printed using paper from registered sustainable
and managed sources.

www.hurstpub.co.uk

Contents

CONTENTS

Part III
Case Studies

Acknowledgments

The chapters in this volume grew out of two Working Group meetings held under the auspices of the Center for International and Regional Studies of Georgetown University's School of Foreign Service in Qatar. Grateful acknowledgment goes to the participants of the Working Groups for their individual and collective intellectual contributions to the project that eventually resulted in this book. Invaluable assistance also came from the capable staff of the Center for International and Regional Studies, namely Zahra Babar, John Crist, Suzi Mirgani, Kasia Rada, Naila Sherman, Nadia Talpur, and Maha Uraidi. I gratefully acknowledge their multiple contributions to the Working Groups and to this volume. Finally, as with so many other projects, I would not have been able to work on this book had it not been for the loving care and support of my wife Melisa and our daughters Kendra and Dilara. It is to them that I dedicate this book.

About the Contributors

Alexis Antoniades is a Visiting Assistant Professor of International Finance at Georgetown University School of Foreign Service in Qatar. Funded by a $1,050,000 grant from the Qatar National Research Fund, Dr Antoniades has undertaken the first micro-study of the Gulf economies that is based on scanner level price data. He also serves as a Senior Advisor to the Qatar National Research Fund at the Office of the Heir Apparent in Qatar.

Christopher Davidson is reader in politics at Durham University. He is the author, most recently, of *Persian Gulf and Pacific Asia: From Indifference to Interdependence* and *Abu Dhabi: Oil and Beyond*. His edited volumes include *Higher Education in the Gulf: Shaping Economies, Politics, and Culture* and *Power and Politics in the Gulf Monarchies*.

Steffen Hertog is a lecturer in comparative politics at the London School of Economics and Political Science. He has published in journals such as World Politics, Review of International Political Economy, Comparative Studies in Society and History and International Journal of Middle East Studies. He is the author of *Princes, Brokers and Bureaucrats: Oil and State in Saudi Arabia* (Ithaca, NY: Cornell University Press 2010).

Mehran Kamrava is Professor and Director of the Center for International and Regional Studies at Georgetown University in Qatar. He is the author, most recently, of *Iran's Intellectual Revolution* and *The Modern Middle East: A Political History Since the First World War*. His edited volumes include *The International Politics of the Persian Gulf* and *Innovation in Islam: Traditions and Contributions*.

ABOUT THE CONTRIBUTORS

Massoud Karshenas is Professor of Economics at the School of Oriental and African Studies at the University of London. His publications include *Social Policy in the Middle East: Economic, Political and Gender Dynamics*, *Industrialization and Agricultural Surplus: A Comparative Study of Economic Development in Asia*, and *Oil, State and Industrialization in Iran*.

Fred H. Lawson is Lynn T. White Jr. Professor of Government at Mills College. He has edited *Comparative Regionalism* (2009), as well as *Explorations in UAE History* (forthcoming 2012).

Ziba Moshaver specializes in international relations and Middle East politics. She obtained her DPhil in International Relations from Oxford University, and is Research Associate at the London Middle East Institute. Her publications include *The State and Global Change: The Political Economy of Transition in the Middle East and North Africa* (co-edited with H. Hakimian), and "Revolution, Theocratic Leadership and Iran's Foreign Policy" in *Analysing Middle East Foreign Policy*, edited by Gerd Nonneman.

Djavad Salehi-Isfahani is Professor of Economics at Virginia Technical University. His articles have appeared in, among others, *Economic Journal, Economic Development and Cultural Change, Journal of Development Economics, Journal of Economic Inequality, International Journal of Middle East Studies, Iranian Studies*, and *Middle East Development Journal*. He has also edited *Labor and Human Capital in the Middle East: Studies of Markets and Household Behavior*, and co-edited *The Production and Diffusion of Public Choice Political Economy*.

Jean-François Seznec is Visiting Associate Professor at Georgetown University's Center for Contemporary Arab Studies. He publishes and lectures extensively on industrialization policy in the Gulf. He has twenty-five years experience in international banking and finance, of which ten years was spent in the Arabian Peninsula. His latest works include a co-edited book *Industrialization in the Gulf: A Socioeconomic Revolution*, as well as a number of journal articles.

Kristian Coates Ulrichsen is a Research Fellow at LSE Global Governance and Deputy Director of the Kuwait Research Programme on Development, Governance and Globalisation in the Gulf States. His most recent books are *Insecure Gulf: The End of Certainty and the Transition to the Post-Oil Era* and (co-edited with David Held) *The Transformation of the Gulf: Politics, Economics and the Global Order.*

Rodney Wilson is Director of the Islamic Finance Programme at Durham University in the United Kingdom. He has authored books on the *Economic Development of Saudi Arabia* and *Islamic Economics: A Short History* (with Ahmed El Ashker). His edited works include *The Politics of Islamic Finance* (with Clement Henry) and *Islamic Perspectives on Wealth Creation* (with Munawar Iqbal).

1

Introduction

Mehran Kamrava

2011 turned out to be a historic year for the Middle East, the full consequences of which are likely to take years and perhaps even decades to manifest. For the foreseeable future, it is unclear whether the "Arab Spring" will usher in a wave of democratization and fundamentally change the nature of state-society interactions in the Middle East, as the Velvet Revolutions of East and Central Europe did in 1989, or eventually reinstate old patterns of non-democratic rule under new guises. What is clear is that the mass-based rebellions that engulfed the Middle East, from Morocco and Algeria in the west, to Bahrain and Oman in the east, all had their roots in fundamental contradictions in the politics and economics of the region. This book explores these contradictions in relation to a subsystem of the Middle East, namely the Persian Gulf region.

At the broadest level, the political economy of the Persian Gulf is characterized by three general sets of developments. First, by and large, Persian Gulf states are engaged in rapid economic growth and efforts at fostering massive infrastructural development. In Chapter 2 of this volume, Fred Lawson chronicles the phenomenal growth of Persian Gulf economies and their increasingly important role in the international arena over the last quarter

1

century. In 2011 the countries of the Gulf Cooperation Council (GCC) were projected to have an economic growth rate of 7.8 percent, with their external current accounts surplus increasing from $136 billion to $304 billion on the back of rising oil prices.[1] In 2009, the value of GCC exports amounted to a total of $473.2 billion, while imports stood at $300.4 billion.[2] Compared to 2004, the total value of GCC exports—meaning oil and gas—had grown by some 203 percent by 2009.[3] As with the preceding two decades, each of the governments used the windfall revenues to invest massively in infrastructural projects. Between 2007 and 2009, for example, the volume of water production across the GCC grew by more than 30 percent, and electricity production saw a concomitant rise of 13 percent.[4] From 2004 to 2009, the number of hotels rose by more than 122 percent during the same period.[5] Iran's economic performance has been far less impressive, as chronicled in Karshenas and Moshaver's chapter in this volume: a product of mismanagement and the steady transfer of economic power from the "legal-rational" arms of the state to less transparent institutions, such as the Islamic Revolutionary Guards Corp.

Second, for all countries of the region—though for some more successfully than for others, and with the exception of Iran—their herculean developmental efforts have been made possible through comparatively high levels of globalization and integration into the global economy, especially when compared with other parts of the Middle East. Significantly, state leaders across the GCC have framed globalization in terms consistent with evolving notions of nationalism. More specifically, they have presented global economic engagement as an integral aspect of the national project. What is key, they have

[1] International Monetary Fund, *Regional Economic Outlook, Middle East and Central Asia* (Washington, DC: IMF, 2011), p. 5.
[2] The Cooperation Council for the Arab States of the Gulf Secretariat General, *GCC A Statistical Glance* Vol. 2 (Riyadh: Gulf Cooperation Council, 2010), pp. 29–30. The previous year, during the global recession of 2008, the trade imbalance had been even more skewed, with $653 billion in exports and only $360.2 billion in imports.
[3] Data collected from Gulf Cooperation Council Secretariat General, *GCC A Statistical Glance* (Riyadh: Gulf Cooperation Council, 2008), p. 36; and, the Cooperation Council for the Arab States of the Gulf Secretariat General, *GCC A Statistical Glance* Vol. 2 (Riyadh: Gulf Cooperation Council, 2010), p. 82.
[4] The Cooperation Council for the Arab States of the Gulf Secretariat General, *GCC A Statistical Glance* Vol. 2 (Riyadh: Gulf Cooperation Council, 2010), p. 26.
[5] *GCC Statistical Bulletins*, 2008 and 2010, pp. 43 and 46 respectively.

maintained, is not necessarily ownership of the process of production and marketing of natural resources—that is, hydrocarbons—but ownership over the outcome after those natural resources are marketed and sold. This framing of nationalism stands in sharp contrast to nationalist conceptions of yesteryear, say of Nasser, or of revolutionaries like Qaddafi and Khomeini, who saw the opening of the economy to outsiders as inviting exploitation by neocolonial powers.[6] The outcome has been comparatively higher levels of global economic engagement among all GCC states. Global investors are attracted to the Persian Gulf, one of the world's most profitable "energy zones," because of the region's business-friendly domestic and policy environments.[7] For their part, the GCC states seek out new, lucrative markets in the West for investing their own sizeable sovereign wealth funds (Seznec's chapter, below). Again, as the chapters by Kamrava and Karshenas and Moshaver demonstrate, Iran, which has been saddled with progressively tighter international economic sanctions since 1995,[8] stands as an exception to this trend.

A third trend characterizing the political economy of most Persian Gulf states has been the effort to lay the foundations for sustainable development once the oil era is over, and hydrocarbon exports can no longer finance development at breakneck speed. To do so, most states in the region, especially the more wealthy ones, have sought to foster knowledge-based economies. These initiatives are discussed at length in Kristian Coates Ulrichsen's chapter, which highlights the sizeable funds that most GCC states have devoted to fostering knowledge economies.

The preliminary results, at least in terms of expanding basic educational infrastructures, are impressive. In merely five years, for example, from 2004 to 2009, the number of students across the Arabian Peninsula shot up by more than 131 percent (from 6,171,252 to 8,384,180), and the number of universities rose from sixty-nine to a hundred and twenty-six, an increase of more than 180 percent.[9] But, as Ulrichsen points out, fostering knowledge-based econo-

[6] For more on these distinct forms of nationalism see Mehran Kamrava, *The Modern Middle East: A Political History Since the First World War*, 2nd edition (Berkeley, CA: University of California Press, 2011), pp. 293–5.

[7] Anoushiravan Ehteshami, *Globalization and Geopolitics in the Middle East* (London: Routledge, 2007), p. 39.

[8] An overview of US sanctions against Iran is available at the US Treasury Department's website, http://www.treasury.gov/resource-center/sanctions/Programs/Documents/iran.pdf.

[9] *GCC Statistical Bulletins*, 2008 and 2010, pp. 22 and 20 respectively.

mies requires more than building impressive edifices and creating educational hubs and enclaves. It also requires structural adjustments in related sectors of the economy, as well as concomitant shifts in cultural values and norms. Accurate empirical data on the phenomenon is also hard to come by. However, anecdotal evidence suggests that changing popular attitudes toward knowledge economy remains a work in progress and may still take a few generations to take effect. For now, motivating high school graduates to pursue (or qualify for) university education continues to be a challenge for high school and university administrators across the region, especially insofar as boys are concerned.[10] Even more challenging is convincing university degree holders to pursue postgraduate studies. Thanks to robust economies, and labor nationalization quotas imposed on most business enterprises operating in the region, university graduates are often enticed to enter the workforce instead of moving on to postgraduate studies.[11] Gainful employment does not always equate to economic efficiency. In one survey in the United Arab Emirates (UAE) conducted in 2002, fully 96 percent of respondents complained about a mismatch between their skills and their actual jobs, which they blamed on systematic deficiencies in the educational system.[12] Not surprisingly, continued reliance on skilled expatriate labor to run the commanding heights of the knowledge economy, as well as on rent income to continue to meet the nationals' employment expectations, tends to circumscribe the effects that knowledge generation initiatives would otherwise have.[13]

[10] In a 2006 survey conducted by the Rand Qatar Policy Institute, 60 percent of female and only 37 percent of male Qatari high school seniors said they wanted to pursue a university degree. Cathleen Stasz, Eric R. Eide, and Francisco Martorell, *Post-Secondary Education in Qatar* (Santa Monica, CA: Rand, 2007), p. 40. Seeking to address these and other similar issues, the Qatari government has launched major reform initiatives both at the K-12 level and in Qatar University. See Kholode Al-Obaidli, *Educational Reform in Qatar: Women ESL Teachers' Perceptions about Roles and Professional Development Needs* (Saarbrücken, Germany: Lap Lambert, 2011); Dominic J. Brewer *et al.*, *Education for a New Era: Design and Implementation of K-12 Education Reform in Qatar* (Santa Monica, CA: Rand, 2007); and, Joy S. Moini *et al.*, *The Reform of Qatar University* (Santa Monica, CA: Rand, 2009).

[11] Jasim Al-Ali, "Emiratisation: Drawing UAE Nationals in their Surging Economy," *International Journal of Sociology and Social Policy* Vol. 28, Nos. 9/10 (2008), pp. 365–79.

[12] Joan Muysken and Samia Nour, "Deficiencies in Education and Poor Prospects for Economic Growth in the Gulf Countries: The Case of the UAE," *Journal of Development Studies* Vol. 42, No. 6 (August 2006), p. 972.

[13] According to one study on the UAE, "whilst Emiratis occupy many of the country's

INTRODUCTION

The three broad developmental efforts characterizing the political economy of the Persian Gulf—rapid economic growth and infrastructural development, integration into the global economy, and the ushering in of knowledge-based economies—have in turn had to contend with three structural features that are endemic to all of the region's political economies. These include rentierism and its attendant consequences, demographic pressures, and other structural deficiencies that exert negative pressures and push back against developmental objectives. All three of these dynamics are analyzed at length throughout the volume. Briefly, since the start of the oil era in the Persian Gulf, the region has witnessed the evolution of rentierism with paradoxical consequences: while rentierism has enabled the state to funnel oil and gas revenues into society and secure a measure of political acquiescence, it has also made the state dependent on maintaining its patronage position for fear of adverse consequences. Insofar as demographic pressures are concerned, the regional states are either far too populous given the state's resources and infrastructural capacities or are, alternatively, heavily reliant on imported labor to carry out their developmental agendas.

Finally, oil wealth in the hands of the state and conspicuous consumption on the part of the populace can mask structural weaknesses arising from dependence on hydrocarbon exports. The volatile growth of Persian Gulf economies from the 1980s to the 2000s, emblematic of those of the rest of the Middle East, demonstrate their captive vulnerability to exogenous trends and directly reflect the turbulent cycle of the international oil market.[14] The grim picture painted by the United Nations Development Program in its 2009 report on Arab economies continues to ring true today and extends to the Persian Gulf region, including Iran:

Oil-led growth has created weak structural foundations in Arab economies. Many Arab countries are turning into increasingly import oriented and service-based economies. The types of services found in most Arab countries fall at the lower end of the value adding chain, contribute little to local knowledge development and lock countries into inferior positions in global markets. This trend has grown at the expense of Arab agriculture, manufacturing and industrial production. ... Overall, the Arab countries were less industrialized in 2007 than in 1970, almost four decades previously.[15]

senior positions, they may not be able to adequately plan or control its future." Al-Ali, "Emiratisation: Drawing UAE Nationals in their Surging Economy," p. 366.

[14] United Nations Development Program, *Arab Human Development Report 2009* (New York: UNDP, 2009), p. 9.

[15] Ibid., pp. 9–10.

As the chapters in this volume attest, although most of the regional states have become major players in the global economy, for many the massive infusion of petrodollars into the economy has only partially masked—at times actually without much success—the pervasive structural weaknesses that continue to characterize their economies.

This volume

The volume is divided into three parts. Part I includes chapters that outline some of the broader trends in the region's political economy, looking at the evolution of their roles within the international economy, their built-in common characteristics, and one of the more significant instruments which they have used to protect themselves from external shocks; sovereign wealth funds. This set of chapters begins with Fred Lawson's analysis of the evolution of the Persian Gulf's role in the contemporary international economy. Lawson traces the evolution of Persian Gulf economies from marginal players in the international arena in the 1980s to pivotal ones today. Financed by hydrocarbon exports, the regional economies have managed to become significant players in the global financial markets, have expanded their own manufacturing base, and have sought new and important trading partners in China, India, and other lucrative emerging markets. Largely buffered from the global recession of 2007–08, Lawson argues, the GCC states found themselves in a position to help resuscitate Western economies, further enhancing their positions in the international arena.

One of most persistent and pervasive features of political economies across the Persian Gulf is rentierism. In Chapter 3, I examine the evolution and institutional configuration of rentierism across the region, looking at ways in which rentier arrangements were superimposed on state institutions as they were beginning to emerge and gain hold over society. These rentier arrangements, I argue, create relations of mutual dependence between state actors and institutions on the one hand, and the social actors and groups on whose compliance the state relies on the other. Needless to say, not all regional economies are alike, rentier arrangements notwithstanding, and the wealthier states of the region have used sovereign wealth funds (SWF) as investment mechanisms. Jean-François Seznec examines Persian Gulf sovereign wealth funds in his chapter, providing detailed calculations of their approximate value. Some of the secrecy that surrounds these SWFs, Seznec argues, especially in terms of their size and management, adds unnecessary mystery to them and—at least insofar as the biggest SWF, the Abu Dhabi Investment Authority, is concerned—can lead to unnecessary, even uncomfortable, questions being asked by local citizens.

Part II examines money, banking, and demography in the Persian Gulf. The common thread running through the three chapters comprising this section is that the political economy of the region tends to be influenced far more by the political considerations of state actors than by economic policies or dynamics. Rodney Wilson analyses the growth of Islamic banking in the region, pointing out that the *étatiste* and top-down nature of Islamic banking in Iran has undermined its potential for growth and efficacy, whereas its bottom-up nature in the GCC has enhanced its popularity and facilitated its growth. This same statist impulse, according to Djavad Salehi-Isfahani, hampers productivity among an increasingly better educated workforce. At least insofar as human resource development is concerned, in the GCC reservation wages have increased without commensurate increases in the workforce's global skills, which instead have relied on imported experts to run the modern, globalizing economies. Along similar lines, lack of substantive moves to bring about monetary union prevents the GCC from realizing its full potential in the global economy. If it were to form a monetary union, the GCC could emerge as an even more significant player in the world economy. Alexis Antoniades outlines halted moves by the GCC to establish a monetary union, potentially the largest such union outside of the Eurozone; various political obstacles and considerations, according to Antoniades, have hampered efforts aimed at establishing a Gulf Monetary Union.

Part III contains chapters that examine three very different case studies, namely those of Dubai, Saudi Arabia, and Iran. In each case, hydrocarbon rent revenues have had specific consequences on the institutional development of the state. Christopher Davidson examines the rise and travails of "Dubai, Inc." and its need for economic diversification and liberalization in order to survive. Davidson questions the very viability of the "Dubai model" given its overt dependence on Abu Dhabi to pull out of the 2008 global financial crisis. Steffen Hertog traces a very different developmental path as pursued by Saudi Arabia. Hertog focuses on the emergence of "islands of efficiency" alongside largely inefficient economic institutions, examining the differential impact of oil revenues on the evolution of state institutions—rent revenues tend to give state actors more leeway to engage in institutional experimentation, which may take different directions in different parts of the state. Only through "very painful adjustments" can the Saudi economy overcome the resulting segmentation and the persistence of inefficiency. In Iran's markedly different economy, as Massoud Karshenas and Ziba Moshaver demonstrate in the volume's final chapter, rent revenues have enhanced the powers of what they call "the informal core state"—state-controlled foundations and other networks of individuals and institutions with various types of links to the state—which tends to be "less transparent and more murky." The formal and informal core states have successfully stymied economic reforms that they have perceived as inimical to their interests.

As the chapters in this volume collectively demonstrate, commensurate with the rise in their incomes from hydrocarbon resources, Persian Gulf economies have grown in significance and influence on the world stage. In addition to oil and gas sales, within the last decade or so sovereign wealth funds have emerged as viable international investment instruments and are meant to sustain economic growth in the post-oil era. But across the Persian Gulf fundamental problems continue to plague the region's economies. Rentierism has locked state and non-state actors into relationships of mutual dependence, led to the segmentation of state institutions into efficient and inefficient ones, and made inefficient political and economic institutions resistant to much needed reforms. The official rhetoric of liberalization notwithstanding, the weight of the state, and the inertia of path dependence, continue to crush what Hertog calls "diffuse innovation and value generation." Oil revenues have so far masked the depth of these problems, and have tended to ameliorate the gravity of deep-rooted economic problems. But, as the rude awakenings of 2008 and 2009 demonstrated, not even the wealthiest are immune from worldwide economic shocks.

There are, nonetheless, a few hopeful signs. There is official recognition that the oil era is finite in duration and that at the very least there is an urgent need to create foundational infrastructures for post-oil, knowledge-based economies. Sovereign wealth funds are being employed to foster economic diversification, and many GCC states have shown the utility and efficacy of Islamic banking as viable alternatives to mostly inefficient state-owned or controlled banks. And, halted as they have been so far, at least the GCC has started discussions on a common currency. Monetary union may be quite some time away, but the GCC has been encouraging policy coordination in other, related areas.

The Persian Gulf is full of economic potential. What remains conspicuously absent is the wherewithal needed to realize this latent potential through difficult policy choices that require significant political capital. Whether the

Arab Spring of 2011 will give the region's old and new political actors the necessary capital to do so remains to be seen. For now, state elites across the region have been able to fend off challenges to their rule and maintain the political status quo through a combination of not-so-latent repression and major economic concessions.[16] But this is not indefinitely tenable. Political change of varying forms and degrees is bound to sweep across the Persian Gulf sooner or later. What form this change will take in relation to the region's countries, and what consequences it will have domestically for each country and collectively for the global economy, remains to be seen.

[16] Wealthier GCC states pledged $20 billion in economic assistance to Bahrain and Oman, the two regional states rocked by Arab Spring rebellions. To placate domestic demands for change, in January 2011 the Kuwaiti government had announced a generous social allowance package for its citizens that included a monthly handout of approximately $3,500 per citizen and comprehensive food subsidies for three months. The following month the Saudi monarch King Abdullah followed suit by promising the injection of $36 billion into the economy in the form of benefits and price subsidies. See, Hala Jaber, "Desert Dictators Try to Buy off Rising Anger at Arab Dynasties," *Sunday Times*, January 30, 2011, pp. 22, 23; and Hugh Tomlinson. "$36bn and a Reshuffle: How an Ailing King Aims to Halt the Tide of Change," *The Times*, February 25, 2011, p. 29.

Part I

Trends in the Political Economy of the Persian Gulf

2

The Persian Gulf in the Contemporary International Economy

Fred H. Lawson

As late as 1985, the Persian Gulf played only a limited role in the international economy. Iran, Iraq, Saudi Arabia, Kuwait and the United Arab Emirates had emerged as major exporters of crude oil, while Oman, Qatar and Bahrain contributed somewhat smaller amounts to the global petroleum pool. Bahrain had taken steps to attract transnational banks as a way to complement its rapidly diminishing hydrocarbon reserves, and Kuwait disbursed substantial amounts of economic assistance to less prosperous countries under the auspices of the Kuwait Fund for Arab Economic Development.[1] Meanwhile, behind the scenes, much of the massive revenue that flowed into regional treasuries after the successive spikes in world oil prices of 1973–74 and 1979–80 was invested in portfolios of blue-chip stocks and government-backed securities in the United States and United Kingdom, helping to prop up an

---

[1] Fred H. Lawson, *Bahrain: The Modernization of Autocracy* (Boulder, Colo.: Westview Press, 1989), pp. 106–109;Ragei El Mallakh, *Economic Development and Regional Cooperation: Kuwait* (Chicago, IL: University of Chicago Press, 1968).

American economy whose predominant position in the global order had started to erode in the mid-1970s.[2]

Over the ensuing quarter-century, however, the importance of the Persian Gulf to the international economy has increased dramatically. The six member-states of the Gulf Co-operation Council (GCC: Saudi Arabia, Kuwait, the United Arab Emirates [UAE], Qatar, Bahrain and Oman) and the Islamic Republic of Iran continue to account for a substantial proportion of both output and total proven reserves of world hydrocarbons. But in addition, the Arab states of the Gulf have undertaken a much more extensive range of activities in the global financial system, while attracting growing amounts of foreign direct investment. Furthermore, the GCC has become a notable producer of such heavy industrial goods as aluminum, plastics and cement, and has started to carve out a niche for itself as a large-scale supplier of these products, particularly to the expanding economies of East and South Asia.

In a broader sense, the Persian Gulf now occupies a pivotal position as the generator-of-last-resort of remittances to the labor-exporting countries of South and Southeast Asia. GCC governments have started to take a more active part in reconfiguring the institutional architecture on which the international economy rests. And the Gulf's Arab states and Iran are making fundamental contributions to sustained growth in the People's Republic of China and India, thereby hastening the tectonic shift in world economic power from west to east.

Hydrocarbon production

Throughout the 1980s, the Gulf Co-operation Council countries were responsible for about one-quarter of the world's total production of crude oil.[3] This proportion remained largely unchanged until the end of the twentieth century, but began to rise in early 2002. By mid-2008, the Gulf Arab states and Iran were contributing just over 28 percent of aggregate petroleum output, although the percentage dropped off during the course of the following year (see Figure 2.1).

Gulf production of natural gas has gained even more ground over the past decade. In 1999, the GCC states and Iran accounted for 8 percent of the

---

[2] David E. Spiro, *The Hidden Hand of American Hegemony* (Ithaca, NY: Cornell University Press, 1999).

[3] A.A. Kubursi, "Oil, Influence and Development: The Gulf States and the International Economy," *International Journal* Vol. 41, No. 2 (Spring 1986), p. 365.

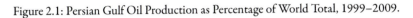

Figure 2.1: Persian Gulf Oil Production as Percentage of World Total, 1999–2009.

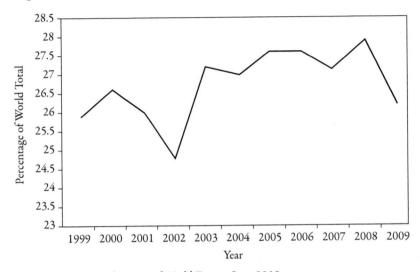

Source: *BP Statistical Review of World Energy*, June 2010.

world's natural gas. This proportion hovered around 10 percent in 2003–04, then rose more sharply to a high of over 13 percent in 2009 (see Figure 2.2). In other words, the ten years from 1999 to 2009 saw the Gulf's share of world natural gas output jump more than 50 percent.

As petroleum prices edged higher and oil-refining technology has improved, a new form of hydrocarbon—natural gas liquids (NGL)—has become a major energy source, particularly in the richer industrial economies.[4] During the years after 1999, global production of NGL has experienced a steady upward trend, from just over 68 billion barrels per day to over 106 billion barrels per day in 2010 (see Figure 2.3). Of this total, Saudi Arabia and the United Arab Emirates (UAE) contributed just under 15 percent in 1999 (see Figure 2.4). These same two countries produced 20.5 percent of world NGL in 2010, while Qatar has entered the field of NGL production in a major—but as yet uncharted—fashion as well.

Gulf producers appear likely to occupy a key position in world hydrocarbon output for the foreseeable future. The GCC states accounted for some 42 per-

---

[4] International Energy Agency, *Natural Gas Liquids: Supply Outlook 2008–2015* (Paris: International Energy Agency, April 2010).

Figure 2.2: Persian Gulf Natural Gas Production as Percentage of World Total, 1999–2009.

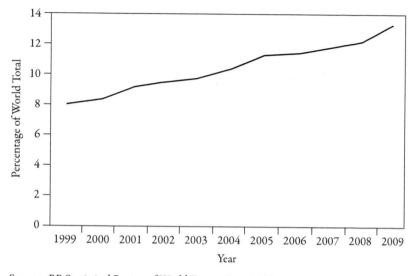

Source: *BP Statistical Review of World Energy*, June 2010.

cent of total proven oil reserves in the mid-1980s and raised that proportion to around 46 percent at the end of the decade.[5] Over the subsequent twenty years, the GCC's share of proven reserves steadily diminished, falling to just under 37 percent by 2009. Meanwhile, Iran's proportion of aggregate proven reserves gradually increased, surpassing 10 percent of the total in 2009. Thanks to the steady rise in Iranian proven reserves, the Gulf is now estimated to account for approximately 47 percent of the world's long-term supply of oil.

Gulf proven reserves of natural gas make up a smaller percentage of the global total, but have exhibited a more pronounced increase over the last two decades. The GCC states were estimated to have held around 14 percent of total gas reserves in 1989, a little over 17 percent in 1999 and just under 23 percent in 2009. Combined with Iran's domestic reserves, the region now contains at least 38.5 percent of the world's natural gas.

Any discussion of hydrocarbons and the Gulf must take into consideration the fact that the region's own consumption of oil and gas is accelerating. Petroleum usage in the UAE jumped 59 percent in the ten years after 1999; Kuwaiti

[5] *BP Statistical Review of World Energy*, June 2010, p. 6.

Figure 2.3: World Production of Natural Gas Liquids, 1999–2010.

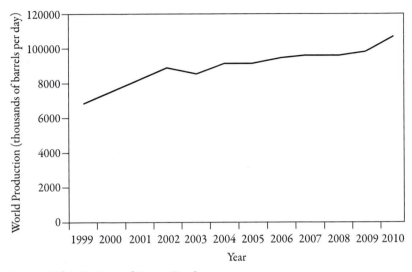

Source: *Oil & Gas Journal* Energy Database.

Figure 2.4: Persian Gulf Natural Gas Liquids Production as Percentage of World Total, 1999–2010.

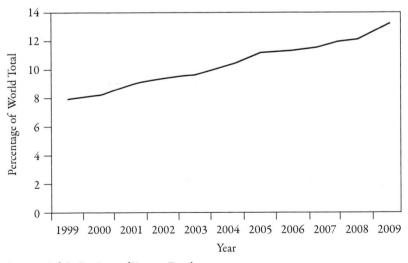

Source: *Oil & Gas Journal* Energy Database.

consumption rose 66 percent during the same decade, while that of Saudi Arabia increased by 70 percent, and Qatar's soared more than 300 percent. Iranian domestic consumption increased by 42 percent from 1999 to 2009, a trend that would be remarkable in the company of any other set of economies besides that of the Gulf states.[6] By 2009 the GCC and Iran together accounted for about 6.6 percent of total world oil consumption. Informed observers have pointed out that burgeoning local consumption, particularly in Saudi Arabia and the UAE, is likely to make it more and more difficult for key Gulf producers to augment supplies of oil to the international market.[7]

Gulf consumption of natural gas has expanded so dramatically that governments in the region have taken extraordinary steps to maintain energy supplies to domestic users. As of 2009, the GCC and Iran consumed more than 11 percent of the world's natural gas.[8] That same year Kuwait received its first shipments of liquefied natural gas (LNG) from Russia through the newly-completed LNG terminal at Mina al-Ahmadi Gas Port. Iran imports some 5 percent of the gas that it uses from neighboring Turkmenistan, and has made arrangements to purchase LNG from Azerbaijan as well.[9] Natural gas has become particularly central to the production of electricity in the Gulf states, more than 90 percent of which comes from gas-fired plants.[10] It is also being used to boost output in depleted oil fields, particularly in Dubai and Sharjah where demand for gas earmarked for re-injection into flagging wells is expected to jump 300 percent by 2020.[11] Moreover, LNG lies at the heart of such heavy industrial activities as aluminum refining and petrochemical manufacturing, which have surged throughout the region in recent years.[12] Anticipated shortages of LNG have pushed the authorities in the UAE to pursue nuclear power as an alternative source of energy, while Oman has announced plans to build a 1,000-megawatt coal-fired generating facility.

---

[6] Ibid., p. 12.

[7] *Middle East Economic Digest*, March 12–18, 2010.

[8] *BP Statistical Review of World Energy*, June 2010, p. 27.

[9] Raed Kombargi, Otto Waterlander, George Sarraf and Asheesh Sastry, *Gas Shortage in the GCC: How to Bridge the Gap* (Abu Dhabi: Booz and Company, n.d.), p. 7.

[10] Ibid., p. 3.

[11] Ibid.

[12] Mina Toksoz, "The GCC: Prospects and Risks in the New Oil Boom," in John Nugee and Paola Subacchi (eds), *The Gulf Region: A New Hub of Global Financial Power* (London: Royal Institute of International Affairs, 2008), p. 92.

Financial activities

Revenues generated from hydrocarbon production play a much more central role in international finance than they did thirty years ago. Two-thirds of the profits generated by the oil price rises of 1973–74 and 1979–80 ended up as long-term deposits in commercial banks or investments in government securities in the richer industrial countries of the Organization for Economic Co-operation and Development (OECD).[13] The remainder was used to fund infrastructure projects in the more dynamic economies of Latin America, purchase real estate in the United States and United Kingdom and provide short-term assistance to "a few industrialized European countries [that were] running current account deficits."[14]

As it became clear that oil monies constituted not simply a one-time windfall but instead a permanent stream of income, Gulf governments altered both the kind and direction of their investment activities. Whereas some 46 percent of GCC overseas investments took the form of bank deposits in 2001, just under 28 percent did so five years later.[15] It is estimated that the GCC countries sank some 24 billion US dollars into shares of stock in private US and European companies in 2005, and another US$24 billion the following year, after allocating less than $1 billion to the purchase of corporate stock in 2004.[16] On the other hand, the diminishing proportion of investments in US government securities masks the continued rise in the actual value of such investments: GCC holdings of long-term US government debt surged from around $50 billion in 2002 to approximately $150 billion in 2006.[17]

More importantly, Gulf investment capital moved into less predictable areas, particularly toward the other Arab countries of the Middle East and North Africa (MENA). By 2006, total GCC investment in the MENA was estimated to equal the amount of GCC holdings in the United States and Europe, and was calculated to match the amount of foreign direct investment

---

[13] Florence Eid, "The New Face of Arab Investment," in Nugee and Subacchi (eds), *Gulf Region*, p. 69.

[14] Ibid., p. 70.

[15] Ibid., p. 71.

[16] Bessma Momani, "Gulf Cooperation Council Oil Exporters and the Future of the Dollar," *New Political Economy* Vol. 13, No. 3 (September 2008), p. 305.

[17] Michael Sturm, Jan Strasky, Petra Adolf and Dominik Peschel, *The Gulf Cooperation Council Countries: Economic Structures, Recent Developments and Role in the Global Economy*, European Central Bank Occasional Paper No. 92, 2008, chart 30.

(FDI) in the MENA coming from all other sources combined.[18] Saudi Arabia, Kuwait and the UAE contributed just under 70 percent of all FDI in the rest of the Arab world in 2006, the great majority of which was targeted at Egypt, Lebanon, Jordan and Tunisia. Projects funded by GCC monies were on the whole more extensive and capital-intensive than ones supported by European capital.[19]

Such investments have dramatically improved the prospects for local industry all across the Arab world. Egypt found itself showered with $3.3 billion in FDI from the GCC during the 2006–07 fiscal year, and in return shipped some $550 million worth of iron and steel products to GCC markets.[20] This trend marked a seismic shift in the direction of Egypt's metals trade: as recently as 2004–05, most Egyptian iron and steel went to the European Union, while shipments to the Arab world approximately equaled those to the US. By 2006–07, however, almost half of Egypt's exports of iron and steel were directed to the Arab countries of the Gulf. It is quite likely that the dramatic rise in industrial exports to the GCC set the stage for the unexpected fall in Egypt's unemployment rate that took place between 2006 and 2008.[21]

On the other hand, the Gulf itself became a greater recipient of investment monies during the first years of the twenty-first century. In 2000, the region accounted for virtually none of the world's foreign direct investment, thanks largely to the negative FDI position occupied by Saudi Arabia. By 2005, however, the GCC countries hosted just over 1.5 percent of world FDI, and after a small downturn in 2007 the figure rose to about 2.5 percent in 2008 (see Figure 2.5). Saudi Arabia attracted most of these monies, particularly after fundamental changes to the kingdom's investment regulations and practices were carried out, beginning in 2005. Some $12 billion in external funding flooded into Saudi projects that same year, with more than $18 billion arriving the year after that.[22] By 2008 the kingdom by itself was the recipient of more than $38 billion in FDI.[23] According to the United Nations Conference on

[18] Eid, "New Face of Arab Investment," p. 71.

[19] Benedict de Saint-Laurent, *Investment From the GCC and Development in the Mediterranean*, Documenti IAI 09/36, Istituto Affari Internazionali, Rome, December 2009.

[20] Eid, "New Face of Arab Investment," pp. 76–7.

[21] Ibid., p. 78.

[22] Sturm, Strasky, Adolf and Peschel, *Gulf Cooperation Council Countries*, Table 6. See also Daniel Hanna, "The Gulf's Changing Financial Landscape," in Nugee and Subacchi (eds), *Gulf Region*, p. 111.

[23] *The Middle East*, December 2010, p. 29.

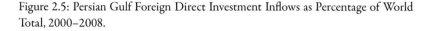

Figure 2.5: Persian Gulf Foreign Direct Investment Inflows as Percentage of World Total, 2000–2008.

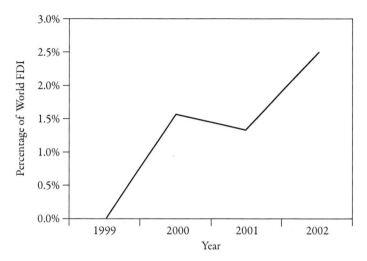

Source: World Bank, *World Development Indicators*, April 2010.

Trade and Development, total FDI inflows into the GCC jumped from $2 billion in 2001 to $6.6 billion in 2003, then to over $14 billion in 2004, more than $39 billion in 2006, almost $47 billion in 2007 and over $60 billion in 2008. Kuwait stood out among the GCC states as the only country that registered a comparatively moderate rise in FDI in the seven years after 2001.

Figures for 2009 indicate that foreign direct investment coming into the Gulf has at last suffered as a result of the global financial crisis of 2007–08. Total FDI in Saudi Arabia fell by 7 percent from 2008 to 2009, while that in the UAE plunged a breath-taking 72 percent to a total of just over $7 billion.[24] By contrast, Qatar enjoyed a 112 percent jump in FDI. Kuwait and Iran showed sharp increases in FDI as well, albeit from comparatively low levels. Iran received some $3 billion in outside investment during 2009, mostly from Chinese companies engaged in oil and gas exploration. For the GCC as a whole, FDI dropped from $60 billion in 2008 to 50.8 billion in 2009.[25]

More active involvement in international finance raises the question of whether or not Gulf Arab governments will maintain their long-standing

[24] Ibid.
[25] Ibid.

commitment to provide stability to the US dollar. So long as it retains its role as the invoice currency for international hydrocarbon transactions, the dollar stands a much better chance of parrying challenges from other world currencies. Furthermore, the GCC states found themselves holding just over 180 billion US dollars by 2005, a figure that represented approximately three-fifths of their total hard currency reserves. Bessma Momani observes that "much of this GCC wealth is either earned, saved or spent in US dollars, and hence the GCC are [*sic*] key players in determining the future of dollar stability."[26]

Despite the appearance of attractive alternatives, in particular the euro, as the twentieth century drew to a close, the Arab states of the Gulf appeared to be uninterested in experimenting with novel ways to denominate and receive payment for hydrocarbon sales. The Organization of Petroleum Exporting Countries (OPEC) considered replacing US dollar valuations with ones based on a basket of major world currencies in the mid-1980s, but backed down in the face of strong resistance by Saudi officials.[27] Iraq, Iran, Libya, Russia and Malaysia have all at one time or another suggested that the euro might serve as a better instrument of accounting than the dollar, but such sentiments have elicited little enthusiasm from GCC member-states. Continued loyalty to the US currency is most likely bound up with political and strategic considerations, rather than arising from calculations of strictly economic profits and losses. Momani points out that since "the GCC's public authorities remain highly dependent on the United States for both internal and external security that cannot be replaced by EU 'civilian power,'" the chances that the euro will supersede the dollar are likely to stay remote for the foreseeable future.[28]

Expanded manufacturing

Decades of halting steps toward economic diversification, combined with underlying shifts in global manufacturing, have culminated in the emergence of a handful of heavy industrial enterprises in the Gulf that look capable of competing successfully in international markets. Among these stand companies engaged in aluminum processing, plastics fabrication and cement production.

Bahrain pioneered the aluminum industry in the region, setting up a modern smelter and a collection of ancillary manufacturing plants from the late

---

[26] Momani, "Gulf Cooperation Council Oil Exporters," p. 295.

[27] Ibid., p. 298.

[28] Ibid., p. 309. See also *Middle East Economic Digest*, May 21–27, 2010.

1960s onwards.[29] In 1979 production commenced in the UAE at a somewhat larger facility, which was operated by the state-affiliated Dubai Aluminum. Oman opened a more modest smelter at Sohar in 2008; Qatar initiated production at a medium-sized plant two years later, at the same time that the UAE announced plans to construct a very large smelter complex under the auspices of Emirates Aluminum. Aluminum Bahrain and Qatar Aluminum have awarded contracts to upgrade existing operations over the next few years. Not to be outdone, Saudi Arabia unveiled plans to bring three massive aluminum smelters on line starting in 2013. The Gulf Organization for Industrial Consulting estimates that aluminum production in the GCC presently constitutes about 9 percent of total world output, and that by 2015 the figure will double to 18 percent. The enhanced role of the GCC in the global aluminum market is indicated by the International Aluminum Institute's decision to create a separate listing for the Gulf in its periodic statistical reports as of January 2010. More important, the Arab Gulf states have set up a Gulf Aluminum Council to co-ordinate future production and distribution of this valuable metal.[30]

Saudi Arabia's refining facility at the new Ras al-Zawr industrial city is projected to become the largest integrated aluminum project ever built. A joint venture between the Saudi Arabian Mining Company (Ma'adin) and US-based Alcoa, the complex is set to consist of a bauxite mine capable of producing 4 million metric tons per year, an alumina refinery able to handle 1.8 million tons, a smelter designed to produce three-quarters of a million tons, and a rolling mill with a capacity of just under half a million tons.[31] The kingdom enjoys domestic proven reserves of bauxite estimated at 126 million tons, which will give Saudi producers a marked advantage over other Gulf producers by 2020.[32] More important, Saudi Arabia expects to step up overseas deliveries as older facilities in Europe, South and East Asia and North America close down in the near future due to high labor costs, more intrusive environmental regulations and increasingly obsolete equipment.[33]

Besides aluminum, plastics makes up a burgeoning component of Gulf manufacturing, which has gained the potential to affect prices and supply chains on a global scale. In 1990 there were 326 factories for plastics products

[29] Lawson, *Bahrain*, pp. 99–101.

[30] *Khaleej Times*, January 22, 2011.

[31] *Saudi Gazette*, September 22, 2010; *Middle East Economic Digest*, March 19–25, 2010.

[32] NCB, "Saudi Aluminum Sector Review," *In-Focus Report*, April 2010, p. 3.

[33] *Middle East Economic Digest*, June 12, 2009; *Saudi Gazette*, November 10, 2010.

in the GCC countries; as of 2007 the figure had risen to 1,223, with 507 located in the UAE alone. Whereas utilization rates at these plants averaged no more than 68 percent of total capacity in 1990, they hovered around 90 percent by 2006.[34] The capacity for polyethylene production in the GCC is due to more than double from 10.7 million tons per year in 2009 to 21.5 million in 2015; at the same time, polypropylene capacity is slated to increase from 4.8 million to 9.5 million tons per year. The proportion of aggregate global output that these figures represent will jump from 13 to 19 percent during this decade.[35]

Complementing the expansion of such basic plastics is a sharp rise in the production of glass fiber reinforced plastics (GRP), a building material that promises to replace more expensive steel and wood components in basic construction over the next few years.[36] GRP plants have recently started operating in Bahrain and Saudi Arabia, while facilities that turn out crucial inputs for GRP have been set up in the UAE. The authorities in the UAE have laid the foundation for further growth by establishing Abu Dhabi Polymers Park to house a collection of integrated plastics companies. At the same time, the GRP industry has been expanding equally rapidly in Iran. As GRP-concrete rebars increasingly take the place of steel rebars in large-scale building projects throughout the world, the prospects for Gulf producers appear bright. Plastics companies based in the UAE were reported to have attracted intense attention at the industry's pre-eminent trade fair in Düsseldorf in October 2010.[37]

On the other hand, local consumption of a wide range of plastics is projected to take off in the near future. The GCC at present makes up about 2 percent of the global plastics market, but the annual growth rate of the regional market is predicted to hover around 10 percent per year.[38] Packaging and construction uses are likely to predominate. To satisfy domestic demand, the Saudi government has approved a variety of manufacturing plants, while the UAE and Kuwait have taken steps to augment local production as well. Kuwaiti plastics, which rely on less efficient inputs than those of Saudi Arabia

---

[34] *AME Info*, March 19, 2008.

[35] *Pudaily*, June 4, 2010; Applied Market Information, *The Plastics Industry in the Middle East*, January 2009.

[36] S. Sundaram, "Oil—Fueling GRP Growth in the Middle East," www.reinforcedplastics.com (accessed October 1, 2008).

[37] MENAFN.com, June 1, 2010.

[38] *Khaleej Times*, September 19, 2010.

and the UAE, are expected to find more profitable markets in the People's Republic of China (PRC) than at home.

Finally, cement has emerged as a major component of Gulf manufacturing. The GCC states combined to produce a little over 27 million tons of concrete in 1997, just under 37 million tons in 2002 and almost 59 million tons in 2007.[39] This represents a 120 percent increase over the ten-year period. Much of this output was targeted at foreign purchasers, who were willing to pay higher prices than government-subsidized developers at home. So much Saudi cement was being siphoned overseas that in June 2008 the ministry of Commerce and Industry imposed a ban on exports. The ban caused local cement prices to fall by some 20 percent. Officials reversed themselves in May 2009 and permitted companies to resume exporting cement, but only under a pair of stringent conditions: that the domestic price of cement must be maintained at a price well below world market levels and that local demand must be fully met before exports can be undertaken.[40]

Generator of remittances

As of 2005, non-citizens comprised more than 80 percent of the labor force in the UAE and Kuwait, about two-thirds in Oman and Saudi Arabia and just under three-fifths in Bahrain and Qatar.[41] According to a report prepared for the Population Division of the United Nations Economic and Social Commission for Asia and the Pacific, "the size of labor migration [to the Gulf is] increasing far beyond the world average."[42] The workforce in the GCC grew by an average of 4.1 percent each year between 1996 and 2007, and immigrant workers are estimated to have constituted more than 25 percent of this increase.[43] By contrast, the total labor force in South Asia during this same period increased by no more than 2.1 percent per year, and that of East Asia by only 1.3 percent per year.

[39] Gulf Organization for Industrial Consulting, *Gulf Statistical Profile 2008* (Doha: GOIC, 2009), p. 183.

[40] *Middle East Economic Digest*, May 7–13, 2010.

[41] Mohammed Ebrahim Dito, *GCC Labour Migration Governance*, United Nations Expert Group Meeting on International Migration and Development in Asia and the Pacific, UN/POP/EGM-MIG/2008/7, September 2008, p. 6.

[42] Ibid.

[43] Ibid., pp. 5–6.

Migrants from India entered the GCC countries in sharply increasing numbers during the first half-decade of the twenty-first century. Some 176,000 Indians relocated to the GCC in 2000, 274,000 in 2002, 397,000 in 2003 and 423,000 in 2004.[44] By 2010 approximately 4.5 million Indian nationals were working in the GCC.[45] These workers helped to push India to the top position among all countries of the world in terms of overseas remittances received.

Reliable data on the actual flow of remittances remain hard to collect, particularly for unskilled laborers. According to figures compiled by the World Bank, remittances accounted for some 6 percent of gross domestic product in the GCC in 2001, just over 3 percent in 2005 and about 1.8 percent in 2008.[46] Given the steady, hydrocarbon revenue-fueled growth that character-

Figure 2.6: Persian Gulf Remittance Payments as Percentage of World Total, 2004–2009.

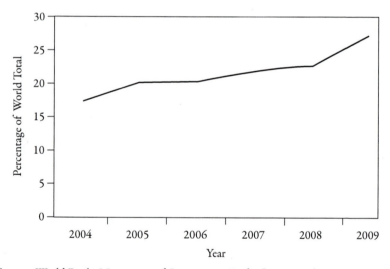

Source: World Bank, *Migration and Remittances Factbook 2011*, and various newspaper reports.

[44] Abdul Azeez and Mustiary Begum, "Gulf Migration, Remittances and Economic Impact," *Journal of Social Science* Vol. 20, No. 1 (2009), p. 57.

[45] Kristian Coates Ulrichsen, *The GCC States and the Shifting Balance of Global Power*, Center for International and Regional Studies Occasional Paper No. 6, Georgetown University School of Diplomacy in Qatar, Doha, 2010, p. 3.

[46] Marga Peeters, *The Changing Pattern in International Trade and Capital Flows of the*

ized regional economies during these years, these percentages translate into a massive increase in outflows for 2005–07, with Saudi Arabia alone contributing approximately $20 billion in overseas remittances in 2008.[47]

Furthermore, remittances from the Arab Gulf states make up a steadily rising percentage of total world income transfers (see Figure 2.6). The proportion of global remittances coming from the Gulf increased gradually from 2004 to 2006, then made a steeper climb from 2006 to 2008. By 2009, remittances from the GCC had exceeded 27 percent of all remittances. These trends demonstrate the importance of the GCC states to the international labor system as employers of last resort. Whenever the world economy expands, migrant labor tends to expand elsewhere, diminishing the overall importance of the Gulf. But whenever the global economy experiences a marked contraction, as it did in 2007–08, the proportion of all migrant laborers and their families that relies on income from the Arab Gulf states surges.

Involvement in international institutions

As the global financial crisis of 2007–08 escalated, GCC governments found themselves entreated to step in and rescue the tottering international financial system. The British Prime Minister Gordon Brown traveled to Saudi Arabia, the UAE and Qatar in November 2008; at each stop he asked his hosts to inject additional resources into the overtaxed International Monetary Fund (IMF).[48] A Saudi delegation arrived in Washington shortly thereafter to represent the GCC states at the annual summit of the Group of 20 (G-20). Instead of offering to bail out the richer industrial countries, King Abdullah bin Abd al-Aziz Al Sa'ud took the occasion to charge that "undisciplined globalization and inadequate control of the financial sector" had caused the current crisis. He went on to recommend that the IMF adopt stricter measures to supervise the risk-taking behavior of influential actors in the OECD.[49] The King's statements reflected a widely-shared attitude in the

---

Gulf Cooperation Council Countries in Comparison with Other Oil-Exporting Countries, Directorate-General for Economic and Financial Affairs, European Commission, 2010, p. 10.

[47] Ibid., p. 11.

[48] Bessma Momani, "The Oil-Producing Gulf States, the IMF and the International Financial Crisis," *World Economics* Vol. 10, No. 1 (January–March 2009), p. 16.

[49] Ibid., p. 17.

Gulf: the Saudi-sponsored newspaper *Arab News* asserted that "Saudi Arabia and the Gulf states do not need the protection of other nations. They should depend on themselves and should not trust anybody but themselves for their protection. How could Saudi Arabia help the US auto industry and not help its own stock market that dropped over 80 percent from its value in the last two years?"[50]

Saudi membership in the G-20 comes at a time when the organization is carving out a pivotal position for itself in the international economic order.[51] The dominant political-economic grouping of the 1980s, the Group of 7 (G-7), consists of increasingly cash-strapped OECD states. When these countries at last mobilized to stabilize the euro in 2010, two things became apparent: not even the OECD economies could raise the financial resources necessary to prop up the sagging European currency, and so long as such key players as China, India and Brazil were left on the outside, global markets were unlikely to believe that any solution to the crisis could be sustained. In an attempt to broaden deliberations about the future of the world financial system, the G-7 turned to the G-20, which had taken shape in 1999 but had lain virtually dormant thereafter. Five key members of the G-20—China, Russia, Brazil, India and Mexico—have emerged as major economic actors in the decade after the organization coalesced. Four others—Turkey, Indonesia, Argentina and South Africa—have become influential diplomatic actors, whose ability to persuade surrounding states to comply with global initiatives made them invaluable as the 2007–08 crisis played itself out.

But it is Saudi Arabia, along with China and a resurgent Russia, that has the potential to give the G-20 a measure of financial clout. US officials clearly had their minds fixed on Riyadh in the winter of 2008–09 when they called for an additional $500 billion to be put into the hands of the IMF. The Saudi Finance Minister Ibrahim al-Assaf responded by promising that the kingdom would "play its role" in restoring the IMF to health, but refused to commit his government to any specific course of action.[52] Ibrahim al-Assaf did, however, take

---

[50] *Arab News*, January 1, 2009.

[51] Eric Helleiner and Stefano Pagliari, "Towards a New Bretton Woods? The First G20 Leaders Summit and the Regulation of Global Finance," *New Political Economy* Vol. 14, No. 2 (June 2009); Andrew F. Cooper and Colin I. Bradford, *The G20 and the Post-Crisis Economic Order*, CIGI G20 Papers No. 3, June 2010; Federico Steinberg, *The Global Governance Agenda and the Role of the G20*, Working Paper 39/2010, Real Iberoamericana de Estudios Internacionales, Madrid, December 15, 2010.

[52] *Financial Times*, March 13, 2009.

the occasion of the 2008 G-20 summit to tell reporters that Riyadh expected the IMF to restructure its governing board in such a way as to accord Saudi Arabia its "appropriate" weight inside the organization.[53] A year later the Saudi delegation to the G-20 summit in Pittsburgh led the push to heighten transparency with regard to hydrocarbon trading and hedge fund speculation.[54]

By the time that the November 2010 summit opened in Seoul, underlying conflicts of interest among the G-20 member-states had begun to sap the strength and prestige of the organization. Saudi officials generally avoided taking sides in the disputes that buffeted the meeting, but threw their weight behind the effort to strengthen the capacity and resources of the G-20's Financial Stability Board, which had been reconfigured in April 2009 out of the earlier Financial Stability Forum.[55] Riyadh also lobbied successfully to restrict the redistribution of IMF voting shares to the advantage of poorer countries, thereby protecting Saudi Arabia's disproportionate representation on the existing board.[56] At the conclusion of the summit, Singapore was invited to play a more direct part in subsequent gatherings, a step that appears likely to enhance the role of Qatar, which along with Switzerland comprises "the 3G group that has positioned itself as a bridge between G20 members and non-members," particularly countries outside of the OECD.[57]

Relations with the People's Republic of China

It would be surprising indeed if no significant relations existed between the Gulf and the world's most dynamic national economy. Trade between the People's Republic of China (PRC) and the Gulf states rests squarely on hydrocarbons: the PRC imported some $1.5 billion worth of petroleum from the GCC in 1991, but pulled in almost $34 billion worth in 2005.[58] Saudi Ara-

---

[53] Momani, "Oil-Producing Gulf States," p. 20.

[54] "Saudi Arabia's Role in Global Economic Leadership: The G20 Summit—A Conversation with Jean Francois Seznec," www.susris.com (accessed 9 November 2009).

[55] Andrew F. Cooper and Eric Helleiner, "Advances in Global Economic Governance amid the Obstacles at the Seoul G20 Summit," *Social Europe Journal* Vol. 5, No. 2 (January 7, 2011).

[56] Claudia Schmucker and Katharina Gnath, *From the G8 to the G20: Reforming the Global Economic Governance System*, GARNET Working Paper No. 73/09, January 2010, p. 8.

[57] Ibid.

[58] Mahmoud Ghafouri, "China's Policy in the Persian Gulf," *Middle East Policy* 16 (Summer 2009), pp. 83–4.

bia's share of the Chinese oil market jumped from 17.5 percent in 2005 to 30 percent in 2009.[59] Iran and Oman each supply another 8 percent of the PRC's imported petroleum, with Kuwait and the UAE together adding another 5 percent.[60] It is projected that the PRC will derive 70 percent of its aggregate oil imports from the GCC by 2015, although recent Chinese activity in Iran may heighten that country's contribution to the flow of Gulf oil into the PRC.[61] In addition, a major Chinese state trading company in March 2004 contracted with the Iranian government to purchase 110 million tons of liquefied natural gas between 2008 and 2033; the state-run petroleum company SINOPEC subsequently concluded a 25-year deal to buy another 10 million tons each year starting in 2009; and a further agreement locks in a further 3 million tons a year for 25 years beginning in 2011.[62] Qatar's LNG sales to the PRC are projected to rise from 5 million tons per year to 15 million tons per year in the next few years.[63]

Total trade between the GCC and the PRC stood at $70 billion in 2009, and is expected to balloon to $500 billion by 2020.[64] Whereas most non-oil imports to the Gulf from the PRC consisted of "cheap textiles" as the twenty-first century opened, the range of goods has since expanded to include automobiles, industrial equipment, construction materials, vehicle tires, packaged

[59] Christopher Davidson, *The Persian Gulf and Pacific Asia* (London: Hurst, 2010), p. 28.

[60] Thomas Strouse, "Constricting Asian Market for Iranian Crude," http://to.pbs.org (accessed 24 September 2010); Zhao Hongtu, "China's Energy Interest and Security in the Middle East," in *China's Growing Role in the Middle East* (Dubai: Gulf Research Center, 2010), p. 46. The figure for Iran marks a drop from 14 percent four years earlier; see John Calabrese, *China and Iran: Mismatched Partners*, Occasional Paper, The Jamestown Foundation, August 2006, p. 7.

[61] John Calabrese, *The Consolidation of Gulf-Asia Relations*, Policy Brief No. 25, The Middle East Institute, Washington, DC, June 2009, p. 2; Theodore H. Moran, *China's Strategy to Secure Natural Resources: Risks, Dangers, and Opportunities* (Washington, DC: Peterson Institute for International Economics, 2010), pp. 26–7.

[62] Calabrese, *Consolidation of Gulf-Asia Relations*, p. 7; Mohamed A. El-Khawas, "China's Link to the Developing World: In Pursuit of Energy Security," *Journal of South Asian and Middle Eastern Studies* Vol. 32, No. 2 (Winter 2009), p. 71; Shahram Chubin, "Iran and China: Political Partners or Strategic Allies?" in *China's Growing Role*, p. 65.

[63] *Financial Times*, May 18, 2010; Christopher Davidson, *Persian Gulf and Pacific Asia*, p. 30.

[64] *Gulf News*, October 10, 2010.

foods and a wide range of higher-value consumer items.[65] For its part, the GCC ships large quantities of bulk metal and metal products to the PRC, including aluminum. The Dubai Chamber of Commerce reports that the UAE's non-oil exports to the PRC in 2010 consisted primarily of plastics, chemicals and rubber goods.

Officials in the UAE have launched a campaign to induce Chinese industrial and commercial enterprises to set up subsidiaries in the seven emirates. Dubai and Sharjah currently host branches of some 2,500 Chinese companies, and the Dragon Mart in Dubai's International City houses an astonishing 3,950 shops devoted to the wholesale and retail sale of PRC-made goods.[66] This mammoth shopping center is supported by eight adjacent warehouses, which boast 30,000 square meters of storage space. In 2010 the Emirate of Ajman opened the rival Chinamall, with outlets for another 600 companies.

To support burgeoning trade between the UAE and the PRC, local branches of HSBC and Standard Chartered banks have put in place innovative mechanisms to settle accounts involving the strictly controlled PRC yuan and the currencies of the GCC states.[67] It is now possible for UAE agents to pay for Chinese-made goods using funds denominated in yuan at certified outlets of the two banks located in twenty provinces of the PRC. Prior to this time, such arrangements had only existed between the PRC and the member-states of the Association of Southeast Asian Nations. Reducing transaction costs for UAE trading companies operating in the PRC can be expected to boost the level of Chinese goods flowing not only into the GCC countries, but into Iran as well.

More important, investment monies from the Gulf have found a growing number of productive outlets in the PRC. Saudi Aramco has undertaken to construct or upgrade oil refineries in the provinces of Qingdao, Guangdong, Shandong and Fujian, while the Kuwait Petroleum Corporation has joined forces with the Chinese National Offshore Oil Corporation to explore promising sites around Hainan island and build a massive new refinery and petrochemical facility in Guangdong.[68] Kuwait also carried out improvements to a

[65] Ghafouri, "China's Policy," p. 87; Steve A. Yetiv and Chunlong Lu, "China, Global Energy, and the Middle East," *Middle East Journal* Vol. 61, No. 2 (Spring 2007), pp. 205–06.

[66] *Gulf News*, October 10, 2010; Davidson, *Persian Gulf and Pacific Asia*, pp. 38–9.

[67] *Gulf News*, October 10, 2010.

[68] John Calabrese, "China and the Persian Gulf: Energy and Security," *Middle East Journal* Vol. 52, No. 3 (Summer 1998), p. 358; Abdulaziz Sager, "GCC-China Relations: Looking Beyond Oil," in *China's Growing Role*, p. 5.

large-scale petrochemical plant in Shandong province, and Saudi Arabia has provided the funds to extend transportation networks and other infrastructure in Xinjiang province.[69] Qatar announced in 2009 that it planned to break ground on an integrated oil refinery, petrochemicals plant and oil terminal in Zhejiang province that was estimated to cost $12 billion.[70] Meanwhile, Dubai Ports World of the UAE has taken charge of day-to-day operations at seven of the PRC's major seaborne freight terminals.[71] Taken together, these projects can be expected to generate a significant increase in the level of "interdependence" between the Gulf and the PRC.[72]

Economic relations between the Gulf and the People's Republic of China in fact represent more than just a basis for greater interdependence between these two parts of the world. The Persian Gulf states have become vital to sustained growth in the PRC, in three ways. First, like the United States before it, the PRC has pinned much of its hope for continued economic expansion on the automobile industry. The focus on automobile production dates to 1994, when state officials pronounced the industry a "pillar" of the country's future economic development. "Undoubtedly," Kelly Sims Gallagher observes, "the Chinese government's decision to make the automobile sector a mainstay of the economy greatly contributed to economic development in China, especially with respect to employment and output."[73] Auto production provided a stimulus for FDI, and "created a strong source of demand in China for raw materials and automotive parts and components."[74] The expansion of the automobile industry gave an impetus not only to the importation of petroleum, but also to domestic production of tempered glass, machine tools, plastics and steel. In the wake of the PRC's 2001 accession to the World Trade Organization, the government has encouraged a fundamental restructuring of the industry that will make it possible for "automobile enterprises [to] grow into large-sized conglomerates, industrial alliances, and special-purpose vehi-

[69] Ghafouri, "China's Policy," p. 88.

[70] Davidson, *Persian Gulf and Pacific Asia*, p. 51.

[71] Christopher Davidson, *Persian Gulf-Pacific Asia Linkages in the 21st Century: A Marriage of Convenience?*, Centre for the Study of Global Governance, London School of Economics and Political Science, January 2010, p. 18.

[72] Luo Yuan, "China's Strategic Interests in the Gulf and Trilateral Relations Among China, the U.S. and Arab Countries," in *China's Growing Role*, p. 25.

[73] Kelly Sims Gallagher, *China Shifts Gears* (Cambridge, Mass.: MIT Press, 2006), p. 22.

[74] Ibid., p. 23.

cle producers to make the Chinese industry more competitive in the world market."[75] Moreover, rising levels of automobile-related pollution have stimulated local companies to carry out technological innovations that may well put the PRC at the forefront of attempts to design practical "hybrid-electric or fuel-cell vehicles."[76]

Less specifically, the PRC's extraordinary economic expansion in the decades after 1990 reflects the leadership's adoption of an "extensive" rather than an "intensive" model of growth. In other words, state officials have pursued a strategy whereby "growth [gets] generated mostly through the expansion of inputs and only marginally through increased productivity."[77] This makes the years after 1990 quite different from the era of the 1970s and 1980s, when planners focused instead on boosting the productivity of various factors. The shift to enlarging industrial capacity and encouraging ever-larger amounts of exports accompanied a steady increase in the flow of crucial inputs, most notably oil and gas. Greater hydrocarbon consumption eclipsed more efficient usage. At the same time, provincial authorities developed "a vested interest in building whatever plant [happened to be] in vogue, whether a steel mill, power station, air-conditioner factory, copper-tube plant, whatever."[78] The influx of Gulf oil facilitated this dynamic. Consequently, the PRC finds itself in an unsustainable position, in which continued economic expansion requires more and more basic resources.

And sustained growth has become increasingly vital politically as widespread popular discontent has started to break into public disorder, particularly in predominantly Muslim areas of Xinjiang province. In the words of Kwang Ho Chun, "the importance of oil in sustaining China's economic growth is perhaps an obvious relationship. Less so is the indirect yet equally important relationship between oil and the maintenance of political and social stability within China itself."[79] On the one hand, sustained growth reflects and reinforces the leadership's "moral authority to rule," so that whenever the economy sputters the regime loses legitimacy. On the other, slower growth constricts opportunities for employment and economic bet-

---

[75] Ibid., pp. 43–4.

[76] Ibid., p. 162.

[77] Jinghai Zheng, Arne Bigsten and Angang Hu, "Can China's Growth be Sustained?" *World Development* Vol. 37 (April 2009), p. 874.

[78] Ibid., p. 878.

[79] Kwang Ho Chun, "Analysing China's Energy Security: A Source of Conflict?" *Journal of East Asian Affairs* Vol. 23, No. 1 (Spring-Summer 2009), p. 94.

terment among the general population. "Thus," Chun concludes, "within China today one can see a complex interdependence between political and social stability, economic growth and oil."[80] Nowhere is this picture more vivid than in Xinjiang.[81]

Popular restiveness in the PRC's far northwest grew more pronounced in the months leading up to the global financial crisis of 2007–08, provoked at least in part by persistent shortages of gasoline and heating oil.[82] Officials in Beijing initially resorted to brute force to restore order, but quickly announced a program of additional government spending for infrastructure and services in an effort to pacify the province.[83] State agencies pledged to double the amount of funds devoted to social welfare, education and agriculture beginning in 2011. Moreover, nineteen cities and provinces were ordered to take part in an innovative "paired assistance" scheme, whereby they were obligated to forward "0.3 percent to 0.6 percent of their annual budget to Xinjiang every year."[84] Maintaining order in the northwest has therefore become intimately connected to sustained growth all across the country. And for the moment, economic expansion in the PRC relies heavily on hydrocarbons and investments originating in the Gulf. It is little wonder that the People's Liberation Army-Navy has taken steps to establish a permanent presence in and around the Arabian Sea.[85]

Relations with India

It is impossible to disentangle the Gulf's role as a generator of workers' remittances from its importance to the expansion of the Indian economy. Almost

---

[80] Ibid., p. 97.

[81] Colin Mackerras, "Xinjiang at the Turn of the Century: The Causes of Separatism," *Central Asian Survey* Vol. 20, No. 3 (September 2001); Graham E. Fuller and S. Frederick Starr, *The Xinjiang Problem* (Washington, DC: Central Asia-Caucasus Institute, 2003).

[82] *Los Angeles Times*, September 30, 2005; *Financial Times*, August 28, 2008; John Chan, "Ethnic Tensions Flare Again in China's Xinjiang Region," www.countercurrents.org, September 10, 2009; Shan Wei, "Explaining Ethnic Protests and Ethnic Policy Changes in China," *International Journal of China Studies* Vol. 1, No. 2 (October 2010), p. 509.

[83] Ibid., pp. 520–21.

[84] Ibid., p. 521.

[85] Philip McCrum, "China and the Arabian Sea," *Middle East Report* no. 256 (Fall 2010).

half of India's total number of unskilled emigrant laborers worked in the GCC as of 2007: the GCC is the source of 27 percent of all remittances coming into India.[86] And within India itself, migration to the Gulf has had the greatest impact on the state of Kerala, whence half of the contract laborers in the region originate. In a broad sense, "migration has affected every facet of life in Kerala—economic, social, political and even religious."[87] Laborers from Kerala have been followed to the Arab Gulf states by workers from Tamil Nadu and Andhra Pradesh, the great majority of whom continue to be uneducated and unskilled.

Thanks to its intimate connections with the GCC states, Kerala boasts two modern international airports. The proliferation of expensive shops, luxurious hotels and well-equipped hospitals "proves the contribution of Gulf migration to the development" of the state's economy.[88] More important, attractive job opportunities in the Gulf have dramatically reduced the rate of unemployment throughout Kerala state and in a limited number of other parts of the Indian subcontinent.[89] The possibility of obtaining work in the oil-producing countries of the Gulf has given government officials and private entrepreneurs a strong incentive to set up a variety of vocational schools, including ones that specialize in "construction-related courses, motor operations, machine operations, welding, computer education, catering, technician, para-medical courses, etc."[90]

On the other hand, the persistent flow of skilled laborers from Kerala to the GCC has ended up elevating labor costs at home. Two factors generate levels of remuneration inside Kerala that turn out to be disproportionately high. First, all sorts of skilled workers—electricians, mechanics, plumbers, welders, vehicle drivers—routinely exit the state's labor market, driving down the supply of such trained personnel. At the same time, expatriates returning home most often make use of their hard-won fortunes to construct new houses, shops and farm buildings, exacerbating shortages of skilled laborers and esca-

---

[86] Samir Pradhan, "India's Economic and Political Presence in the Gulf," in *India's Growing Role in the Gulf* (Dubai: Gulf Research Center, 2009), pp. 21–3.

[87] Azeez and Begum, "Gulf Migration," p. 56.

[88] Ibid., p. 58.

[89] K.P. Zachariah, E.T. Mathew and S. Irudaya Rajan, "Consequences of Migration: Socio-Economic and Demographic Dimensions," in K.C. Zachariah, K.P. Kanna and S. Irudaya Rajan (eds), *Kerala's Gulf Connection* (Thiruvananthapuram: Centre for Development Studies, 2002).

[90] Azeez and Begum, "Gulf Migration," p. 59.

lating prices of construction materials. The general cost of living inside Kerala is thus considerably higher than it might otherwise be, had lucrative jobs in the Gulf never existed.

More broadly, India's sustained growth has become bound up with developments in the Gulf. Harsh Pant puts the matter succinctly: "As a group, the GCC is India's second largest trading partner. It is the largest single origin of imports into India and the second largest destination for exports from India."[91] The total value of goods exported from India to Saudi Arabia soared 600 percent from 2000 to 2008.[92] In addition, the Arab Gulf states have become major destinations for Indian foreign direct investment, involving a wide range of ventures in "software development services, engineering services, tourism, readymade garments, chemical products, agricultural and allied services."[93] Furthermore, officials in New Delhi have been actively courting GCC governments to provide the $500–600 billion necessary to upgrade India's crumbling infrastructure.[94]

Hydrocarbon imports from the Gulf are only marginally less crucial to India's economic expansion than remittances, trade and investments. Again Pant puts the point most cogently: "Burgeoning population, coupled with rapid economic growth and industrialization[,] has propelled India into becoming the sixth largest energy consumer in the world, with the prospect of emerging as the fourth largest consumer in the next 4–5 years. Energy," he concludes "is clearly the driving force in Gulf-India relations."[95] GCC producers supply 65–70 percent of India's petroleum imports, with Iran contributing another 8 percent and Qatar acting as "India's exclusive supplier of natural gas" until a five-year contract to purchase Iranian natural gas begins to take effect.[96] Iran also supplies 15 percent of India's oil imports, although recurrent economic sanctions threaten to interrupt this particular energy stream.[97] India's

[91] Harsh Pant, "Looking Beyond Tehran: India's Rising Stakes in the Gulf," in Gulf Research Center, *India's Growing Role*, p. 46.

[92] *Middle East Economic Digest*, March 26–April 1, 2010.

[93] Pradhan, "India's Economic and Political Presence," p. 28.

[94] Dietmar Rothermund, *India: The Rise of an Asian Giant* (New Haven, CT: Yale University Press, 2008), Chapter 11; Pant, "Looking Beyond Tehran," p. 47; *New Indian Express* (Chennai), April 30, 2008.

[95] Pant, "Looking Beyond Tehran," p. 47.

[96] Ibid., p. 48; N. Janardhan, "What Oils the Wheels of GCC-Indian Cooperation?" *Daily Star* (Beirut), August 12, 2005; *Financial Times*, May 18, 2010.

[97] *Gulf Times*, January 6, 2011; Uddipan Mukherjee, *The Oil Payments: New Twist in*

growing vulnerability to disruptions in the flow of hydrocarbons from the Gulf no doubt explains the Indian navy's increasing activism in the waters of the Arabian Sea.[98]

Conclusion

Writing in the spring of 1986, A.A. Kubursi observed that the influence of the Persian Gulf states in the international economy appeared to be waning, due to their over-reliance on hydrocarbon production and evident lack of success in diversifying domestic industry. Consequently, "the tables have now been turned. GCC countries are more dependent on the West for food, technology, capital goods, and markets for oil and petrochemicals than the West is dependent on Gulf oil, dollars, and markets." Only if the Arab states of the Gulf managed to forge alliances with the larger Arab states, perhaps under the auspices of the Arab League, might the GCC countries gain the capacity to protect and further their strategic interests.[99]

Things look very different twenty-five years later. Persian Gulf states continue to occupy a pivotal position in the global oil and gas order and the revenues that governments in the region derive from hydrocarbon exports now play a major role in shaping trends on world stock markets, while at the same time providing desperately-needed investment capital to the rest of the Arab world. Regional manufacturing has moved into lucrative products that enjoy burgeoning markets overseas. Meanwhile, remittances paid to workers from South and Southeast Asia provide income and savings to hundreds of thousands of families whose members can find few if any alternative employment opportunities. The GCC has won an active voice among the world's economic powers, thanks to Saudi Arabia's membership in the Group of Twenty. Finally, the GCC states and the Islamic Republic of Iran have carved

---

India-Iran Relations, Institute of Peace and Conflict Studies, New Delhi, January 13, 2011; Harsh V. Pant, "India's Relations with Iran: Much Ado about Nothing," *The Washington Quarterly* Vol. 34, No. 1 (Winter 2011), p. 63.

[98] Pant, "India's Relations with Iran," p. 68; Ed Blanche, "Looking East, Indian Naval Power Grows in the Arabian Sea," *Daily Star* (Beirut), January 24, 2004; David Scott, "Strategic Imperatives of India as an Emerging Player in Pacific Asia," *International Studies* Vol. 44, No. 2 (April–June 2007); Walter C. Ladwig, "Delhi's Pacific Ambition," *Asian Security* Vol. 5, No. 2 (2009).

[99] Kubursi, "Oil, Influence, and Development," p. 381.

out key positions in the commercial and industrial sectors of Asia's two most dynamic economies—the People's Republic of China and India. The region's long-standing connections to Europe and North America remain in place, but it is expanding ties to these industrial and financial powerhouses that indicate most clearly the waxing influence of the Gulf in the contemporary international economy.

Invaluable research assistance was provided for this chapter by Patricia Baker, Suzan Boulad, Sahar Momand, and especially Nicole Beckerman.

3

The Political Economy of Rentierism in the Persian Gulf

Mehran Kamrava

Across the Persian Gulf region, state-building processes began in earnest at a time of scarce resources and relative lack of autonomy of social actors with aspirations of acquiring political power. State-building involved two simultaneous processes. On the one hand, it included the creation of various institutions of the state through which political power could be wielded and perpetuated. These institutions included, among others, the army and the internal security forces, the bureaucracy, and commanding heights of power such as the position of chief executive. At the same time as these institutions were being created, and often through these very institutions, a second process of state-building was unfolding. In most, but not all, places this process involved the incorporation of one or more groups of social actors into the state, who in turn would become key stakeholders in the maintenance of the evolving political system. These social actors often included resource-rich elites—usually merchants and wealthy industrialists, but on rare occasions also landlords—or the growing masses of the middle classes who became the primary occupants of the countless civil service positions that were becoming available in the burgeoning state bureaucracy.

In consolidating their power, emerging state actors relied on the incorporation of these key stakeholders into the orbit of the state. By the time oil revenues started flowing into the coffers of the state at unprecedented levels, in some cases decades after patterns of state-society interactions had already been forged, political elites were already firmly in control of state resources. The additional rent revenues derived from oil enabled state actors to deepen their incorporation of the different social groups into the orbit of the state, and to devise new ways in which this incorporation took shape.

Not all states, alas, were equally endowed with oil in relation to their population base or geographic size. Iran and Iraq might have had a lot of oil, but they had millions more mouths to feed and salaries to pay, whereas most of the states of the lower Persian Gulf had far smaller populations and much smaller landmasses to worry about. Differences in size—in geography and demography as well as in oil deposits—reinforced differences in pre-existing and emerging patterns of state-society relations. By necessity, as bonds developed between the state on the one hand, and the social groups it intended to incorporate on the other, the rentier arrangements that took hold in Iran and Iraq became more indirect, more fragile, and less solid. Across the Arabian Peninsula, however, overlaid on historical patterns of "sheikhly rule,"[1] rentier arrangements took far more direct forms by strengthening the pre-existing bonds of patronage and clientelism between rulers and the ruled, and creating new linkages between them.

This chapter calls for a more nuanced conception of rentierism and posits three main points. First, despite fluctuations in revenue sources and significant differences in income levels and sources, rentier political economies remain firmly established across the Persian Gulf, encompassing the six states of the Gulf Cooperation Council as well as Iran and Iraq. These states have little in common in terms of history, institutional make-up, and ideological dispositions and legitimacy. But they do have in common rentier political economies, albeit to varying degrees. Second, the chapter argues that emerging rentier dynamics were superimposed on evolving institutional arrangements as state-building processes were already underway. The overlaying of the two has influenced the nature and manner in which the states in question have subsequently evolved. The third argument revolves around state autonomy. Even in cases where rent-reliant states enjoy tremendous wealth, rentier arrangements

---

[1] James Onley and Sulayman Khalaf, "Shaikhly Authority in the Pre-Oil Gulf: An Historical-Anthropological Study," *History and Anthropology* Vol. 17, No. 3 (September 2006), pp. 189–208.

tend to place both the states and their social beneficiaries in positions of mutual dependence on one another, curbing the autonomy of both. That pervasive rentierism tends to inhibit social autonomy is well known. What is important to note is that it also inhibits the autonomy of the state.

Rentier arrangements shape and inform—and in turn restrict—the policy choices and options open to state elites. The starting points of analysis here are the political arrangements and institutions through which Persian Gulf states maintain themselves in power and on which rentier arrangements were later superimposed. Rentierism does not create political arrangements from scratch, especially at earlier stages in the state-building process. It reinforces preexisting arrangements, enabling authoritarian political establishments to enhance their coercive capacities, and deepen their hold on power. It facilitates the development of new *modus operandi* and institutions that enable the state to more effectively maintain its authoritarian hold on power, placate potential opponents, share its largesse with key social allies, and mold social institutions in ways it prefers.

The relationship is a mutually reinforcing one. Once rentier arrangements take hold, they also exert an important influence on the structure of state institutions and the choices open to state actors. As Terry Lynn Karl maintains, "dependence on a particular export commodity shapes not only social classes and regime types...but also the very institutions of the state, the framework for decision-making, and the decision calculus of policymakers."[2] In the process, a relationship of mutual dependence develops between the state and the social groups that become the prime beneficiaries of rentier arrangements, tying the two together in ways neither anticipated.

So far, the literature on rentierism has largely focused on two broad questions: whether or not rentierism impedes democracy, and whether a decline in rent revenues causes political instability in rentier states.[3] Variations within

---

[2] Terry Lynn Karl, *The Paradox of Plenty: Oil Booms and Petro-States* (Berkeley, CA: University of California Press, 1997), p. 7.

[3] For a small sampling of the rich and diverse literature on rentierism see Hazem Beblawi, "The Rentier State in the Arab World," in Giacomo Luciani (ed.), *The Arab State* (Berkeley, CA: University of California Press, 1990), pp. 85–98; Kiren Aziz Chaudhry, *The Price of Wealth: Economies and Institutions in the Middle East* (Ithaca, NY: Cornell University Press, 1997); Michael Herb, "No Taxation Without Representation? Rents, Development, and Democracy," *Comparative Politics* Vol. 37, No. 3 (April 2005), pp. 297–316; Ivar Kolstad and Arne Wiig, "It's the Rent Stupid: The Political Economy of the Resource Curse," *Energy Policy* Vol. 37, No. 12 (2009),

rentierism and the consequences of such variations on a number of important developments, such as class formation, patterns of institutional growth and state building, and political instability, have generally been overlooked in the literature.[4] Also, most studies of rentierism have either been case specific (focusing usually on Saudi Arabia) or have looked at a large n, or else have compared two cases.

This chapter presents a meso-level comparative study of the phenomenon across the Persian Gulf. In rentier states, the chapter argues, the political outcomes of fiscal crises are not uniform, and the institutional responses of states to rent-related developments, such as sudden revenue declines, are likely to vary considerably between states with different sources of legitimacy. The types of state political responses to rent-related economic crises are likely to depend on one or more developments, such as the depth and extent to which rentier arrangements inform the *modus operandi* of the state; the direct or indirect ways in which state revenues are funneled to society; the exact nature of the groups in society that are beholden to the state through rentier arrangements (for example merchants or the salaried middle classes); and independent variables such as national cleavages or pre-existing tensions that predate the emergence of the rent-allocating states. Also important to consider are the ways in which rent channels have evolved in different states, along with the evolution of rentier arrangements, and the differing consequences they are likely to have on politics.

Rentierism in the Persian Gulf

Despite the diversity of state types found in the Persian Gulf basin, the one constant in the region is the rentier state. Differences in patterns of political

---

pp. 5317–25; Gerd Nonneman, "Rentiers and Autocrats, Monarchs and Democrats, State and Society: The Middle East Between Globalization, Human 'Agency', and Europe," *International Affairs* Vol. 77, No. 1 (2001), pp. 141–62; Gwenn Okruhlik, "Rentier Wealth, Unruly Law, and the Rise of Opposition: The Political Economy of Oil States," *Comparative Politics* Vol. 39, No. 3 (April 1999), pp. 295–315; Michael Ross, "Does Oil Hinder Democracy?" *World Politics* Vol. 53 (April 2001), pp. 325–61; and Richard Snyder and Ravi Bhavnani, "Diamonds, Blood, and Taxes: A Revenue-Centered Framework for Explaining Political Order," *Journal of Conflict Resolution* Vol. 49, No. 4 (August 2005), pp. 563–97.

[4] A notable exception is Michael Herb's "A Nation of Bureaucrats: Political Participation and Economic Diversification in Kuwait and the United Arab Emirates," *International Journal of Middle East Studies* Vol. 41, No. 3 (2009), pp. 375–95.

evolution and state-building notwithstanding, these rentier states all share a number of fundamental similarities in their domestic political economies. Most fundamentally, all earn relatively high profits from economic activities that do not require proportionately high levels of productivity. This, as will be argued presently, is the essence of rentierism. What differs from one case to another is the extent of the states' reliance on rentier arrangements to govern, the nature and types of the classes whose development and growth these states are able to foster, and the nature of the relationships that the states are in turn able to create and maintain with these classes over time.

Let us begin with a definition of rentierism. Rents are generally defined as exports earned or income derived from value added products or services, or, more commonly, from a gift of nature—hydrocarbons being the most lucrative, courtesy of international demand.[5] Hence, although not derived from the productive sectors of the domestic economy or from taxes, institutional structures emerge that encourage rent-seeking behavior, and, by doing so, significantly shape the overall nature and profile of the domestic political economy. The resultant rentier state is one dependent largely on extractive resource rents, taxes and royalties paid by multinational corporations, and on profits derived from its equity stakes in international investments.[6] In rentier states, the amount and accessibility of rent revenues do not depend on the state's mediation with domestic private actors, but are instead derived from the availability of natural resources, the proportion of rents to the population, bargains with foreign firms, and returns on international investments. For rentier states, in other words, "their economic power and ultimately their political authority rest on their dual capacity to extract rents externally from the global environment and subsequently to distribute these rents internally."[7]

Similarly, rentierism shapes "prevailing notions of property rights, the relative powers of interest groups and organizations, and the role and character of the state vis-à-vis the market."[8] This has important consequences for the ways that states draw on their main source or sources of revenue—in the form of

---

[5] Kenneth Omeje, "Extractive Economies and Conflicts in the Global South: Re-Engaging Rentier Theory and Politics," in Kenneth Omeje (ed.), *Extractive Economies and Conflicts in the Global South: Multi-Regional Perspectives on Rentier Politics* (Burlington, VT: Ashgate, 2008), p. 5. Along similar lines, economists define "rent" as income derived from demand-determined prices above the minimum price required to call forth a given supply of a natural resource such as land, oil, or diamonds.

[6] Ibid.

[7] Karl, *The Paradox of Plenty*, p. 49.

[8] Ibid., p. 7.

taxes or rents from a commodity—and how they in turn distribute them to the population. Heavy reliance on rent revenues instead of taxes tends to insulate states from societal demands for political accountability and responsiveness.[9] Nevertheless, as Steffan Hertog has demonstrated, state autonomy derived from rent is not static and can change over time, and "different parts of [the rentier state] can follow different trajectories, some developmental, some regressive."[10] The rentier states' ability to placate societal pressures and maintain its autonomy from society may be eroded over time, exposing its vulnerabilities to certain groups.

At the same time, political choices cannot be relegated to the back seat. In Saudi Arabia, for example, both Hertog and Okruhlik have shown that elite decisions are enormously important in the shaping of the state and that the rentier framework needs to take into account "more explicit linkages between state strategies of expenditure and the political consequences for particular social groups."[11]

With the exception of Iran, all states of the Persian Gulf rely overwhelmingly on the export and sales of hydrocarbons as the primary mainstays of their economies (Figure 3.1). Subject to comprehensive international sanctions that have become more rigorous over the last few years, since the mid-2000s Iran has found it increasingly difficult to find international markets for its oil and gas products.[12] For the rest of the region, however—minus Iraq, for

---

[9] The debate concerning the causal connection between rentierism and democracy is rich and beyond the scope of this chapter. Michael Ross, for example, argues that rentierism impedes democracy and makes the following argument: "governments that fund themselves through oil and have larger budgets are likely to be authoritarian; governments that fund themselves through taxes and are relatively small are more likely to become democratic." Michael Ross, "Does Oil Hinder Democracy?" p. 335. Michael Herb finds the relationship more nuanced. "While the possibility that rentierism harms democracy cannot be dismissed," he argues, "it is clear that it has a smaller substantive impact than region, Muslim share of the population, and income." Michael Herb, "No Representation without Taxation?" p. 310.

[10] Steffan Hertog, "Shaping the Saudi State: Human Agency's Shifting Role in Rentier-State Formation," *International Journal of Middle East Studies* Vol. 39 (2007), p. 541.

[11] Steffan Hertog, *Princes, Brokers, and Bureaucrats: Oil and the State in Saudi Arabia* (Ithaca, NY: Cornell University Press, 2010); Gwenn Okruhlik, "Rentier Wealth, Unruly Law, and the Rise of Opposition: The Political Economy of Oil States," Comparative Politics Vol. 39, No. 3 (April 1999), p. 295.

[12] "Sanctions Begin to Bite Iran's Economy," *The Economist*, October 9, 2010, p. 67.

Figure 3.1: Oil & Gas as a Percentage of Total State Revenue.

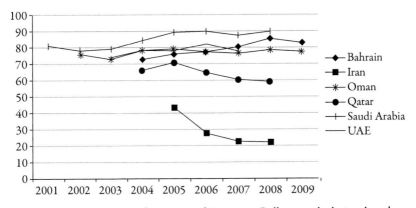

Source: Central Bank Annual Reports and Economic Bulletins; calculations based on Central Bank reports.

which data are not available—hydrocarbon sales account for an average 70 percent of total state revenues.[13] Inversely, direct and indirect forms of taxation and other socially-extracted revenues, such as licensing fees and fines, remain exceedingly low across the region, again with the exception of Iran (Figure 3.2).

As these figures indicate, Iran is clearly an outlier case, with declining oil revenues being steadily replaced by increasing reliance on taxation. Nevertheless, overall levels of taxation in Iran remain comparatively low. Whereas the total amount of taxes collected in Iran has seen a steady increase since 2003–04, as a percentage of the gross domestic product (figure 3.3) the tax burden in Iran, while the highest in the region at 7.5 percent in 2008, remains exceedingly low by international standards. In the four countries of the Persian Gulf for which tax data are available, including Iran, the tax burden hovers at no more than 5 percent, whereas the unweighted average in the Organization for Economic Cooperation and Development (OECD) is around 35 percent (figure 3.3).

[13] Persian Gulf average excludes Iraq and is based on central bank figures, except for Kuwait. Kuwait data come from Rabobank country risk research report, http://overons.rabobank.com/content/images/Kuwait200911_tcm64–75091.pdf (accessed October 22, 2010).

Figure 3.2: Taxes, Fees, & Fines as a Percentage of Total State Revenue.

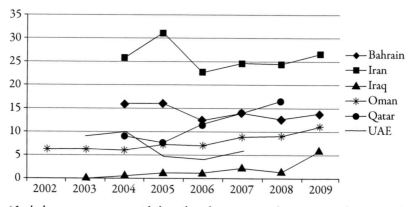

* Includes taxes on state-provided goods and services, penalties, customs, duties, "social contributions."
Source: Central Bank Annual Reports and Economic Bulletins; calculations based on CB reports.

Figure 3.3: Tax Burden in the Persian Gulf vs. the OECD.

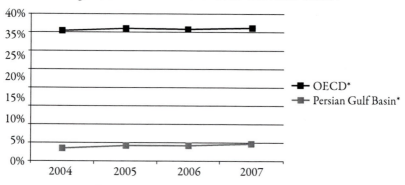

* unweighted average of OECD member countries.
† average for Bahrain, Iran, Oman, Qatar.
Source: OECD.Stat Extracts; Central Bank Annual and Economic Reports; calculations.

The comparatively low percentage of state revenues derived from hydrocarbons, and relatively heavier reliance on taxation, raise the question of whether Iran, especially since the early 2000s, can still be classified as a rentier state. The Islamic Republic may have had increasing difficulty in recent years finding international buyers for its hydrocarbons, but, as figure 3.4 indicates, it still manages to raise significant capital through the sale of other assets in the domestic and international markets. Thus it still remains a rentier state. The other Persian Gulf country with equally substantial capital revenues, Qatar, raises them primarily through returns on domestic and especially international investments.

Rentierism and state evolution

Across the Persian Gulf, different patterns of state incorporation of various social classes emerged. Broadly, the emergence of contemporary states in the Persian Gulf has followed one of two patterns. In Iran and Iraq, where formal instruments of political power have existed for centuries in one form or another, state institutions have evolved, or mutated, through and often because of the vicissitudes of history. Even through the ravages of tectonic disruptions brought on by wars and revolutions, today's Iranian and Iraqi state institutions are as much products of path dependency as they are of agency

Figure 3.4: Capital Revenues as a Percentage of Total Revenue.

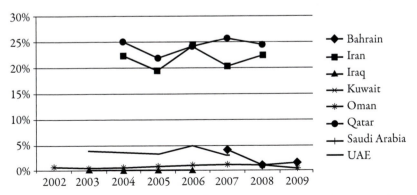

Source: Central Bank Annual Reports and Economic Bulletins, calculations based on Central Bank reports.

and elite decisions.[14] Throughout the Arabian Peninsula, however, the inflexible manner of Ottoman administration and its inability to control bitterly divided tribes, coupled with its hasty retreat back to Istanbul, left the territories with few if any formal instruments of power.[15] This exigency was left unredressed during British colonial hegemony.[16]

With the swift arrival of independence in the 1960s to 1970–71, state-building had to occur almost overnight, and institutions had to be crafted and populated to facilitate the running of the ostensibly independent and modern state. At least initially, bureaucratic proliferation in the Arabian Peninsula was less a product of path dependency than elite decision-making. And the mismatch between human resources capital on the one side, and financial resources and ambitions on the other, necessitated the importation of armies of expatriate workers, foreign advisors, and entire industries under the auspices of import-substitution industrialization, leading to the emergence of "islands of efficiency" within often "flabby" bureaucracies.[17] In Iran and Iraq, alongside bureaucratic mechanisms designed specifically to distribute rent-generated wealth, rentierism had to adapt itself to the existing institutions of the state. In the Arabian Peninsula, the connections between emerging state institutions and rent wealth were more direct and immediate, enabling ruling families to expand and strengthen the clientelist ties on which they relied in more direct and targeted fashions.

In Iran, beginning in the 1960s the pre-revolutionary state embarked on concerted efforts to bring various popular strata of society into its orbit of supporters, a campaign that started in earnest in 1963 and grew into what the state popularly billed as the White Revolution. This so-called "revolution of the Shah and the people" was initially meant to strengthen the state's ties to the peasantry, and to neutralize the potential for a communist-inspired revolution by turning the countryside into the regime's base of support.[18] As the state expanded its bureaucratic network and its developmental agendas throughout the 1960s, and as the mobilizational promises of the White Revo-

---

[14] Mehran Kamrava, "Preserving Non-Democracies: Leaders and Institutions in the Middle East," *Middle Eastern Studies* Vol. 46, No. 2 (March 2010), pp. 251–2.

[15] Fredrik F. Anscombe, *The Ottoman Gulf: The Creation of Kuwait, Saudi Arabia, and Qatar* (New York: Columbia University Press, 1997), pp. 169–72.

[16] Zahlan, *The Making of the Modern Gulf States*, p. 15.

[17] Hertog, *Princes, Brokers, and Bureaucrats*, pp. 28–9.

[18] Ervand Abrahamian, "The Structural Causes of the Iranian Revolution," *MERIP Reports* No. 87 (May 1980), p. 23.

lution failed to yield concrete results, the state turned its attention to the urban middle classes, in 1975 establishing an all-encompassing state party, the Rastakhiz, in which membership was compulsory for state employees. Again, the assumption was that the Rastakhiz would satisfy the middle classes' thirst for political participation by providing them with an outlet for political expression and participation while keeping intact their ties to the state.[19] But the farcical nature of the party did not take long to manifest itself, and before long it was viewed as another arm of an ever-expansive but ineffective state.[20] In the meanwhile, buoyed by the massive infusion of oil revenues in the aftermath of the 1973 Arab oil boycott of the West, the state expedited the expansion of its administrative and bureaucratic networks, hiring civil servants in droves, and compensated for the failures of its White Revolution and the Rastakhiz by expanding its supposedly omnipresent security and police agencies. By the late 1970s, the Iranian state had emerged as a full-blown neo-patrimonial dictatorship.[21]

That the bonds tying the social classes to the Iranian state were tenuous became dramatically obvious beginning in 1977, when a mass-based revolution, this one of the people against the Shah, swept the regime aside and ushered in a new political order in 1979. The political system that succeeded the monarchy, both early in its life and today, has been only marginally more successful in using its populism to keep the popular classes, or any one consistent subgroup within them, tied to itself. Established in the aftermath of the revolution, the Islamic Republic Party was disbanded by Ayatollah Khomeini out of fear that it had become too fractious an organization.[22] The streets, instead, soon became the primary venue for political mobilization, and choreographed displays of mass loyalty to the cause of the revolution and devotion to its leaders became so common as to lose meaning. The primary institutional link between the state and social actors remained none other than the bureaucracy, which by now had been expanded and complemented to include an array of state-owned enterprises and foundations (*bonyads*) that

---

[19] Parvin Merat Amini, "A Single Party State in Iran, 1975–78: The Rastakhiz Party: The Final Attempt by the Shah to Consolidate His Political Base," *Middle Eastern Studies* Vol. 38, No. 1 (January 2002), pp. 131–2.

[20] Ibid., p. 163.

[21] Said Amir Arjomand, *The Turban for the Crown: The Islamic Revolution in Iran* (Oxford: Oxford University Press, 1988), p. 73.

[22] Maziar Behrooz, "Factionalism in Iran Under Khomeini," *Middle Eastern Studies* Vol. 27, No. 4 (October 1991), p. 597.

were meant to deliver on the revolution's many promises to the deprived and the downtrodden.[23]

Throughout, what kept the Iranian state functioning, and enabled it to employ and cater to the urban middle classes, were the rent revenues accrued from oil exports. In fact, once the "imposed war" with Iraq was over in 1988, and the revolution's founder had passed away from the scene in 1989, the state bureaucracy and continued repression remained as the only viable substitutes for receding populism. Ironically, the long-term effects of the revolution featured little or no substantive changes to the means of connection and interaction between the state and the larger social classes, while the bureaucracy still remained as one of the only viable institutional links between the two.[24] The fragility of these bonds once again came to the surface in 2009, when in the aftermath of a presidential election widely believed to have been stolen mass demonstrations reminiscent of the late 1970s rocked Tehran and the country's other cities.

Broadly similar patterns of state-society interactions, albeit with a different flavor and under markedly different political circumstances, unfolded next door in Iraq. For a few good years after its appearance in the country in the late 1940s and the 1950s, the Iraqi Ba'ath Party did serve as more of a popular institution for the expression of political aspirations.[25] But its steady transformation into the principal organ of the state throughout the 1970s, and a concomitant reliance on the authoritarian impulse of the state by its emerging leaders, eroded any meaningful potential that might have existed for the emergence of electoral or even ideological legitimacy for the state. The state ruled through fear, maintained by a plethora of "institutions of violence" and led by a supposedly larger-than-life Saddam Hussein.[26] Similarly to Iran, by the late 1970s the Iraqi state's "ruling bargain" revolved primarily around a combination of guaranteed state employment, coercion and fear of the omnipotent Mukhaberat, and whipped-up nationalist sentiments.[27] The 1980–88 war with

---

[23] Ali A. Saeidi, "The Accountability of Para-Governmental Organizations (*bonyads*): The Case of Iranian Foundations," *Iranian Studies* Vol. 37, No. 3 (September 2004), p. 480.

[24] Arjomand, *The Turban for the Crown*, pp. 173–4.

[25] Kanan Makiya, *Republic of Fear: The Politics of Modern Iraq* (Berkeley, CA: University of California Press, 1998), p. 236.

[26] Ibid., p. 38.

[27] For more on "ruling bargains" in the Middle East see Mehran Kamrava, *The Modern Middle East: A Political History Since the Second World War*, 2nd edition (Berkeley, CA: University of California Press, 2011), pp. 346–7.

Iran did provide some relief insofar as demands for political accountability were concerned, but the state strained under the weight of prosecuting the war against an unrelenting foe, checking the anti-centralist aspirations of the Kurds and the Shi'a, and keeping the domestic economy immune from the effects of the war.[28] Rent revenues, to which massive infusions of direct foreign cash assistance were added in the 1980s—estimated at $75 billion from the West and the Gulf states[29]—became the primary lifeline of the state. Beginning in the early 1990s, and especially after its disastrous invasion of and ejection from Kuwait in 1990–91, with international isolation and comprehensive sanctions in full force, all the state could do was to keep the civil service and its expansive coercive machinery going in the hope of fending off implosion. Rent revenues might have declined to a nadir, but they remained the only sustenance keeping the wounded state alive.

For both Iran and Iraq, as the number and percentage of state employees expanded beginning in the 1950s and the 1960s, the state's dependence on maintaining the civil service employed and therefore pliant also increased proportionately. According to one estimate, the percentage of Iran's public sector employees as a total of the urban work force shot up from one third in 1976 to one half in 1986.[30] As the following section will demonstrate, that proportion has continued to grow since. This has resulted in a steady deepening of the rentier trap, whereby the state has to keep the expansive civil service going while providing an increasing array of services to compensate for its lack of electoral or ideological legitimacy. Political institutionalization occurs under the auspices of a bloated bureaucracy whose innate inefficiency is only of secondary importance as compared to its safety-valve function as a primary provider of guaranteed employment and what state services exist. The revenues needed to keep the state machinery going could not possibly come from taxes or fees even if the state could politically afford to levy them in meaningful degrees. On the contrary, they are often kept to a bare minimum. The revenues come instead from hydrocarbon exports and take the form of rents. The state needs rents to provide employment and services, and needs to pro-

---

[28] Gareth Stansfield, *Iraq* (London: Polity, 2007), pp. 118–20.

[29] The CIA's 2004 *Iraq Survey Group Final Report* estimates financial assistance from Western creditors at $35 to $45 billion and an additional $30–$40 billion from Saudi Arabia, Kuwait, and the United Arab Emirates during the 1980s (https://www.cia.gov/library/reports/general-reports-1/iraq_wmd_2004/index.html).

[30] Saeidi, "The Accountability of Para-Governmental Organizations," p. 487.

vide employment and service in order to survive. It is, simply put, fully trapped in its own web.

A generally similar relationship of dependence between the state and rent revenues developed in the countries of the Arabian Peninsula. But here vast differences in scale—of revenues in proportion to people—and emerging patterns of ruler-ruled ties combined to fundamentally change the dynamics involved. In all cases the key factor was, and remains, the incorporation of comparatively powerful social actors into the orbit of the state. In Saudi Arabia, Heretog has shown that "the way the state grew was an outcome largely of royal elite decisions unconstrained by larger political forces," facilitated largely by a society that was deeply fragmented geographically and the absence of any experience of national politics or formal mechanisms for political participation.[31] Elsewhere in the Peninsula, emerging ruling families found it necessary to forge strategic alliances with other prominent families, through marriages and business relations, and with foreign patrons, in order to secure initially tenuous holds on power. With Britain as the overall overseer and guarantor of the region's developing diplomatic map and domestic political orders, ruling families set out to create local alliances of their own that appeased and placated potential rival claimants and reinforced their own status of preeminence.[32] Rent revenues began flowing into the coffers of the Peninsula states in the late 1950s and the early 1960s, and by 1971 when independence finally came to the Peninsula's nine smaller emirates, seven of which coalesced into one country, an embryonic bureaucracy was beginning to deliver state services and provide middle class employment. But unprecedented increases in oil revenues beginning in the 1970s, in the face of what remained comparatively very small populations, freed the state from the need to keep expanding the civil service as a tool for catering to middle class demands. Instead, the state continued to cement its domestic alliances with awards of contracts and outright grants, encouraging the entrepreneurial classes to capitalize on opportunities presented by significant cash supplies to invest in real estate ventures and establish monopolies in imports.[33] What civil service jobs there were went initially to those urbanites left out of the private sector for one reason or

---

[31] Hertog, "Shaping the Saudi State," p. 542.
[32] Rosemarie Said Zahlan, *The Making of the Modern Gulf States: Kuwait, Bahrain, Qatar, the United Arab Emirates*, and Oman (London: Unwin Hyman, 1989), pp. 12–13.
[33] Chaudhry, *The Price of Wealth*, pp. 153–5.

another, or, especially beginning in the 1970s, to expatriates and imported workers from across the Arab world and south Asia.[34] Only in the early 2000s, when discrepancies in the percentage of foreign to domestic workers became too glaring, did there appear pressures across the region to start nationalizing the labor force.[35] So far, however, the results of labor nationalization schemes, often premised on unrealistic assumptions, have been highly uneven.[36]

In Iran and Iraq, the state struggles to keep up with the manifold economic and infrastructural needs and the ever-increasing demands of the urban population. Its principal solution for doing so has been the bureaucracy and the civil service, and, wherever possible, strategic concessions to social actors that can lend it support in times of need or at least stand aside in moments of crisis—Iran's bazaari merchant classes being a prime example.[37] There are far too many mouths to feed, too many jobs to create, too many salaries to pay, and too many roads and hospitals and schools to build for the revenues the state has at its disposal. The rent monies the state accrues go into enhancing its institutional capacity—that is, beefing up what is already a bloated bureaucracy—and then trickle down to society in the form of state employment and subsidies in housing and consumer goods. True to rentier form, the state does retain its role as the ultimate provider of goods and services thanks to rent revenues. But it does so indirectly, by channeling the rent through a maze of institutions and networks, and not always very successfully. Not surprisingly, it remains vulnerable to bouts of instability and political turmoil, many of which may not necessarily be economically rooted but can be due to exogenous shocks—say, a US invasion—or internal political upheavals, as in popular anger over a stolen election.

---

[34] Andrzej Kapiszewski, "Arab Versus Asian Migrant Workers in the GCC Countries." Paper presented at the United Nations Expert Group Meeting on International Migration and Development in the Arab Region, Beirut, May 15–17, 2006, p. 6.

[35] Ingo Forstenlechner and Emilie Rutledge, "Unemployment in the Gulf: Time to Update the 'Social Contract,'" *Middle East Policy* Vol. 27, No. 2 (Summer 2010), p. 40.

[36] In 1995, for example, the Central Bank of Oman issued a circular stipulating that by the year 2000, 75 percent of senior and middle management positions in commercial banks, 95 percent of clerical positions, and 100 percent of all other positions had to be held by Omani nationals. Onn Winckler, "Labor and Liberalization: The Decline of the GCC Rentier System," in Joshua Teitelbaum (ed.), *Political Liberalization in the Persian Gulf* (New York: Columbia University Press, 2009), p. 75.

[37] Arang Keshavarzian, *Bazaar and State in Iran: The Politics of the Tehran Market Place* (Cambridge: Cambridge University Press, 2009).

Seldom is there such a struggle within the Arabian Peninsula states, however. These states by and large do not have any difficulty providing necessary services for their citizen populations, and, in fact, they have invariably succeeded in establishing comprehensive, cradle-to-grave welfare systems that cater to most conceivable needs of their subjects.[38] The middle classes staff what bureaucracy there is, but they are assisted at every level, from secretaries and scribes to street cleaners, by an army of imported workers who are often segregated and at times even sequestered from the rest of the population.[39] From their early beginnings, bureaucracies in the Arabian Peninsula have served as important mechanisms for rewarding loyalty and perpetuating clientelist networks, especially insofar as commoners are concerned.[40] The larger civil service also continues to serve as a primary network for the funneling of rent revenues to the urban middle classes in the form of state salaries. Nevertheless, to augment their income, many civil servants enter into private sector partnerships as well, often becoming involved in one or more small or medium-sized businesses.

At the same time, the dispersal of rent revenues from the top to the rest of society often occurs in more direct ways as well, sometimes in the form of land grants handed out by none other than the Amiri Diwan itself, as in the case of Qatar, and sometimes through agents and other interlocutors working for wealthy sheikhs and landlords. Since the distinction between the budget of the state and the purse of the ruling family is often blurred at best and nonexistent at worst, in the Arabian Peninsula it is existing patrimonial links that rentierism tends to permeate and reinforce, instead of the webs of administrative linkages that it helps solidify in Iran and Iraq.

There are, of course, notable differences within the Arabian Peninsula itself, and the seven states that comprise it differ markedly from one another in a number of respects.[41] With an estimated population of around 25 to 28 million people, and occupying by far the Peninsula's largest landmass, Saudi Arabia's administrative and bureaucratic resources are far more stretched than

---

[38] Christopher Davidson, *Abu Dhabi: Oil and Beyond* (New York: Columbia University Press, 2009), p. 128.

[39] Syed Ali, *Dubai: Gilded Cage* (New Haven, CT: Yale University Press, 2010), pp. 81–2.

[40] Hertog, "Shaping the Saudi State," p. 544.

[41] Given its distance from the Persian Gulf, Yemen is generally not considered to be a part of the region, and therefore none of the chapters in this volume deal with it in any direct way.

any of the region's other states. The Kingdom's economy has a number of inherent structural factors that perpetuate high rates of unemployment.[42] Intensified inequalities in the distribution of wealth have created pockets of poverty amid seas of opulence and conspicuous consumption.[43] At the same time, size and resources have necessitated less direct means of channeling rent revenues into the local economy than is possible in the smaller neighboring sheikhdoms. Nevertheless, at the macro-level, the Al Saud family has been able to leverage bureaucratic and royal largesse to create a system of "segmented clientelism"—"a heterogeneous system of formal and informal, rent-based clientelism in which vertical links dominate."[44] As "monopolistic distributors of rent" members of the Saudi ruling family have "kept their clients separate and avoided substantive delegation of policy powers to any collective."[45]

Greater wealth and much smaller populations have strengthened other similarly allocative states elsewhere in the Peninsula. In Abu Dhabi, for example, state allocations may take the form of direct transfers of wealth and free services, low-cost or even free housing, and employment and business advantages.[46] In Dubai, although the ruling Al Maktoums have not had direct access to oil revenues, state largesse often takes the form of "soft loans" for entrepreneurs, the free provision of utilities and services for nationals, and, more recently, state initiatives that have turned previously worthless land into highly valuable real estate, leading to the emergence of extremely wealthy landlords.[47] The "rentier elite" that has emerged as a result has been sustained through an

---

[42] Paul Rivlin, *Arab Economies in the Twenty-First Century* (Cambridge: Cambridge University Press, 2009), pp. 223–5.

[43] Daryl Champion, *The Paradoxical Kingdom: Saudi Arabia and the Momentum of Reform* (New York: Columbia University Press, 2003), p. 142.

[44] Hertog, *Princes, Brokers, and Bureaucrats*, p. 5.

[45] Ibid., p. 248. Hertog is careful to point out that this has had varied consequences for the Saudi bureaucracy, creating "islands of efficiency" amid oceans of bureaucratic inefficiency. "While Saudi royals have on many occasions used their fiscal authority to build personal fiefdoms or to employ veritable armies of idle bureaucratic clients," he argues, "on others they have used their resources to build efficient administrative bodies by purchasing international expertise and offering attractive career paths to ambitious nationals. If anything, large increments of oil have *increased* the menu of institutional options available to the elite, resulting in a state apparatus with a highly varied component" (original emphasis), p. 3.

[46] Davidson, *Abu Dhabi*, p. 128.

[47] Christopher Davidson, *Dubai: The Vulnerabilities of Success* (New York: Columbia University Press, 2008), pp. 149–50.

elaborate "patrimonial network" with the Al Maktoums at its core and surrounded by a host of prominent families.[48] In Qatar a similarly comprehensive cradle-to-grave welfare state provides citizens with free or low-cost services, land grants and generous loans, guaranteed employment in the civil service, favorable investment opportunities, and lucrative licensing and contract opportunities that reinforce the benevolence of the ruling Al Thanis through networks and direct ties to the ruling family.

Not surprisingly, individual variations notwithstanding, public sector employment as a total percentage of the economically active population remains comparatively high throughout the Persian Gulf. According to official figures, across the Persian Gulf on average only about 22 percent of the economically active population is employed in the public sector (Figure 3.5), compared to the 14 percentage average in the OECD.[49] But official statistics do not take into account two important sources of state-sponsored employment, namely employment in joint-venture companies and the many state-owned enterprises that nominally reside in the private sector, and state-mandated schemes and quotas in all Gulf Cooperation Council (GCC) states

Figure 3.5: Public Sector Employees as a Percentage of Economically Active Population.

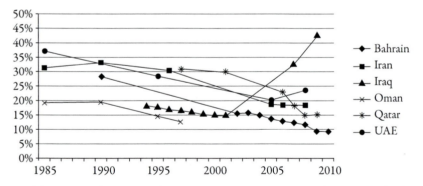

* Public Sector includes general government units, social security funds, and publicly owned enterprises.
Source: ILO LABORSTA Labour Statistics Database; Country Labor Force Surveys.

[48] Ibid., pp. 153–6.
[49] OECD average from, OECD, OECD *Government at a Glance*, 2009 (Paris: OECD, 2009).

aimed at nationalizing the labor force in the private sector. Michael Herb has gone so far as to estimate that as many as 90 percent of nationals in the lower Persian Gulf states are in the employ of the state.[50]

The distinction between the phenomenal growth in the wealth of the state and the purse of the ruling families has never been made quite clear. At the same time, through their control over the national income and ever-expanding instruments of power, the ruling families have enhanced their position of patronage, so much so that even in times of economic slowdown they are well positioned to withstand fluctuations in the inflow of rent revenues. In fact, in times of economic downturn, ruling family clients do not agitate against the ruling family, but are likely to look to it to help pull them out of recession.[51] Across the region, in fact, since the dawn of independence in 1971, there has been little or no correlation between bouts of economic downturn on the one hand and instances of domestically-generated political instability or state responses to perceived internal threats on the other. Nevertheless, societal responses to fiscal and political crises in rentierism have varied across the Peninsula and have been historically and institutionally contingent. In Kuwait, the economic slowdown of the 1980s and the political crisis of the early 1990s, precipitated by the Iraqi invasion and occupation, enabled the private sector to capitalize on state vulnerabilities to enhance its increasingly corporate political interests and platforms.[52] In Dubai, however, the economic meltdown of 2008 has not, so far at least, changed existing patterns of state-merchant or larger state-society relations in any precipitous ways.[53]

[50] Michael Herb, "A Nation of Bureaucrats: Political participation and Economic Diversification in Kuwait and the United Arab Emirates," *International Journal of Middle East Studies* Vol. 41, No. 3 (2009), pp. 375–95, p. 382.

[51] Sabri Zire Al-Saadi, "The Global Financial Crisis and the Hidden Crisis of the Oil-Rentier Economies: Back to Basics," *Strategic Insights*, Center for Contemporary Conflict at the Naval Postgraduate School, Monterey, CA, pp. 6–7.

[52] Pete Moore, "Rentier Fiscal Crisis and Regime Stability: Business-State Relations in the Gulf," *Studies in Comparative International Development* Vol. 37, No. 1 (Spring 2002), p. 44.

[53] Even before the 2008 meltdown, Hvidt noted that the relationship between Dubai's ruler and the business community was one of dependence: "The ruler is under constant threat that parts of the business elite might leave the country in order to seek better opportunities elsewhere. And as such the ruler is forced to accommodate the wishes of the new internationalized business class in policy formulation and execution." Martin Hvidt, "Governance in Dubai: The Emergence of Political and Economic Ties Between the Public and Private Sector," Center for Contemporary

Equally important is the exact location of state assets and their position in relation to the formal mechanisms of power. Precisely where state assets are located, the kinds of formal checks and balances to which they are subject, who has control and dispersal authority over them, and the formal and informal mechanisms through which wealth can be channeled down from them are all important predictors of the entrenched nature and effectiveness of rentier arrangements within the state. In most states of the Arabian Peninsula, despite the mystery surrounding them and the reversals they appear to have suffered in recent years, sovereign wealth funds are emerging as important investment vehicles, and one would assume important sources of revenues, for the state and more specifically the ruling family.[54] At the state level the institution of the Amiri Diwan, and after that the informal *majlis*es or *diwaniyya*s that perpetuate successive rungs of clientelism, serve to pass down rentier benefits in more direct ways to what ultimately amounts to a wider circle of social actors. In Iran, the two primary organs for the distribution of the state's wealth, the Islamic Revolutionary Guards Corps and the various *bonyad*s, face little formal oversight from other state agencies such as the parliament, cater to specific constituencies within the state, and continue to expand their base of domestic economic activity in the face of tightening international sanctions.[55] For those outside of the state bureaucracy, and outside certain circles and agencies within the bureaucracy, the benefits of rentierism remain mostly hidden and largely indirect.

Clientelism fosters a two-way relationship of mutual dependence. The client's dependence on the patron is obvious. What is often less obvious is the growing dependence of the patron on the services provided by the client in return and the overall pattern of the relationship that emerges between the two. This limits the range of options open and available to the patron regardless of the amounts of wealth involved or the precise nature of the channels through which that wealth is being distributed. Rentierism, in other words, tends to inhibit not just the independence of the social actors that have come

---

Middle East Studies, University of Southern Denmark, Working Paper No. 6 (June 2006), p. 15. For some of the financial fallouts of the meltdown see Eckart Woertz, "Implications of Dubai's Debt Troubles," *Gulf Research Center Reports*, December 2009.

[54] Brad Setser and Rachel Ziemba, *GCC Sovereign Wealth Funds: Reversal of Fortune*, Council on Foreign Relations Working Paper (New York: CFR, 2009).

[55] Saeidi, "The Accountability of Para-Governmental Organizations," p. 496.

to rely on it, but also that of the state that perpetuates it as its primary or ideal *modus operandi.*

Rentierism and state autonomy

The fact that states control large portions of the national economy, and can allocate inordinate wealth to their clients, has further entrenched and enhanced their stature as the guarantors of the prosperous domestic order. As evident from Figure 3.6, Arabian Peninsula countries have some of the highest per capita GDPs in the world, especially when the non-national population is taken out of the equation—Qatar's per national GDP is just below $450,000 a year and the United Arab Emirates' (UAE) is slightly less than $300,000 a year. In the meanwhile, armies of temporary, migrant workers do much of the required labor (Table 3.1).

Figure 3.6: GDP per Capita and per National in the Persian Gulf Basin 2008.

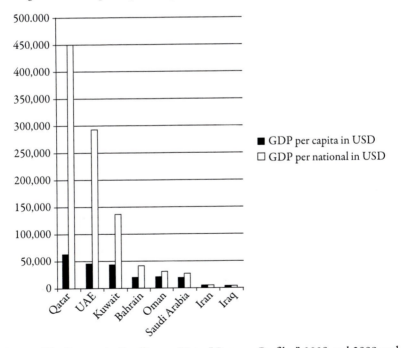

Source: The Economist Intelligence Unit, "Country Profiles," 2008 and 2009 and "Country Reports," April and May 2010.

Table 3.1: GDP and Population Measurements, 2008.

Country	GDP in USD, 2008	GDP per capita in USD, 2008	GDP per national in USD, 2008	Total Reported Population	Nationals	Non-nationals
Bahrain	21,902 million	19,911	41,526	1,100,000	527,433	572567
Iran	337,343 million	4,602	4,685	73,300,000	72,000,000	1300000
Iraq	84,719 million	2,815	2,815	30,100,000	N/A	
Kuwait	148,169 million	43,579	135,935	3,400,000	1,090,000	2310000
Oman	60,299 million	21,010	30,609	2,870,000	1,970,000	900000
Qatar	100,407 million	62,754	448,246	1,600,000	224,000	1376000
Saudi Arabia	475.1 billion	19,157	26,857	24,800,000	17,690,000	7110000
UAE	254,394 million	45,427	292,407	5,600,000	870,000	4730000

Source: The Economist Intelligence Unit, "Country Profiles," 2008 and 2009 and "Country Reports," April and May 2010.

In the Arabian Peninsula, the domestic political economy has been largely shaped by, and today revolves around, a benevolent ruling family, tied directly or indirectly to successive social clients whose wealth and social stature is derived largely from their position in the hierarchy of patronage linkages. Qatar and the UAE, for example, which are the richest of the lot, are governed by seemingly enlightened despots most eager, so far successfully so, to implement social experiments of unfathomable magnitude.[56] Turning the sea into artificial islands, and the barren desert into wellsprings of knowledge, requires more than just visionary leadership; it needs just as much a steady hand unimpeded by the nuisances of accountability and checks and balances.

The current Qatari and Emirati models, in fact, could not have been far from his mind when James C. Scott described the "high modernist state": "a particularly sweeping vision of how the benefits of technical and scientific progress might be applied—usually through the state—in every field of human activity."[57] "Working, representative institutions," Scott continues, would enable a "resistant society" to make its influence felt, and are thus vehemently resisted by high modernist states.[58] With its deeply authoritarian nature and its disdain for politics, "the temporal emphasis of high modernism is almost exclusively on the future."[59] This transformative vision of the future often manifests itself in the form of new, planned cities, of which Scott sees Brasilia as a prime example. Doha, Dubai, and Abu Dhabi, and the multiple planned cities within each—Education City and Dohaland in Doha, Knowledge Village and International City in Dubai, and Masdar City in Abu Dhabi being just some examples—resemble massive state-led efforts at fostering visions of an ideal, progress-oriented future.

---

[56] In articulating his vision of the country's future, the Qatar Emir writes: "Wise political leaders know the direction in which they would like their societies to develop, balancing the interests of present and future generations." *Qatar National Vision 2030* (Doha: General Secretariat for Development Planning, 2008), p. i.

[57] James C. Scott, *Seeing Like a State: How Certain Schemes to Improve the Human Condition Have Failed* (New Haven, CT: Yale University Press, 1998), p. 90. According to Scott, high modernist leaders, from Lenin and Trotsky to Julius Nyerere and the Shah of Iran, "envisioned a sweeping, rational engineering of all aspects of social life in order to improve the human condition" (p. 88). Along similar lines, "the high modern state began with extensive *prescriptions* for a new society, and it intended to impose them" (original emphasis), p. 90.

[58] Ibid., p. 102.

[59] Ibid., p. 95.

But by itself wealth does not necessarily enhance the state's autonomy. Particularly in Qatar and in the richer emirates of the UAE, the state has been able to use its massive wealth to enhance its instruments of control—through either patronage, or surveillance and coercion, or both—and has developed a variety of highly effective, often very polished regime maintenance mechanisms. The media, relying mostly on non-national reporters kept on short leashes, have been effectively muzzled.[60] Al Jazeera and its imitator Al Arabiya have become perfect examples of "modernizing" forms of state control of the media. In the meanwhile, that state has been able to significantly shrink private space. But, while related and synergetic, state capacity is not the same as state autonomy. Capacity is a state's ability to "implement official goals, especially over the actual or potential opposition of powerful social groups or in the face of recalcitrant socioeconomic circumstances."[61] Autonomy, however, revolves around a state's pursuit of "goals that are not simply reflective of the demands or interests of social groups, classes, or society."[62] Many of the GCC states, for example, have tried to push through reforms to the sponsorship (*kafala*) system regarding migrant labor, but their efforts have met with the resistance of local Chambers of Commerce and other semi-organized or informal business groups. Despite much discussion about the desirability of changing or altogether abandoning the system, therefore, the *kafala* system remains in force across the GCC.[63] Similarly, in both Qatar and the wealthier emirates of the UAE, notably Dubai and Abu Dhabi, state actors often have to temper their enthusiasm for rapid change and modernization with attention to the sensibilities of more conservative prominent families and even higher ranking bureaucrats. Wealthy Persian Gulf states may have tremendous capacity for control and transformative change. But by the very pursuit of those transformative goals, and in order to maintain the rentier arrangements that sustain them in power, they unintentionally sacrifice some autonomy.

---

[60] Daniel Byman and Jerold Green, "The Enigma of Political Stability in the Persian Gulf Monarchies," *Middle East Review of Internatiomal Affairs* Vol. 3, No. 3 (September 1999), p. 28.

[61] Theda Skocpol, "Bringing the State Back In: Strategies for Analysis on Current Research," in Peter Evans, Dietrich Reuschmeyer, and Theda Skocpol (eds), *Bringing the State Back In* (Cambridge: Cambridge University Press, 1985), p. 9.

[62] Ibid.

[63] See, for example, B. Izzak, "Labor Bill Gives New Rights for Workers," *Kuwait Times*, 30 January 2009. "Making the Case for Flexible Employment in GCC," *Oman Observer*, September 29, 2010; "UAE Leaps Forward," *Khaleej Times*, December 21, 2010.

Overall, in both the Persian Gulf's richer and poorer states, rentierism appears to have had a generally corrosive effect on state autonomy. The precise nature of the relationship between a state's wealth and its distributive capacities on the one side, and its autonomy from social actors and pressures on the other, needs to be contextualized. Again and again, critical examinations of rentierism have demonstrated that agency matters, and that elite decisions and historical and social developments need to be considered alongside path dependent institutional dynamics.[64] State autonomy—defined as state ability to articulate and execute policy preferences without being unduly restrained by social pressures—is contingent on a number of factors. There does not appear to be a consistently linear relationship between extensive rent wealth and state autonomy. If anything, the more reliant a state becomes on rent revenues, the more dependent it appears to become on groups with increasing corporate identities that can begin to act as its junior coalition partners.

The evolution of rentier arrangements across the Arabian Peninsula prompted merchants and other new entrants into the orbit of the state to develop a keener sense of their own corporate interests and a sharpening of their political instincts for furthering those interests. In Saudi Arabia, it was initially through the growth of the state bureaucracy that "more or less random networks of commoners within and around the administration" developed, albeit always under royal patronage, and provided opportunities for wealth accumulation and upward mobility.[65] In Kuwait, the "ruler-merchant pact" that has been in place since the early emergence of Al Sabah rule has in more recent years found expression in the two allies' common interests in curtailing the influence of the Islamist groups that are influential in the country's parliament.[66] In Qatar, unlike Kuwait, historically merchants have not been a corporate group in themselves, but much less powerful partners to the ruling elite.[67] In recent decades, however, they have emerged as key players in

[64] Gerd Nonneman, "Rentiers and Autocrats, Monarchs and Democrats, State and Society: The Middle East between Globalization, Human 'Agency', and Europe," *International Affairs* Vol. 77, No. 1 (2001), p. 145; Hertog, "Shaping the Saudi State"; Moore, "Rentier Fiscal Crisis and Regime Stability."

[65] Hertog, "Shaping the Saudi State," p. 548.

[66] For more on the ruler-merchant pact in Kuwait see Jill Crystal, *Oil and Politics in the Gulf: Rulers and Merchants in Kuwait and Qatar* (Cambridge: Cambridge University Press, 1990), pp. 7–9. On state-merchant common interests in curtailing Islamist groups in the country's parliament see Moore, "Rentier Fiscal Crisis and Regime Stability," pp. 46–8.

[67] Crystal, *Oil and Politics in the Gulf*, p. 9.

the state's frantic drive to create a modern infrastructure and to catch up with the rest of the region in terms of development. With the state—the ruling minority within the Al-Thani family—remaining as the senior partner and the ultimate patron, a number of other families have achieved great prominence thanks to lucrative contracts and import licenses (for example the Al Attiyahs, the Al Misnads, and the Al Kuwaris, and, of course, the Al Thanis more distant from the center of power). Importantly, many of the country's wealthiest merchant families are Shi'ite, some of them of Iranian descent—the Al Fardan, Jaidah, and Darwish families being prime examples.[68] With anywhere between 10 to 20 percent of the population composed of Shi'as, the ruling family is keenly aware of these families' clout and, also, of the importance of their implicit and explicit economic and political support. A similar though more pronounced situation has developed in Dubai, with the ruler dependent on international capital and investors, Emirati and otherwise, who can vote with their feet and seriously impact the Emirate's growth. Rentierism, even when underwritten by fabulous wealth, appears to produce a situation of co-dependence, one in which private capital and the state rely on one another for maintaining and perpetuating a mutually beneficial status quo.

Elsewhere in the Persian Gulf, in poorer rentier states, different dynamics have led to similarly dependent relationships with similar outcomes of curtailed state autonomy. In these states the networks of patronage tend to be less obvious, less direct, more diffuse, and often less lucrative. The economic and financial bonds that tie the different social actors to the state tend to be more fragile, and therefore more readily subject to strain in times of fiscal and/or economic difficulty. At times, in fact, rentierism appears to be masked and hidden. Here the state's autonomy is curtailed not because of the success of its rentier arrangements but actually for the opposite reason—because they are a work in progress. The state is constantly seeking to enhance and deepen its patronage ties to multiple social actors—the urban middle classes, the clergy, merchants and entrepreneurs, the intelligentsia, etc.—with success that is often spotty and easily reversed in times of crisis. Extreme examples in this category include Iran and (pre-2003) Iraq, where, given a chance, politically restive populations challenge the dominant political order despite their indirect or even direct financial dependence on it. Two recent examples illustrate

---

[68] Other prominent Qatari Shi'as include Ali bin Ali, the proprietor of the FMCG conglomerate, Abdulla Abdul Ghani, owner, among other interests, of a lucrative Toyota dealership, and the real estate baron Ahmad Hassan Bilal.

the limited autonomy of each state. Already bereft of legitimacy over accusations of election thievery, the government of President Ahmadinejad has been unable to impose a value added tax on the country's merchants and bazaaris without politically troublesome pushback.[69] Also, the Iraqi state, or whatever of an Iraqi state there is, was not able to muster up enough autonomy from bickering social actors to constitute a viable, functioning government for more than eight months in 2010.[70] For comparatively wealthier states, their curtailed autonomy often manifests itself in different ways. That the Saudi leadership has had to scale back its ambitions of pushing reforms through the system speaks of its limited autonomy in relation to powerful actors that it has not been able to placate.[71]

There is broad agreement among scholars that in the absence of institutionalized political accountability, "resource curse" tends to undermine long-term economic efficiency and increases resource misallocation in the economy.[72] But the relationship between resource endowment and the evolution of authoritarian versus democratic institutions needs to be contextualized. The precise nature of the relationship between the two depends in large measure on pre-existing circumstances and dynamics that predate the emergence of rentier arrangements. Undeniably, access to rent resources enables the authoritarian states of the Persian Gulf to stay in power. But in itself rentierism did not lead directly to authoritarianism, nor does its absence lead automatically to democracy. Rent wealth is but one of a number of tools at the disposal of

---

[69] Nazila Fathi, "Tax Delay Fails to Quell Iranian Protests," *New York Times*, October 13, 2010, p. 10.

[70] Leila Fadel, "Still Struggling to Form Government, Iraq Breaks World Record," *The Washington Post*, October 1, 2010, p. 11.

[71] For an analysis of the travails of the Saudi reforms see, Champion, *The Paradoxical Kingdom*, Chapter 4.

[72] See, for example, Mohsen Mehrara, "Reconsidering the Resource Curse in the Oil Exporting Countries," *Energy Policy* Vol. 37 (2009), pp. 1165–9; James Robinson, Ragnat Torvik, and Thierry Verdier, "Political Foundations of the Resource Curse," *Journal of Economic Development* Vol. 79 (2006), pp. 447–68; Peter Maas, *Crude World* (New York: Vintage, 2010); and, Michael L. Ross, "The Political Economy of the Resource Curse," *World Politics* Vol. 51, No. 2 (January 1999), pp. 297–322. Not everyone agrees, however. "Contrary to long-entrenched intuition," claim two economists, "'nonrenewables' can be progressively extended through exploration, technological progress, and investments in appropriate knowledge." Gavin Wright and Jesse Czelusta, "The Myth of the Resource Curse," *Challenge* Vol. 47, No. 2 (March/April 2004), p. 35.

the state as it responds to developments from within and beyond its borders and charts its evolutionary course. Sometimes it can be used effectively to blunt pressures for accountability and opening up, and sometimes it cannot.

In those instances in the Arabian Peninsula where endogenous or external dynamics did not place domestic political institutions or practices under stress—as in Saudi Arabia, Qatar, the emirates of the UAE, and Oman—rentier arrangements reinforced existing patterns of sheikhly rule, so much so that today the basic patterns of clientelism and patronage remain pretty much as they have been for decades with little or no modification, except for the ostensibly modern guises and institutions through which they are distributed (that is, employment in the bureaucracy and state-owned enterprises, licenses for new business enterprises, and the like). Wealth did in fact enable these states to buy political complaisance and to strengthen ruling bargains that rested on non-democratic premises from the very beginning. But wealth strengthened existing ruling bargains rather than creating bargains from scratch. Elsewhere in the Peninsula, in Bahrain and Kuwait, states developed institutional features designed to address stresses and crises that were not necessarily revenue-related. In both states, representative political institutions, such as elected parliaments, evolved in response to a combination of stresses that were both internal (sectarian tensions in Bahrain, "ruler-merchant pacts" and a vibrant class of intellectual activists in Kuwait) and external (the Iranian revolution for both, and the Iraqi invasion for Kuwait). A case could be made that in Bahrain the parliament is a political necessity for the state in order to make up for the comparative lack of wealth that characterizes other states in the region. But a similar argument cannot be made in relation to Kuwait, where on average citizens earn around $140,000 a year. The relationship between rentierism and the prevailing political economy needs to be contextualized and the causal outcomes between them are not uniform.

Conclusion

Across the Persian Gulf basin, the evolution of state institutions has occurred concurrently with, and has been reinforced by, profound changes in domestic political economies. Two simultaneous and mutually reinforcing developments have occurred: at the same time as the state has proliferated its institutional structures and has sought to establish contact with various social groups, either through direct incorporation or by indirectly addressing their needs, it has had access to rent revenues of varying size and consistency. The monarchical sheikhdoms of the Arabian Peninsula, in which patronage and clientelism have long been part and parcel of sheikhly rule, happened to have much smaller population bases and relatively much larger rent revenues. From the beginning of the state-building process, rulers fostered a relationship of direct dependence on the part of other clans and families on whose support they relied in times of need. The massive infusion of rent revenues into state coffers, thanks almost exclusively to hydrocarbon exports, has deepened these pre-existing relationships of dependence. This dependence has been mutual, bonding patrons to the relationship with their clients as much as the clients are tied to their patrons. For the much less wealthy Iranian and Iraqi states, the pervasive rentier arrangements the state hopes to carve out remain largely elusive, keeping the state in a condition of trying to constantly play catch-up with the promises and premises that rentierism implies. In both instances—whether there is tremendous wealth flowing into society or assumptions that it will flow if there is proper management and distribution mechanisms—rentierism curtails state autonomy.

Iran and Iraq share a number of underlying similarities with the other rentier states of the Middle East, Algeria and Libya and also Egypt and Jordan. These similarities are found especially in the mechanisms for resource alloca-tion, the levels of resources available in proportion to the population, and the general evolution and profile of state distributive networks. The conclusions drawn from the Persian Gulf appear generalizable to the rest of the Middle East region. Miriam Lowi has demonstrated, for example, that similarly to Iran and Iraq (and Indonesia), in Algeria "institutional frameworks that con-solidated politicized distributional arrangements were elaborated."[73] Ulti-mately, she argues, "the outcome of challenges to political stability hinges squarely upon the decisions of leaders, and their ability to mold and manipu-late, to their advantage, structural features of the context they find themselves in."[74] These states can sustain themselves only through resort to considerable violence as they face near-chronic challenges to their power and authority. As a panacea for lack of political legitimacy, rentierism works only if it can over-whelm the system with its magnitude and scale, as is the case in the small sheikhdoms of the southern Persian Gulf. Elsewhere, in both the Persian Gulf and beyond, so long as the system lacks other sources of political legitimacy

---

[73] Miriam R. Lowi, *Oil Wealth and the Poverty of Politics: Algeria Compared* (Cam-bridge: Cambridge University Press, 2009), p. 155.
[74] Ibid., p. 176.

that give it a halo of legitimacy before society, it needs to be complemented with polished regime maintenance methods, complemented with hefty doses of violence if necessary, to compensate for the curtailed autonomy of the state.

For all its pitfalls, and the official discourse of preparing for the post-oil era by fostering knowledge-based economies, rentierism does not appear to be departing the Persian Gulf anytime soon. Back in 2003, an observer of Saudi Arabia confidently declared the impending demise of rentier arrangements. "The unsustainability of the Saudi rentier-distributive political economy has been apparent for many years," he wrote, "and the era of rentier opulence is drawing to a close."[75] Today that closing is yet to come. Rentier arrangements have trapped ruling elites and their clients in relations of mutual dependence, and so far the price of terminating or stepping out of these relations has been too high for either side to meaningfully initiate. Even for the Iranian state, which is far more reliant on taxation than any of its counterparts elsewhere in the region, the risks of abandoning or even curtailing dependence on indirect and hidden rentier arrangements are far too great to take. One month the state imposes a VAT on gold merchants, the next month it doles out cash payments to anyone claiming to need it.[76] For the time being, Persian Gulf rentierism is here to stay.

[75] Champion, *The Paradoxical Kingdom*, p. 168.
[76] William Yong, "Iranian Officials Warn of Unrest Tied to Subsidy Cuts," *New York Times*, October 11, 2010, p. 10.

4

The Sovereign Wealth Funds of the Persian Gulf

Jean-François Seznec

In the past few years, the concept of "sovereign wealth funds" (SWFs) seems to have appealed to numerous economists, consultants, journalists and academics. The idea that a country could place funds for management with institutions not directly under the control of the central government or a council of ministers is nothing new. Kuwait has been investing some of its earnings from oil outside Kuwait, at first under the control of a British company, the Kuwait Investment Office (KIO), and now under the control of Kuwait-based Kuwait Investment Authority (KIA), since 1953. What seems to have inflamed the interest and imagination of observers was the sheer size and secrecy of the funds. There seems to always be a fear in the Western financial centers that the "Arabs" will take over their main institutions. When various reports from McKenzie and Deutsche Bank came out in 2008, the funds appeared to be absolutely huge and growing to a quasi-unmanageable size fueled by the increasing flow of funds out of the West into the coffers of the oil producers in the Persian Gulf, Russia, Venezuela—altogether countries often presented as less than friendly to the West and the United States in particular.

A number of major banks and consultants put the sovereign wealth funds of the Persian Gulf at a total of about $1.5 trillion.[1] This amount, of course was estimated in 2008, when oil prices passed over the $147/b mark in New York and seemed to be on the increase with no end in sight. McKinsey is quoted to show an accumulation of oil income in the Gulf Cooperation Council (GCC) countries at $2.4 trillion by 2010 and $8.8 trillion by 2020.[2] In spite of the significant expenses within the GCC, McKinsey expected in 2008 that the GCC states would be able to invest up to $5.0 trillion overseas through their use of SWFs by 2020.[3]

It does appear that some of the fears in the West have been fanned by the systematic secretive approach of the main SWFs in the Gulf. Without much study of the actual income of the Gulf states, fabulous amounts were bandied about and increased exponentially with time, fanned by various iconic transactions such as the acquisition of 4.9 percent of Citicorp for $7.5 billion by the Abu Dhabi Investment Authority (ADIA) in 2007, the investment of $7 billion in the Carlyle Group by Mubadala, also of Abu Dhabi, or the support of Credit Suisse by the Qatar Investment Authority (QIA) to the tune of $15 billion. The power of secretiveness made many observers feel that the managers of funds, especially in Abu Dhabi, were obtaining very high returns on investments, higher than all others, as if secretiveness allowed funds managers to invest in high return low risk items unavailable to others.

Of course the reality is different. In fact now the reverse appears to be taking place. It seems to be common currency to evaluate the SWFs in light of the large losses of the many hedged funds in 2008 and 2009 and of the substantial decline in the world stock markets since then.

This chapter will attempt to present the main SWFs of the Gulf and try to demystify them. Detailed information for some of the funds, like Mubadala or TAQA, has been made available for the past two years. However, for the larger ones like ADIA, no financial information has been forthcoming so far.

---

[1] Nimrod Rapheali and Bianca Gersten, "Sovereign Wealth Funds: Investment Vehicles for the Persian Gulf Countries," *Middle East Quarterly*, Spring 2008, Volume 15, No. 2, pp. 45–53.

[2] Simeon Kerr, "Gulf tipped to ride wave of soaring prices," *Financial Times*, January 24, 2008 (http://www.ft.com/cms/s/0/a634c13e-ca09–11dc-b5dc-000077b07658.html?nclick_check=1).

[3] Diana Farrell and Susan Lund Diana Farrell and Susan Lund, "The New Role of Oil Wealth in the World Economy," McKinsey Global Institute, February 7, 2008 (http://www.euractiv.com/en/euro/new-role-oil-wealth-world-economy/article-170187).

This chapter will propose a methodology to go from the actual cash income of the countries earned from oil sales to the amount placed in the SWFs and evaluate the size of those funds that do not disclose it. I will also theorize on what are the possible political and economic reasons that limit the transparency of many of the Gulf's funds, and especially question who actually owns the funds. It is relatively easy to know who technically control the funds, but it is not clear, in some cases, whether the funds are owned by the states on behalf of the people, by the ruling families of the Gulf, or by the people directly but managed by the royal families as fiduciary agents for it, through the SWF management structures.

Definition and description

No two Sovereign Wealth Funds are alike, and therefore it can be challenging to find one definition that fits all. The main differences between the various definitions have to do with the actual control of the funds by the government. One observer defines SWFs as "a government vehicle, which is funded by foreign exchange assets, and which manages these assets separately from official reserves."[4] A private report by Deutsche Bank for its part says that SWFs have the following characteristics: 1-Sovereign, 2-Independently managed from the Central Bank reserves, 3-Have a higher foreign currency exposure, 4-Have no explicit liabilities, 5-Have a higher risk tolerance, 6-Have a long-term investment horizon, 7-Potentially could make strategic investments to promote reciprocity back to the country.

The Sovereign Wealth Fund Institute's website states that a SWF is a "state-owned investment fund composed of financial assets such as stocks and bonds...funded by foreign exchange assets... SWFs exclude the foreign currency reserve assets held by monetary authorities ...[and] government pension funds."[5]

The secretive nature of many funds has triggered a guessing contest between academics, consultants, and bankers to figure out how much each fund is worth, who manages them, and what type of instruments are being bought and sold. In fact, it is unclear among the observers which of the Gulf funds are SWFs. Indeed, it seems that many writers agree with the definitions above, but

---

[4] Clay Lowery, Acting Under Secretary for International Affairs at the US Treasury, quoted by Deutsche Bank in their report Sovereign Wealth Funds-GCC Perspective, September 26, 2007.

[5] www.swfinstitute.org/what-is-a-swf/

Table 4.1: Sovereign Wealth Funds of the Gulf: Estimated Portfolios as per Various Institutions, in Billions of USD.

Date of est.		Date of Inception	Deutche Bank[1] 2008	Monitor[4] 2008	McKinsey[5] 2008	CFR[2] 2009	Carnegie[3] 2008	SWF Institute Sep-10	SAMA[6] Dec-10	JF Seznec Dec-10
Kuwait	RFFG/KIA	1953	264	250	200	222	213	203		
Qatar	Qatar investments	2000	60		40-60	58		85		
Saudi Arabia	NA	NA	365			501	330	627	392	392
UAE	ADIA	1976	874	874	500-875	328	500-875			363
	Mubadala	2002	10	10	10-15			13		27
Bahrain	Mumtalakat	2006	10					9		
Oman	SGSF	1980	8					NA		
Iran	Oil Stabilisation Fund	1999	13	15				23		

[1] Deutche Bank: Sovereign Weath Funds, Overview, October 2008.
[2] Council on Foreign Relations, CGS-Working Paper, Brad Setser and Rachel Zale, January 2009.
[3] Carnegie Papers. When Money Talks", Swen Behrendt October 2008.
[4] Monitor Group, Assessing the Risks: The Behavior of Sovereign Wealth Funds in the Global Economy, June 2008.
[5] McKinsey Global Institute, The Coming Oil Windfall in the Gulf, January 2008.
[6] SAMA Monthly Statistical Bulleting December 2010 Table 8A NB. This figures includes only Foreign Securities held or managed by SAMA for itself and for the Independent Organizations [SR1,181,916M and SR289,239M respectively].

promptly forget them when actually listing and speculating about the funds themselves. Below is a table of the main funds of the Gulf and the estimates mentioned by some of the best observers of the financial markets of the region.

The Qatari Investment Authority and the five major funds of the United Arab Emirates (UAE) are the only funds that would follow most of the criteria listed in the definition above. Other investment funds in the Gulf—such as the Kuwait Investment Authority (KIA), which manages the Reserve for Future Generation in Kuwait, Mumtalakat in Bahrain, and is the holding company for the investments of the State of Bahrain in their local companies, or the Oman fund—are hardly free from the interference of the state, the central banks or the ministries of finance. They are often told where and how to invest. Further, they are managed directly by their own state's employees, some are entirely invested in their local industries, others like the KIA have very widespread ownership in numerous firms worldwide. In all cases, however, their independence is minimal.

Saudi Arabia

The investments of the Kingdom are wholly managed by the Saudi Arabian Monetary Agency (SAMA), the central bank of the Kingdom. They are not invested through a separate fund, and according to the definitions of SWFs should not be viewed as a SWF. On the other hand, SAMA, which invests between $300 and $500 billion, depending on the income and expenses of the Kingdom, is always mentioned as one by observers like the Arab Financial Forum, McKinsey, the SWF Institute. Therefore, this chapter will cover SAMA, but with the understanding that the amounts managed are disclosed, and technically not to be considered comparable to funds like the UAE's ADIA or the Qatar Investment Authority (QIA). The Central Bank centralizes the amounts received from oil and other state-managed exports, such as refined products and natural gas liquids sold by Saudi Aramco. Some observers even mention the Public Investment Fund (PIF) of Saudi Arabia as a SWF.[6] However, PIF uses SAMA, the Central Bank, to invest all its cash dollar funds. It is very likely that all of PIF's balances get invested by SAMA in similar instruments to those used to invest its own dollar balances—short term government obligations, mostly US treasuries. In the same manner, SAMA invests the dollar funds of the two pension funds of the Kingdom, the

[6] Deutsche Bank in a 2008 private report.

Public Pension Fund and the General Organization for Social Insurance (GOSI). SAMA invests its "Wealth" on behalf of the "Sovereign," but is not investing as a true SWF. Indeed, SAMA is the central bank and the funds have no independence from it. Moreover, SAMA has no tolerance for risk. At one point, before the market crash of 2007–08, many in the Kingdom were complaining that Saudi Arabia was too conservative and was not taking advantage of potential gains in the stock markets of the West. After 2008, SAMA turned out to be admired by everyone when many funds lost from 30 to 60 percent of the value of their investment on the stock markets and in hedge funds.

In 2008, Saudi Arabia announced that a $6 billion fund, to be called SANABEL, would be established for foreign investments. This fund would have been established as a trial balloon by the Saudi government to evaluate the ability to follow the example of ADIA and other SWFs reputed to earn very large returns. However, by and large, it appears that SAMA and the Ministry of Finance are happier keeping the state's fund under their management and in their traditional short-term virtually risk free, albeit low return, investments. After the world financial debacle of late 2008 and 2009, no word has come from Saudi Arabia about the establishment of this fund. One can only think that the project has been stillborn.

Qatar

The Qatar Investment Authority manages the funds of the State of Qatar not used for the budget and running expenses. QIA, which is quite secretive, is independent from the Central Bank and invests overseas. The total assets of the fund are estimated to be between $40 billion and $60 billion [see Table 4.1]. This fund has received some press because it took a 25.07 percent share in Sainsbury Plc, the well-known British supermarket chain, for £732 million.[7] It has a stake of 10.58 percent in the London Stock Exchange. In June 2008, it bought 6.2 percent of Barclays Bank for £432 million, now reduced to 5.8 percent. It is the largest shareholder of Credit Suisse, the second largest Swiss Bank, with 10 percent of its capital. It owns 6 percent of Lagardère, the very large French defense contractor.[8] Of course, the fund lost very large amounts on its purchases of shares in 2008 and Spring 2009, when the shares of most financial institutions, especially the banks like Barclays and Credit Suisse,

---

[7] BBC News 5 June, 2007 (www.news/bbc.co.uk/2/business/6755497.stm).

[8] *Sovereign Wealth Fund Institute*, "Qatar Investment Authority," http://www.swfinstitute.org/fund/qatar.php.

declined enormously. However, if QIA did not panic and kept its holdings, as is probably the case, the values have by and large come back. For example, Credit Suisse, which was worth $78.59 per share on April 27, 2007, plunged to $20.11 on March 6, 2009 but recovered to $46.15 as of February 4, 2011.[9]

The QIA has been expected to grow exponentially due to Qatar's extensive growth in Liquid Natural Gas (LNG) exports. Qatar is blessed with the largest dry gas field in the world, the North Dome, which is shared with Iran (and called the South Pars on the northern side of the maritime border). Qatar decided many years ago to monetize this gas by becoming the largest producer in the world of LNG. Qatar's capacity for LNG has now reached 77 million tons per year (ts/y), up from 33 million ts/y in 2009. Qatar's income has been expected to grow in proportion to the new capacity. However, the price of gas, unlike that of oil, is under severe pressure. Qatar has borrowed over $68 billion to manage its gas industry. Qatar was the recipient of not less than twenty-seven different large syndicated facilities to build its LNG plants, buy the vessels needed for transport, expand existing refineries, build its Gas-to-Liquids plants, etc.[10] The new 77 million ts/y capacity is by far the largest in the world. It was built with the aim of selling a large portion of this LNG to Europe and the US. When the plants were started, the price of gas was increasing and shortages were expected in the US in particular. However, prices in the US have declined very substantially since 2009. For decades, the price of gas was directly linked to the price of oil. However, with the expectation of shale gas coming into production massively in the next few years in Europe, with even greater production expected in North America, the price of gas has tumbled. It hovers around $4.0 per million btu (British thermal units), when parity with an $80 per barrel (/b) oil would put it at about $13.3 per million btu.

Fortunately for Qatar, many of its contracts have been signed with East Asia users. These contracts are usually based on a price computed using parity with oil, but with a ceiling and a floor. The ceiling protects the buyer from oil at the levels of the summer of 2008 ($147/b), and a floor maintains enough cash flow to allow the banks to be repaid. Today, most of the East Asian buyers are paying in the range of $10 to $11 per million btu.[11]

---

[9] Google.com/finance, under CS

[10] A few consulting firms will compile a list of project loans for use by their clients. However, one can also go through the trade newsletters and magazines (MEES, MEED, etc.) and arrive at similar figures.

[11] OAPEC *Quarterly Report* Vol. 36, no. 10, p. 13.

The East Asian formula guarantees substantial income for Qatar, but it is putting pressure on buyers in Korea and Japan. China is buying LNG from other suppliers for as low as $6 per million btu, hurting Japan's and Korea's competitiveness. It is likely that Korean and Japanese companies will seek modifications to their contracts, for which we can expect very tough negotiations, but which most likely will end up with decoupling of the price of Qatari gas from that of oil. Further, much of the production that was intended for the US is now either going to stay underground, at great cash losses for Qatar and its joint venture partners, mainly ExxonMobil, or will be produced for buyers that will not pay more than a market rate strongly influenced by the low prices of gas in the US. Altogether, the lack of demand for LNG in the US, and the potential pressure for lower prices in Asia, will hurt Qatar's income from gas.

Furthermore, the expenses related to LNG are vastly superior to those related to oil, so that the net income of Qatar from its LNG will be much lower than originally computed. The banks have to be reimbursed with capital and interest, the plants have to be run, maintained, and accounting-wise depreciated. Qatar still makes over $23 billion per year from its small production of crude oil of about 750,000 barrels per day (b/d),[12] but its income from LNG may be very disappointing. A couple of years ago, Qatar could have been expected to earn as much as $53 billion from its LNG, if sold at parity with oil at $13.3/million btu. However, if contracts are negotiated or renegotiated at prices closer to those prevailing in the main gas markets of the US and China, gross income could decline to $8 billion/y.[13] Qatar is unlikely to lose cash from its LNG investments, but is unlikely to make money on them until the demand for LNG increases to the point when the gas prices get re-coupled to those of oil.

Thus, it would appear that the net amount of funds from oil and gas used to make Qatar a leading state in the region may be sufficient for the very large

[12] www.jodidb.org, the very detailed database provided by JODI, the Riyadh based organization that manages the dialogue between producers and consumers of oil, list Qatari oil production at 733b/d in December 2010.

[13] Should Qatar produce LNG at 100 percent of its capacity, i.e. 77 million ts/y, and sell it at par with oil at $80/b, this would correspond to $53billion/y, using a conversion of 52 trillion btu per ton of LNG. Should the price of LNG decline to $6.5, which is the price paid by China, it would cut the income by half. Further, the total cash needed by Qatar, including costs of production, interest payments, payments on principal, etc., could be as high as $4.0 per million btu. This would cut income to $2/mmbtu, which would correspond to $8 billion per year.

expenses of the budget, the social projects and the great plans to hold the 2022 football World Cup; also, however, that the amount of funds available for QIA will be limited, and perhaps even reduced.

Kuwait

Kuwait has had a sovereign wealth fund since 1963. The original concept of the fund was to take 10 percent of all gross oil revenues and invest them overseas. To this day, the Kuwaiti state computes its annual income from oil and places the 10 percent in a special purpose vehicle called the Reserve for Future Generations (RFFG). This is a gross amount. In other words, whether or not the state's budget is in deficit or in credit, the amount is taken before any state expenses or budget requirements. By 1991, Kuwait had over $100 billion in assets and was earning more from its investments than from the oil itself. Until late 1992, it was not clear how the money was invested and by whom. After the country's invasion by Saddam Hussein's forces, it became public that the money had been held and managed by the Kuwait Investment Office (KIO) out of London. It was managed quite secretly and no one except the Amir and a few of his closest associates knew how the fund operated and how the funds were invested.

The RFFG became something of a savior to the Kuwaiti people. Indeed when Saddam Hussein invaded and took over Kuwait and all its institutions, he could not get access to the main moneys of the Emirate, as the investments were being held in the UK. The night of the invasion the UK authorities, like all the other governments in the world, blocked all Kuwaiti accounts so that Saddam Hussein could not have access to them. Thus, with substantial funds in a UK-based company and the support of the Bank of England, the Amir could access the funds of the RFFG managed by KIO and used them to pay each exiled Kuwaiti family a proper allowance. This allowed the Kuwaiti exiles to wait for the US and its allies to liberate the country. Of course, this reduced the size of the RFFG. Furthermore, Kuwait had to use the RFFG to fund the repairs of the sabotaged oil fields and state infrastructure. Today, the RFFG has, by and large, recovered, having benefited from the steady increase in oil prices since 1999. The fund is currently estimated at about $220 billion, perhaps even higher depending on the value of the investments during the present economy recovery. The detailed results are not public, but information on the fund is not limited to the Amir. The RFFG is no longer supervised by the KIO, as it was in 1991. After some very questionable investments in Spain in the mid-1990s, which prompted an extensive parliamentary inquiry at the request of the Prime Minister, the supervision and management of the investments were handed over to the Kuwait Investment Authority (KIA), which is under the supervision of the Ministry of Finance. This limited the influence of the Amir on the SWF and transferred the supervision of this critical financial asset to the Prime Minister and his cabinet. Now, the KIA by law has to report regularly to the Council of Ministers, and at times the ministers will inform parliament, which greatly increases the level of transparency regarding the amounts involved.

Similarly to Abu Dhabi, Kuwait does not seek to take controlling interests in companies. Among the KIA's largest investments are 6.93 percent of Daimler Benz and 6 percent of Citibank. Kuwait recently arranged to take a 4.8 percent share, worth about €600 million, in the French company Areva, the leading provider of nuclear energy and technology in the world.[14] In the 1980s, Kuwait did attempt to take a major stake in British Petroleum, but was forced by Margaret Thatcher to sell half of its stake of 15 percent, and since then has sold most of its shares in the oil giant. Kuwait made a great deal of money on the transaction as BP's shares rose substantially during this incident, but Kuwait was somewhat burned in the process, appearing to have learned to avoid aiming again for a major stake in such a strategically important Western company.

UAE

There are five main funds in the UAE, all located in Abu Dhabi. Dubai also has a couple more minor funds, as does Ras al-Khaimah. The Dubai funds are somewhat difficult to estimate, as they are part and parcel of Dubai, Inc., a euphemism for the overall control of the economy of Dubai by Sheikh Mohamed bin Rashid. The various holding companies and state controlled semi-private firms in Dubai have received funds from the Dubai SWFs, but overall Dubai Inc. has borrowed most of the money it has invested. In the process, the authorities of Dubai have managed to build a harbor, transshipment center, and manufacturing zone among the most successful in the world, not mention impressive new neighborhoods and iconic buildings. It also boasts one of the largest aluminum plants in operation worldwide. However, the money flows are not clear. We know that Dubai's oil resources are very limited and that the net income from successful ventures is notable but not

---

[14] *Middle East Economic Survey* Vol. 53, No. 51 (December 20, 2010), p. 17.

comparable to Qatar's or Abu Dhabi's. It appears much of the money has come from borrowings from international and local banks, as well as accounts payable to contractors, but altogether, the debt level may be around $120 billion. One could then assume that Dubai's SWFs are funded mostly by debt, and thus not technically SWFs at all. The level of information in this field is so scattered and unreliable that the writer has decided not to include the Dubai funds in this study of SWFs in the Gulf. For similar reasons the fund of Ras al-Khaimah will not be studied here either.

By and large, four of the five funds of Abu Dhabi are likely not funded by large amounts of debt. One of the funds, TAQA, does have strong leverage, funding itself through the banks and floating shares on the stock market. However, the other four funds are supported directly by the treasury of Abu Dhabi, which in turn gets its income from oil and gas revenues. Each of the funds is managed by a board of directors, which represent the interests of one or more clans within the royal family. Within each board, the chairman represents the royal clan that is most vested in the fund. Despite inherent family ties, each of these funds has a highly professional management, which proposes investment policies and implements them when agreed by the boards. Nevertheless, there seems to be a major effort to include the various clans and the major Abu Dhabi merchant families in all the funds. For example, Sheikh Mohamed bin Zayed is on the board of ADIA, even though the main power there appears to reside with Sheikh Khalifa, the Emir of Abu Dhabi and President of the UAE Federation. In a somewhat different approach, Mubadala is a Public Joint Stock Company (PJSC), but the company is wholly owned by the government of Abu Dhabi and therefore is often viewed as being under the control of Sheikh Mohamed bin Zayed. However, it also has a board composed mostly of young talented representatives of the main non-royal trading families of Abu Dhabi. Mubadala in its reports refers to "its shareholder," meaning the government of Abu Dhabi, and its board members, who come from the main merchant families in the UAE and act as trustees for the government.

At this time the main funds are:

> *ADIA (The Abu Dhabi Investment Authority)*. ADIA is usually considered to be the largest SWF in the world. It has traditionally kept a very low profile and remained extremely secretive. No one, outside the top management of the fund, seems to have a precise idea of how much money is actually being managed. Amounts are reported as being anywhere between $250 billion and over $1 trillion. A great part of this chapter will be used to provide a tentative

methodology in estimating this figure. As will be shown below, I estimate that ADIA in 2011 manages approximately between $311 billion and $392 billion. Even at this figure, which is much lower than what is often estimated, the amounts involved are simply staggering.

In the past year and a half, ADIA has started to release some information on its operations. In early 2010, ADIA published its *Annual Review 2009*.[15] The report, shows that 80 percent of the money it holds is managed by outside funds managers and that 60 percent of the funds are used to replicate indexes worldwide. The fund has 1,200 employees. Perhaps the most newsworthy revelation is that the fund has returned 6.5 percent per annum for the past twenty years and 8 percent if we go back for 30 years. These are excellent returns and higher than could be expected considering the large losses that were undoubtedly incurred in 2008/2009.

> *Mubadala.* Unlike most of the other SWFs in the Gulf, Mubadala started in 2008 to disclose its assets, liabilities, profits and losses, as well as some detail on its portfolio mix and philosophy. Mubadala now has total assets of $23.4 billion with a long-term debt level of $7.4 billion.[16] If short-term debt is included, Mubadala would have a leverage of almost one to one (one part equity for one part debt). Mubadala discloses profits as well as losses incurred in the 2008/2009 downturn in a series of figures audited by KPMG, then published and distributed through the internet. The fund is involved in many different areas, but most actively in the oil and gas, industrial investments, aerospace and real estate sectors.

Mubadala has a stake in the Carlyle Group, a well known US private equity company, and in Mediobanco and Lease Plan, both of Italy. Of some importance in today's high price for commodities, it owns an 8.3 percent stake in Guinea Alumina Corporation, a joint-venture with BHP Billiton, which transforms some of the bauxite of Guinea to alumina. The alumina, in turn, is shipped to Bahrain, Dubai and other aluminum producing countries. As Mubadala is planning a 1.4 million t/s aluminum plant in Abu Dhabi, this stake appears highly strategic.

Until Mubadala issued its annual report, most observers estimated the fund as holding $10 billion in assets. Interestingly, the fund is also somewhat leveraged, something unusual for SWFs which normally operate solely out of their

---

[15] http://www.adia.ae/En/pr/Annual_Review_Website2.pdf
[16] mubadala.ae/images/upload_images/2010_HY_Results_Presentation.pdf

own capital. This could indicate that Mubadala's management is much more aggressive in its approach than ADIA's. However, it does appear, from the financial statements and the notes attached to them, that Mubadala has extensive relations with the government of Abu Dhabi and that the "shareholder" is providing extensive funding, some even listed as interest free. Furthermore, the fund owns a very large portfolio of real estate in the UAE, which is listed but not valued, and which undoubtedly would be worth very large amounts if the properties were passed on the books at their real value, thereby easing overall financial leverage down to an extremely low, and healthy, ratio.

Mubadala is managed similarly to a very large hedge fund. Deals are looked at constantly, sometimes almost frenetically. The corporate culture is akin to that of investment companies in New York or London. However, it does have a large interest in developing advanced technology projects, which are expected to benefit Abu Dhabi. Mubadala enjoys strong leadership by the Crown Prince and a visionary board of directors consisting of young and very active merchants. Hence, unlike ADIA, which invests worldwide and very conservatively, Mubadala tends to champion large industrial projects in the emirate, which ultimately benefit all Emiratis.

> *Other Abu Dhabi funds.* Sheikh Mansour bin Zayed al Nahyan, a highly respected member of the royal family, often said to be non-political and mainly interested in business ventures, heads The International Petroleum Investment Company (IPIC). IPIC owns 9.1 percent of Daimler Benz, 3.3 percent of Atlantia S.p.A. (a large Italian operator of highways) and AABAR real estate in Abu Dhabi. It is building the new 1.5 million b/d pipeline between Abu Dhabi and Fujairah, which will allow oil shipments from Abu Dhabi to bypass the Straits of Hormuz by the end of 2011. IPIC owns 17 percent of OMV AG of Austria, which is a prime technology company in the petrochemical industry, and has control of Borealis, a well-known chemical manufacturer originally from Norway. It also acquired NOVA chemicals in Canada in 2009, a company reputed for its ethylene technology. The acquisitions in the chemical and energy areas attest to its very strategic approach to investing, allowing Abu Dhabi to control the technology needed for the development of its large ethylene and downstream plant, Borouge.

When added to those of Mubadala, IPIC's investments show the determination of the Abu Dhabi leadership to make strategic acquisitions by taking important participations in firms that will contribute to Abu Dhabi's industrial development and ensure procurement and control of advanced technologies. Unlike the Saudi model developed by Saudi Basic Industries Corporation (SABIC), where SABIC develops its own technology, Abu Dhabi is also seeking control of the technologies used in its productions, but will do so in a more indirect manner through financial control.

Hence, it would seem that while ADIA is in charge of protecting the overall assets of Abu Dhabi by investing in index-related overseas markets, the smaller but more aggressive funds of IPIC, and especially Mubadala, seek to invest in industries and services located in Abu Dhabi or those profiting the actual development of Abu Dhabi, not only in the short term but also in the long term, by controlling firms whose technologies are essential to Abu Dhabi's internal economic growth.

Table 4.2: International Assets of TAQA, in Millions of USD.

Investment	Purpose	Amount
Pioneer Canada	Oil & Gas	$540
Northrock Resources-Canada	Oil & Gas	$2,000
ABB JV in Morocco & India	Power Generation	$490
CMS Generation Co. ME, Africa, India	Power Generation	$900
Talisman Energy	Oil—North Sea	$550
IL&FS India	Power	$1,000
BP Netherlands	Oil	$694
PrimeWest Energy-Canada	Oil & Gas	$5,000

Source: *MEES* 53:36 September 7, 2010 p. 3.

The Abu Dhabi National Energy Company, known as TAQA PSJC, is one fund that actually issues annual and quarterly financial reports.[17] It is owned by ADWEA, the electricity and water utility of Abu Dhabi, the Farmer's Fund, and to some extent the public, by way of the Abu Dhabi stock exchange. The company has invested in utility development in the Emirate with 13,794 MW and 654 million gallons per day of desalinated water, and additionally, in gas storage facilities and a gas terminal. Some of the international assets of TAQA are listed below.

As of June 30, 2010, the total assets of TAQA were about $25 billion but with an equity of only $3.4 billion. The equity is much lower than it should be due to substantial markdowns in a number of investments, largely due to

[17] www.taqa.ae

the recession of 2008/2009. Nevertheless, the company's very high leverage renders TAQA more like a private equity company than a SWF, and judging from the low level of capitalization, it does not appear to have overwhelming and overt support from the government of Abu Dhabi.

Methodology in computing size of funds

Any effort to establish estimates of how much money is flowing into the SWFs of the Gulf has to be based on evaluating how much is received from oil sales by the Gulf countries. Of course estimating the value of oil sales is somewhat like shooting a moving target, as the price of oil fluctuates widely, from $147/b in New York in July 2008 down to $30 by January 2009, and then back up again reach a modicum of stability around $70/b to $80/b from the summer of 2009 to the winter of 2010. More importantly, the actual volume of sales of oil also vary. For instance, in 2008 the Saudis produced over 9 million b/d, but in 2010 shrank production by about one million b/d. Nevertheless, the estimates below are an educated guess of what amount to large flows of funds. The main points discussed below are presented in table form in Appendices A, B and C attached.

Income computation

The amount of money earned by the Saudis can be estimated with a reasonable margin of error. The Kingdom does not invest its funds in shares or stocks. Nor in essence does it have any sovereign wealth funds. However, we do know that SAMA invests the foreign assets of the Kingdom on behalf of the state and on behalf of major independent state organizations like the Public Investment Fund or the General Organization for Social Insurance, and the equivalent fund for public servants. The amounts, held mainly in US short-term treasury bills, rise and fall according to state budgetary needs. As of December 2010, the total amount managed by SAMA was $315 billion of state funds and $77 billion for the "independent organizations," that is, those entities that manage the pension funds and development banks of the Kingdom, the management of which is fully controlled between SAMA and the Ministry of Finance.[18]

The Saudi model, however, demonstrates how oil sales proceed in the oil countries of the Gulf, as geography, geology, proximity to markets, and quality

[18] SAMA Monthly Statistical Bulletin, December 2010 (SAMA.gov.sa).

of products are quite similar across the region. Hence, if the Saudis produce a given quantity of heavy crude, the percentage of this heavy crude relative to the overall output and sales is likely to be similar in Abu Dhabi or Kuwait. Thus, the computations of income estimates have been based on what this writer knows from Saudi production and practices, applied to the other countries of the Gulf.

The countries of the Gulf produce about 17 million b/d and about 2.5 million b/d of Natural Gas Liquids (NGLs). The largest producer is Saudi Arabia, which extracts 8.32 million b/d.[19] The Gulf crudes are a mix of light, medium and heavy crudes. Light crudes are close in quality to the WTI crude sold on the NYMEX market in New York or the Brent on the IPE in London, the two markets that form the base of most oil pricing in the world today, including much of the Persian Gulf. However, Saudi Aramco and the State Organization for Marketing Oil of Iraq (SOMO) base their pricing formula on the Houston based index for Argus sour crude, which they say is closer on average to their own mix of crude exports. The Far Eastern buyers see their price computed on the average of Oman-Dubai crudes, a type not commonly traded on major markets, making the priced defined by the average transactions computed and reported daily by Platt's.

On average the Gulf crudes will be priced lower than the similar crudes of the US, Europe, West Africa, or Venezuela. The difference is due to the need for Gulf producers to keep their crudes competitive with those that originate much closer to their main buyers in Europe and the US. Hence, when oil is traded at $80/b in New York at NYMEX for WTI, the actual price paid to the Saudis for similar grade oil will be about $71.86, using the average discount of 9.04 percent of the past eleven years.[20] Estimates of income based on a price of $80/b in New York on WTI would imply that the Gulf producers were earning about $1,077 million per day, or $393 billion per year.[21] However, computing oil earnings without taking into account the difference

[19] "OPEC Crude Oil Production," *Middle East Economic Survey* Vol. 51, No. 5, February 2, 2008, pp. 2 and Vol. 53, No. 37 (September 13, 2010), p. 7.

[20] The discount is computed by the author by comparing the average daily price for WTI and Arabian Light between 1999 and 2010 as published by the EIA at www.eia.doc.gov.

[21] It should be noted that the price difference between Brent and WTI may vary according to the daily supply and demand for local crudes as well as the international ones. In fact, at times, as is the case in late 2010 and early 2011, Brent can be substantially higher than WTI.

between Gulf crudes and similar African or American crudes would exaggerate inflows by over $47 billion per year.

Furthermore, over time, shipments of crude will include a mix of light, heavy or medium crudes—the last two being often sold at a substantial discount. Overall, the computation of income for Gulf productions and shipments assumes a mix of oil based on the writer's estimate of the Saudi mix at 10% heavy crude, 20% medium crude, 55% light crude, 15% ultra light, products and NGLs.

One must also point out that the Gulf countries produce 17.42 million b/d[22] of crude but do not export this much, as some of it is refined and used domestically. In fact, the Gulf producers refine about 5.2 million b/d[23] themselves, and most of the refinery products are consumed locally. Saudi Arabia, which refines about 2.5 million b/d, consumes about 2 million b/d locally. Thus, the actual net exports of oil, including the exports of products such as diesel or gasoline, total about 15.3 million b/d.[24] As mentioned, the Gulf countries also export about 2.5 million b/d of Natural Gas Liquids (NGLs),[25] mainly propane and butane, which are sold often at a premium but presently are relatively depressed due to the low natural gas prices worldwide.

Expenses

Production costs

Our model also considers that gross oil income of the Gulf States must be adjusted for a number of cash expenses, which will remove funds from being potentially added to the SWFs. The first item is cost of production. Oil in the Gulf is relatively easy to produce, but still requires extensive expenditures in

---

[22] Saudi Arabia 8.32, Iran 3.7, UAE 2.3, Kuwait 2.3, Qatar 0.80. The figure does not include Oman at 0.80 million b/d and Bahrain at 0.15 million b/d, who are not members of OPEC and not listed by MEES.

[23] Saudi refine about 2.5 million b/d, Iran = 1.4, Qatar = 0.3, UAE = 0.4, Kuwait = 0.5, Bahrain = 0.3

[24] Saudi Aramco. http://www.saudiaramco.com/irj/portal/anonymous

[25] It is important to note that Liquid Natural Gas (LNG) is composed of CH4, Methane, which represents the bulk of gas production in the world. NGLs are different; they consist mostly of heavier molecules, C3H8 and C4H10, Propane and Butane and a much smaller proportion of gas production. Ethane, C2H6, which provides the bulk of the petrochemical feedstock in the Gulf, represents about 2.5 percent of all the gas produced, and in the case when the methane is made into LNG, the Ethane is not removed and included in the liquefaction and export.

equipment, personnel, training and maintenance. In fact, this cost has been increasing as of late, since large national oil companies in the Gulf have been pouring funds into infrastructure modernization, oil exploration, oil field maintenance and further resource exploitation. Many years ago, it was the prevalent wisdom to assume that Saudi oil cost about $1.50/b to produce. Today, some oil engineers will estimate the cost at nothing less than $4/b, a figure which will likely rise as newly developed fields swing into full production. The estimate of $4 applies to countries like Kuwait and Qatar, but is more realistically up to $6 in countries like the UAE, which has large offshore fields offshore, traditionally demanding more amounts of capital to exploit.

Military expenses

Military expenditures are increasingly incurred by the Persian Gulf states and demand funds which could otherwise be available for investments. These actual expenses are not disclosed by the states and are not usually included in yearly state budget announcements. In this model, we used the figures published each year by the Stockholm International Peace Research Institute (SIPRI). Military expenses have ballooned over the past years as the Gulf region has become marred by wars, insurrections, terrorism and invasions. Saudi Arabia spent $39 billion in 2009 and the UAE (with a local population of less than one million) spent $13 billion.

Evaporation

Another cash expense, which seems to extract sizeable amounts out of the SWFs is payments made to the royal families. This of course is not publicly disclosed, but it is well known that the monarchies pay a stipend to each of their royal family members every year. The only hint we have of the amounts actually paid comes from an interview given by Prince Al Walid bin Talal to the *New York Times* in 2001.[26] There, the Prince stated that he received an allowance of $180,000. If we extrapolate that information, and assume that the average princely income is analogous, it follows that Saudi Arabia's Royal Diwan distributes to the royal family about 4 percent of the gross oil income.[27]

---

[26] "A Saudi Prince with an Unconventional Idea: Elections," *New York Times*, November 28, 2001.

[27] I assume here a number of about 15,000 princes and princesses, which include the collateral branches going to Mohamed bin Saud, the founder of the dynasty in 1745.

This figure is not easy to confirm and has not been externally verified, and of course is not appearing in the Kingdom's accounts. The quality of the estimate is a further limited by the fact that the number of royal family members is unknown outside the Royal Diwan. It would seem that this "evaporation" takes place between the moment the oil company receives payments on oil shipments in its New York account and before the bank transfers the amount to the central bank and the Ministry of Finance. If that is the case, the transfers are probably effected by standing instructions to the financial institutions receiving the oil money, principally JP Morgan Chase and Citibank, and sent to the Royal Diwan's accounts, perhaps located in Switzerland or some other fiscal paradise with a strong history of confidentiality.

The "evaporation" out of oil income may be happening in every Gulf state, hence we have applied it at the level of 4 percent of gross oil income to the computation of net income for each state in the Gulf. This percentage could be higher or lower, but imperfect as it may be, the estimate is too significant to sweep under the rug entirely. If the amounts were much higher, it would be relatively simple to see a major difference between what may be flowing into the accounts of Saudi Aramco or ADNOC, and what actually enters the accounts of the state. If the amounts were too low, it is likely that there would be some tension within the families, which would permeate the political sphere and put at risk the general acceptance of the leadership.

Budgeted expenses

Besides the cost of production, military expenses, and evaporation, the states of the Gulf have large expenses related to the day-to-day running of the state. Employment in the civil service in Saudi Arabia is one of the ways the government provides jobs for its youth. For the past ten years, the Arab countries of the Gulf have seen a level of economic growth unheard of in their history, all driven by oil income and resulting in booming state budgets.

Naturally, the budgets of the Gulf states are public and published. They are computed by the governments using estimated future oil prices. In reality most budgets of the past four or five years have predicted lower oil prices than those achieved. Hence, in many cases, the amounts actually spent were higher than the budgets, but lower than the actual income, thereby contributing positively to the cash balances of the states and swelling their ability to invest in SWFs. The actual expended budget figures shown in the appendices are the ones provided by the Central Banks of the region.

Finally, the amounts left over after these deductions are not all delegated to SWFs. We assumed, perhaps arbitrarily, that only 70 percent would be placed in SWFs and that, in the case of Abu Dhabi, only another 70 percent would find its way to the ADIA.

The power of compounding interest

ADIA was created in 1976 and has had invested income ever since, although this has varied quite substantially from year to year. ADIA's 2009 Annual Review recorded earnings averaging 6.5 percent over the past twenty years and up to 8 percent if we look back as far as thirty years ago.

As mentioned in the methodology above, we computed the expected net income from oil in Abu Dhabi. We assumed that 70 percent of the net income went to the SWFs, and that 70 percent of these SWFs went to ADIA. We computed the present value of the expected flows of funds since ADIA's first annual inflow in 1977. For the years when the cash flow of the state was negative, we assumed that some amounts were taken from ADIA and placed back into the state's coffers.

Using the above method, the writer estimates the level of ADIA funds in late 2010 to be between $312 billion and $396 billion,[28] including an average return of 6.5 percent to 8 percent per year.[29] To come closer to some of the estimates published in 2008, ADIA would have to return about 15 percent per annum for the past thirty-three years, a rare achievement among fund managers, especially for funds of such magnitude, which must be spread across a number of different assets and currencies. ADIA's report states that 60 percent of their assets seek to emulate the indexes of the world, corroborating return rates between 6.5 and 8 percent, as mentioned in the Annual Review. In fairness to the reports written by McKinsey and Deutsche Bank in 2007 and 2008, their calculations were made before the major stock market crashes in many of the shares and bonds that ADIA possibly invested in. Even if average income had been in the double digits, a loss of 40 percent on many of ADIA's portfolio and the spiraling of numerous hedge funds might have cost a great deal to the Abu Dhabi SWFs, thereby shrinking the return on the McKinsey and Deutsche Bank numbers.

---

[28] The net present value of the fund for the given average returns shown in Appendix A, B, C and D was computed by Ms Radhika Khrisnaswami, MBA candidate at the McDonough School of Business, Georgetown University.

[29] ADIA, Annual Review, 2009 (ADIA.ae/EN/News/media_review.aspx).

This study does not run a similar analysis for Saudi Arabia. It uses the Saudi figures to estimate the net oil revenues to the state after all expenses, but has not done a discounted cash flow analysis. Indeed, the Saudi state earns funds from many other sources besides oil, such as income from the petrochemical industry and other parastatal firms. Additionally, the actual amount of foreign funds held by SAMA and various agencies of the state is disclosed and published monthly, which removes the need to estimate the level of funds available for investments based on calculated oil income. On the other hand, the model could be checked by comparing actual amounts published in SAMA's monthly statistical bulletin, with those generated by running the estimation methodology on SAMA's level of investments taking into account the amounts taken out or earned above and beyond the budgets for the past twenty years.

Weaknesses of the model

The model used above in estimating the present level of funds at ADIA succeeds in being more than a simple estimate. Indeed, ADIA is a very large fund with numerous investments made using a substantial number of managers that specialize in all manner of industries and markets. We have assumed that the amount of funds received by ADIA is directly related to the oil income of Abu Dhabi. Whereas this assumption is logical considering that oil is the main source of revenues to the Emirate, the actual net income could change drastically depending on the immediate needs of the government or the royal family.

The calculation of oil income is also merely an estimate. It is not based on an exact knowledge of the mix of oil actually sold by ADNOC, the oil company of Abu Dhabi. The estimated mix is based on what we understand about the composition of Saudi oil. Of course, the exact Saudi proportions are not entirely sure either, and thus the entire estimation framework must be taken with a grain of salt.

Another possibility for error is in the calculated of cost of production. We have used the figure of $6/b for production of oil after 1998. This is indeed somewhat above the Saudi costs, but on average Abu Dhabi should have costs higher than Saudi Arabia due to larger production from offshore wells. By the same token, however, the actual cost of Saudi production is unknown; the $4/b used here is what some oil engineers with experience in the Gulf comfortably guess, but it is no audited truth.

The military expenses computed by SIPRI may include some of the budget lines entered by Gulf governments in the expenses of various ministries. For example the SIPRI figures may be counting portions of the funds spent on the various military groups such as the police forces or the border guards under Ministry of Interior command in Saudi Arabia, for which some of the expenses may actually be accounted for in the regular budget as well. Especially in the case of Saudi Arabia, this double-counting of expenses could possibly be substantial, as the Ministry of Interior forces today are larger than the regular military forces of the Army, Navy and Air Force combined.

The 4 percent assumed to be "evaporation," that is, payments to the royal diwans for redistribution to the ruling families, may be lower or, in fact, much higher. This information is by and large unknown and should be viewed only as a guess, albeit perhaps a conservative one.

A major methodological flaw may be to accept that the Abu Dhabi funds are received and expended in a way somewhat similar to those of Saudi Arabia. Indeed, there is much in common between Abu Dhabi's political structure and Saudi Arabia's. There is one family in charge of the main decisions in each country and both are quite dependent on oil revenues. Their oil is on average of similar quality and price. Both states spend liberally on military build-up, both have very large civil services and, thus, budgeted state expenses. On the other hand, there are notable differences, namely the size of each country, the number of locals involved in the production of oil, and the development of the respective countries.

It is the hope of this writer that the unavoidable inaccuracies in applying the Saudi model to Abu Dhabi's income, expenses and subsequent investments will cancel each other out, just as the errors which undoubtedly exist in the computation of oil income in Saudi Arabia and Abu Dhabi may also neutralize each other.

Conclusion and some unanswered questions

It seems to be taken for granted by most observers of the Gulf SWFs that details of the funds, their management and their returns are cloaked in secrecy. There seems to be a move afoot in the UAE to start providing more information, as was seen when discussing Mubadala above. However, the largest of all the funds, ADIA, has only given a slick brochure with some information on its investment philosophy and the rate of return for the past twenty and thirty years. Its absolute failure to give any disclosure regarding how much is actually managed is the reason why this chapter attempted to build a model estimating the amount managed by ADIA. ADIA actually stated that it supports the

Santiago principles in September 2008, which were established by twenty-six of the largest SWFs. "The goal was to create an agreed framework of Generally Accepted Principles and Practices that reflected appropriate governance and accountability arrangements, as well as the conduct of investment practices by SWFs on a prudent and sound basis." This was achieved in September 2008 when the IWG's members signed the so-called "Santiago Principles" in Santiago, Chile. The Principles are underpinned by the following guiding objectives for SWFs:

1. To help maintain a stable global financial system and free flow of capital and investment;
2. To comply with all applicable regulatory and disclosure requirements in the countries in which they invest;
3. To invest on the basis of economic and financial risk and return-related considerations; and
4. To have in place a transparent and sound governance structure that provides for adequate operational controls, risk management and accountability."[30]

ADIA in the same document goes on saying that the principles are "voluntary," thereby explaining why it does not need to provide any details, like Mubadala or the Government Pension Fund of Norway Sovereign Fund does. There appears to be no valid reason for the secrecy surrounding ADIA's management to continue, except perhaps for two important factors.

First, the management of ADIA has traditionally been very tight lipped, and as was seen above, this policy contributed to a rumor mill that resulted in vastly overblown estimates of the investment authority's assets. However, this inflation could establish a major advantage for ADIA. It made every funds manager in the world eager to deal with ADIA and seek to add it in his list of clients. Fund management is a very competitive industry and managers always find a way to present their past results as the best in that industry. It is merely a question of playing with the dates and periods during which the managed investments have taken place. ADIA, which is probably visited by every funds manager in the world, can compare and contrast the various products available, thus selecting a number of managers that offer similar products, their styles, probity and success, and then choose which ones to work with according to the level of fees charged. The hedge funds are known to charge very high fees and include profit-sharing, but not loss-sharing. Regular funds

[30] http://www.adia.ae/En/Governance/Santiago_Principles.aspx

managers will also present very positive returns until their fees are subtracted, but by allowing the amount of its assets to become so inflated, ADIA could simply play on managers' eagerness to enter into business and therefore perhaps accept much lower fees than these managers would otherwise demand. After all, every manager wants to be able to tell its clients in private that they work with the largest and most fabulously successful SWF in the world. They are likely to seek work from ADIA on the most competitive terms on the assumption that the volume of business will be huge, at least if the reports of consultants and the press are to be believed.

Second, and perhaps more important, is the fact that it is not clear who ultimately owns and controls ADIA's funds. Technically, the government of Abu Dhabi owns ADIA, but does the government itself own the funds, or does it just manage them on behalf of the people of Abu Dhabi? If the latter is true, are the funds managed by ADIA entrusted to it as fiduciary for the people of Abu Dhabi, and if so why does the royal family seemingly have the ability to make major decisions as to the type of investments without disclosure to the ultimate owners, the Abu Dhabi citizens? The difference is not merely academic. Indeed, if the funds are owned by the state and managed by ADIA on its behalf, then funds are the property of the citizens of Abu Dhabi. The people of Abu Dhabi would then have a right of regard on the source of the funds, their amount, the risk level, the profits and losses incurred, the type of investments, and ultimately their distribution. In other words, gains and losses would have to be fully disclosed, like those of the Norwegian or Alaskan SWFs. At this time, however, many outsiders see ADIA as being under the full control of the royal family. This perception is of course too simplistic, but it is understandable, considering the lack of disclosure and transparency. This question of control, transparency and fiduciary responsibility is at the very core of ADIA's and Mubadala's management styles. At this time, one can only speculate that ultimately the funds managed by ADIA and Mubadala and the other SWFs of Abu Dhabi are actually state funds, managed on behalf of the citizens of Abu Dhabi by the board of directors of each of the funds. However, these boards are controlled by the royal family, which makes the main members of the family fiduciaries to the people. It is clear that Mubadala has chosen to open its books and keep the public fully informed. On the other hand, it is not clear that ADIA's board has fully accepted its fiduciary responsibility to the public at large. Presumably, if it did, the subsequent transparency would substantially rein in the ability of the Abu Dhabi leadership to have unfettered access to the funds and ultimately change somewhat its political power in the country.

Complicating the story is the fact that Abu Dhabi is part of the United Arab Emirates. It is of importance to understand whether the funds comprise part of the wealth of the country as a whole or only the wealth of the single Emirate of Abu Dhabi. Until now, this question had been overwhelmingly answered by the assumption that the SWFs of Abu Dhabi are fully owned and managed by Abu Dhabi alone. However, as the Federation becomes more closely integrated, and some emirates become increasingly dependent upon Abu Dhabi's wealth to fund their own development, some inside and outside of the emirate may start wondering if the oil income and, by extension, the SWFs, are not in fact the income and savings of the whole country.

5

Knowledge Based Economies in the GCC

Kristian Coates Ulrichsen

In recent years, the six Gulf Cooperation Council (GCC) states have embraced the concept of knowledge economies as integral to their ambitious programs of economic diversification. These in turn represent a crucial element of their adaptation to the broader processes of structural change in the global economy based on accelerating flows of information, knowledge, capital and humans across state boundaries. Policymakers in the Persian Gulf states used a large share of their capital accumulation during the 2002–08 oil price boom to invest in high-profile and frequently headline-making initiatives in higher education and scientific research. Underlying these moves toward a knowledge-based economic transition is official acknowledgment of the necessity of producing well-educated and qualified workforces able to compete in internationally competitive labor markets and alleviate pressing problems of un- and under-employment. Some of the results have been eye-catching as hubs of agglomeration for knowledge-intensive goods and services impart an added-value dimension to the strategies of economic diversification underway throughout the region.

Nevertheless, the strategy to translate oil wealth into human capital integral to the shift toward knowledge economies raises significant questions for the political economy of rentier-state structures in the Gulf States. Central to this is whether the transition toward a knowledge economy is compatible with the maintenance of public sector-dominated redistributive mechanisms of governance. Can the present enclave-based strategies translate into broader cross-sectoral linkages that strengthen autonomous private sector-led developments and institutional capacity-building in the GCC states? Might existing examples of knowledge-creation provide the building-blocks for deepening and widening the economic transition? Is the East Asian model of knowledge-intensive economic development applicable to the different socio-economic context in the Persian Gulf? Is the "revolution" in higher education in the Gulf[1] underpinned by systemic reforms to systems of primary and secondary education and other indicators of human development? What implications might the rise of knowledge-based goods, services and "economic cities" have on stratified labor markets and the imbalance between the public and private sectors in Gulf states? Will a highly-educated and skilled workforce emerge as agents of transformative change that challenges regime-led top-down patterns of gradual political reform?

This chapter begins with a definitional overview of knowledge economies. The opening section assesses the state of the transitions underway in each GCC state and contextualizes them within national economic diversification visions and plans. It also lists existing knowledge-production and value-added enclaves that represent examples of the knowledge economy on a micro- and meso-level. A second section moves beyond the empirical framework to examine a number of challenges—and opportunities—that may arise out of the embedding and maturation of initial openings. It describes how an enabling environment must be constructed if knowledge-based economic transitions are to achieve takeoff and spread beyond their present enclaves of expertise. The third and concluding section links the analysis to the social and political characteristics of the GCC states and offers a preliminary assessment of the moves toward knowledge economies in the region.

Overview of knowledge economies

Transitioning toward a knowledge economy involves a shift from reliance on physical capital and low cost labor for competitive advantage toward the rise of

---

[1] Vincent Romani, "The Politics of Higher Education in the Middle East: Problems and Prospects," Brandeis University Crowne Center for Middle East Studies Brief 36 (May 2009), p. 1.

technology and knowledge-based industries as major generators of value-added, exports and new jobs. In the Organization for Economic Cooperation and Development (OECD) countries, the number of people working in knowledge-intensive and technologically-advanced industries trebled from 50 million in 1970 to 150 million in 2005.[2] Although definitions of the term *knowledge economy* vary across organizations and institutions, its underlying tenets are well captured by the Economic and Social Research Council in the United Kingdom, which in 2005 defined it as an "emerging economic structure" in which "economic success is increasingly based on the effective utilization of intangible assets such as knowledge, skills, and innovative potential as the key resource for competitive advantage." This approach emphasizes how the knowledge economy affects every sector within an economy, whether knowledge-intensive or not, and that it is a process of continuous adaptation rather than a one-off acquisition or step.[3] Dominique Foray, meanwhile, identified a series of structural transformations in the "economics of knowledge" that radically altered the conditions of production and transmission of knowledge and information and created an economy characterized by "the accelerating (and unprecedented) speed at which knowledge is created and accumulated."[4]

Embedded in this process of change is the emergence, or expansion, of a highly-educated and qualified workforce. This reflects the fact that education and the production of, and access to, knowledge are the great dividers in the modern information-based society. They encompass a range of tangible and intangible factors feeding into cumulative policy reforms that create the enabling environment and institutional infrastructure within which this transition can take shape. Moreover, as countries around the world, from global first-movers such as South Korea (which formed a dedicated Ministry for the Knowledge Economy in 2008), Singapore (frequently cited in the Persian Gulf as a model to follow) and the Scandinavian states to regional latecomers, develop explicit knowledge economy strategies, the opportunity cost of falling back becomes greater.[5] This is particularly the case in the comparatively high-

---

[2] Ian Brinkley, Kristian Ulrichsen, Will Hutton, and Philippe Schneider, "Kuwait and the Knowledge Economy," The Work Foundation & LSE Global Governance (July 2010), p. 15.

[3] Ian Brinkley, "Defining the Knowledge Economy," The Work Foundation Knowledge Economy Report (July 2006), p. 4.

[4] Dominique Foray, *The Economics of Knowledge* (Cambridge, Mass.: MIT Press, 2004), pp. ix–x.

[5] In February 2008 South Korea relabeled its Ministry of Commerce, Industry and

income developing states in the GCC, where the scale and intensity of investment in the knowledge economy has grown considerably since 2000.

National approaches toward building knowledge economies thus vary, as do the exact definitions of what precisely is encompassed within them. In the United Kingdom, the National Endowment for Science, Technology and the Arts (NESTA) has identified an "Innovation Index" of factors it deems necessary for knowledge-creation and entrepreneurship to occur. These include a skilled labor force, greater openness to new ideas, higher expenditure on public research and collaboration with industry, and a culture of entrepreneurship within a competitive and demand-led business environment that encourages and rewards innovation.[6] Building on this, research led by Will Hutton, also in the United Kingdom, has emphasized the importance of investment in these knowledge-based "intangible" assets in contributing to successful transitions: "the knowledge economy is the future, but this is not just about science, technology, digitalization and the onward march of creativity...It is a revolution of the mind."[7]

Creating knowledge economies requires greater and sustained level of engagement on multiple fronts, rather than merely a focus on qualitative improvements to education or institutional or regulatory reform, critical though these are. To have any chance of success, a complex enabling environment must emerge that interlinks reforms to institutional and capacity-building infrastructure, market development and appropriate legal frameworks (particularly over intellectual property rights), a financial system capable of mobilizing and channeling investment to firms whose innovatory outputs may encompass a lengthy start-up phase, all underpinned by the intangible values inherent in nurturing a meritocratic business culture of productive entrepreneurship. Within this enabling environment are two issues of pivotal relevance to prospects of successful knowledge economy transitions in the Gulf States: the alignment of standards of educational attainment (and the value-system attached to this) with local labor markets and the balance between the public and private sectors.

Energy as Ministry of Knowledge Economy, http://www.mke.go.kr/language/eng/about/message.jsp (accessed October 21, 2010).

[6] "The Innovation Index: Measuring the UK's Investment in Innovation and its Effects," NESTA Index Report, November 2009, p. 21, http://www.nesta.org.uk/library/documents/innovation-index.pdf (accessed October 24, 2010).

[7] Will Hutton, *Them and Us: Politics, Greed and Inequality—Why We Need a Fair Society* (London: Little, Brown and Company, 2010), p. 34.

The MENA context

In December 2009, a high-level international conference organized by the Islamic Educational, Scientific and Cultural Organization emphasized the need—and the urgency—to develop the knowledge economy in Middle Eastern states. In its concluding *Tunis Declaration on "Building Knowledge Economies"* the participants drew attention to the urgency of transforming their economic base: "In view of the pressing need of States to start preparing for the post-petroleum and post-carbon future, as well as for major water, energy, food, and climate change in the decades to come...the majority of States need to diversify their economies instead of over-dependency on petroleum revenues for some countries, or on the agricultural sector for others.[8]

This aspiration notwithstanding, two years earlier a seminal report issued by the World Bank entitled *The Road Not Traveled: Education Reform in the Middle East and North Africa* identified the broader challenges and obstacles in the way of successful reform. Focusing on the provision and quality of education as the integral core of any larger strategy, the report found that the region as a whole, including the GCC states, faced a misalignment between the educational standards and skills sets required in modern labor markets. Moreover it highlighted the tenuous linkages between investment in education and economic and social development as compared with similarly-placed countries in Latin America and East Asia.[9] Significantly, however, it emphasized the importance of embracing knowledge economies, as well as the dangers of falling further behind, as it concluded that modern global competitiveness "depends on firms that employ a well-educated, technically skilled workforce and are capable of adopting new technologies and selling sophisticated goods and services."[10]

This statement of the need for qualitative changes to the provision of, and access to, educational systems in itself built on the second *Arab Human Development Report* issued by the United Nations Development Program in 2003. Entitled *Building A Knowledge Society*, it called for the creation of an "Arab knowledge society" but acknowledged a mismatch between ineffectual

---

[8] "Tunis Declaration on "Building Knowledge Economies,"" Islamic Educational, Scientific and Cultural Organization, December 3, 2009.
[9] MENA Development Report, "The Road Not Traveled: Education Reform in the Middle East and North Africa," The International Bank for Reconstruction and Development/The World Bank (Washington, DC, 2007), p. 5.
[10] Ibid., p. 8.

demand for, and production and dissemination of, Arab knowledge and the abundance of Arab human capital available. Consequently, it advocated "a pressing need for deep-seated reform in the organizational, social and political context of knowledge," the embedding of science in Arab educational systems, and the development of "an enlightened Arab knowledge model that encourages cognitive learning, problem solving and creativity while prompting the Arabic language, cultural diversity and openness to other cultures."[11]

GCC states' visions and plans

The GCC states' higher levels of GDP and income per citizen mean that they are better positioned than other Middle East North Africa (MENA) countries to undertake the deep structural reforms implicit in any knowledge economic transition. In 2010, a report prepared by the former British Prime Minister Tony Blair entitled *Vision Kuwait 2030* starkly laid out the policy options facing Kuwait, as a regional laggard in economic reform and diversification; it warned that "Put simply, Kuwait cannot sustain its current path. It changes direction or it declines...there is no point in dressing this message up; there has to be a thorough, deep and radical set of changes introduced."[12] In Kuwait, as in other GCC states, local discourse on knowledge-based economic transformations has entered policymaking debates, and these have informed new approaches that seek to embed it in strategies of human capital development.

This is evident in the national visions adopted in each GCC country and in the pronouncements of international and non-governmental organizations, think-tanks and consultancy reports.[13] Oman was the first GCC state to formulate an economic diversification plan with the launch of *Oman 2020: Vision for Oman's Economy* in June 1996. This comprehensive approach was designed to run in conjunction with an ongoing series of five year development plans that focused directly on economic diversification and expanding the private and non-oil sectors.[14] In Bahrain, which like Oman faces depletion of hydro-

---

[11] *The Arab Human Development Report 2003: Building a Knowledge Society* (New York: United Nations Development Program, 2003), p. iv.

[12] "Vision Kuwait 2030" Final Report (2010); Foreword by Tony Blair, p. 4.

[13] These include Tony Blair Associates and The Work Foundation in Kuwait and the RAND-Qatar Policy Institute in Doha.

[14] Marc Valeri, *Oman: Politics and Society in the Qaboos State* (London: Hurst and Co., 2009), p. 202.

carbon reserves much sooner than other GCC states, a package of measures introduced in the early 2000s included labor market reform, economic reform, and educational and training reform. These fledgling reforms were spearheaded by the newly-created Economic Development Board that promotes a pro-business agenda based around the branding of *Business Friendly Bahrain*, and which adopted the *Economic Vision for Bahrain 2030* in 2008.[15]

These early movers in diversification have since been surpassed in order of magnitude by Qatar, the United Arab Emirates and Saudi Arabia. In 2008, the General Secretariat for Development Planning in Qatar unveiled its ambitious *Qatar National Vision 2030*. This outlined five major challenges facing Qatar, including meeting the needs both of the current and future generations and aligning economic growth with social development and environmental management.[16] Its emphasis on human and sustainable development is evident in the rapid expansion of Ras Laffan Industrial City. Since its launch in 1996, Ras Laffan has emerged as one of the fastest growing industrial cities in the world and an integrated hub for the production and export of liquefied natural gas (LNG) and gas-to-liquid (GTL).[17] Already by 2009 it employed more than 100,000 people in twenty-two local and international companies, and developed a reputation for being one of the world's leading green industrial zones through its focus on clean gas.[18]

Abu Dhabi has, to a degree, emulated the Qatari approach by prioritizing a combination of high technology heavy industries and future energy industries within the framework of its *Abu Dhabi Economic Vision 2030*. The establishment of the Abu Dhabi Future Energy Company in 2006 and its ambitious plans to develop Masdar City are largely intended to create the infrastructural basis for an enormous "free zone" concentration of renewable energy companies and researchers.[19] In addition to facilitating joint ventures with major international partners and stimulating substantial flows of foreign

[15] Christian Koch, "Gulf States Plan for Day that Oil Runs Dry," *Jane's Intelligence Review* Vol. 18, No. 12 (December 2006), pp. 23–4.

[16] "Qatar National Vision 2030," http://www.gsdp.gov.qa/portal/page/portal/ GSDP_Vision_Root/GSDP_EN/GSDP_News/GSDP%20News%20Files/ QNV2030_English_v2.pdf (accessed October 29, 2010).

[17] "Ras Laffan Industrial City Investment Reaches $70 Billion," *The Peninsula*, September 23, 2009.

[18] Ibid.

[19] Christopher M. Davidson, *Abu Dhabi: Oil and Beyond* (New York: Columbia University Press, 2009), pp. 82–5.

direct investment, the initiative will also position Abu Dhabi as a global leader in the field of renewable and sustainable energy research and development.[20] Recent announcements (in 2010) of delays to, and downsizing of, the development may affect the eventual outcome of the project, but if completed it can play a significant role in a transition from an oil-dependent economy to a productive, value-added and knowledge-based one.[21]

In Saudi Arabia, the creation of economic cities as hubs of agglomeration and diffusion of knowledge forms a major element in the Kingdom's economic diversification and job creation strategy. A series of major initiatives have been launched, notably the construction of six economic cities, including the showpiece King Abdullah Economic City on the Red Sea coast north of Jeddah, containing an integrated seaport, industrial center and financial sector.[22] These build on the Kingdom's long-delayed accession to the World Trade Organization in 2005 and the privatization of key economic sectors by the Supreme Economic Council in order to attract foreign investment.[23] More importantly, the cities are also designed to bypass cumbersome and ossified bureaucratic structures by creating parallel economies based on regulatory frameworks conducive to private sector investment.[24] Together with the large-scale petrochemical projects underway at Ras Tanura, Jubail Industrial City and the Petro Rabigh Refinery, these initiatives are expected to generate 10.8 million jobs within the Kingdom. However, a report compiled by the National Bank of Kuwait in 2009 estimated that suitably-qualified Saudi workers would only fill about half, or 5.45 million, of the positions, leaving the remainder to expatriate laborers.[25]

This demonstrated how ongoing lags in indices of human development may act as constraining factors if reforms are implemented piecemeal and unevenly

[20] Kristian Ulrichsen, "Rebalancing Global Governance: Gulf States' Perspectives on the Governance of Globalisation," *Global Policy* Vol. 2, No. 1, 2011, forthcoming.

[21] Ed Attwood, "Masdar to Delay Final Completion Until at Least 2020," Arabian Business.com, October 10, 2010.

[22] http://www.kingabdullahcity.com/en/Home/index.html (accessed October 31, 2010).

[23] Rodney Wilson, "Economic Governance and Reform in Saudi Arabia," in Anoushiravan Ehteshami and Steven Wright (eds), *Reform in the Middle East Oil Monarchies* (Reading: Ithaca Press, 2008), pp. 137, 144.

[24] Ibrahim Saif, "The Oil Boom in the GCC Countries, 2002–2008: Old Challenges, Changing Dynamics," *Carnegie Middle East Paper* No. 15 (March 2009), p. 14.

[25] "Saudi Arabia to Generate 10.8 million Job Opportunities by 2014," *Saudi Gazette*, August 10, 2009.

across the economy. Others include networks of familial political-economic alliances that complicate the transition to a market economy with high standards of corporate governance.[26] Meanwhile Dubai's experience offers a cautionary tale, as its fast-track, grandiose government-led development model to transform the Emirate into an international center for the service and logistics industries proved unable to withstand the global economic slowdown. Although the "Dubai model" constituted the most radical attempt in the Gulf to move toward a post-oil economy, and initially succeeded in reducing the oil sector's GDP contribution to 5.1 percent by 2006,[27] its implosion in 2008–9 demonstrated its inherent weaknesses, based on an unsustainable expectation of a constant supply of easy credit and rising real estate prices. Ironically, in light of its objective of diversifying Dubai's economy away from oil, it was ultimately resuscitated by emergency transfers of (oil-derived) capital from Abu Dhabi.[28]

The following section will examine in detail the processes of transition and the changes that have already occurred in the Gulf States. Large-scale prestige projects have caught global attention but require support from reforms to educational systems at the primary and secondary levels if they are to develop organic roots within society. Education, in turn, requires an enabling environment that provides the legal and institutional framework for moving from a comparative to a competitive economic advantage. Underpinning the entire transformational process must be the growth and nurturing of the range of intangibles associated with productive notions of entrepreneurship and innovatory capability, and a shift in socio-cultural attitudes toward the value of educational attainment interlinked with belief in the work-reward causation. For this to occur, the GCC states must embed a knowledge culture that values high returns on the acquisition of knowledge and development of human capital. This requires going beyond top-down government-led approaches, which are far better suited to building physical (rather than human) capital, to a bottom-up reformulation of rentier mindsets and value systems.

---

[26] "The Gulf as a Global Financial Centre: Growing Opportunities and International Influence," *Chatham House Report*, London, 2008, p. 48.

[27] Martin Hvidt, "The Dubai Model: An Outline of Key Development-Process Elements in Dubai," *International Journal of Middle East Studies* Vol. 41, No. 3, 2009, pp. 401–402.

[28] Christopher M. Davidson, "Dubai and Abu Dhabi: Implosion and Opportunity," *Open Democracy*, December 4, 2009.

Progress toward knowledge economies in the GCC states

Although the above-mentioned MENA-wide regional reports were largely pessimistic in their analysis of current efforts to transition toward knowledge economies, the GCC states' economic diversification plans demonstrate how the scale and intensity of change are far from uniform across the Arab and Islamic world. Their higher levels of oil revenues and per capita GDP mean that the Gulf States possess comparatively greater resources to undertake this shift than resource-poorer states in the Maghreb or the Levant. This is reflected in the succession of large-scale and prestige projects unveiled in recent years in the Gulf, which has fundamentally reshaped the regional knowledge-creating landscape. Moreover, the GCC states already possess examples of knowledge-intensive hubs that have created a web of linkages tying them into networks of sophisticated value-creation. The most successful of these localized instances of the knowledge economy in the Gulf, the Saudi Basic Industries Corporation (SABIC), employs high-quality local personnel and has established its own research centers and petrochemical affiliates that increasingly design the products it goes on to sell across the globe.[29]

A clear example of these direct "backward linkages" at work is the construction of a massive acetone plant in Jubail Industrial City by the Saudi Kayan Petrochemical Company, an affiliate of SABIC. In January 2011 it commenced the first Middle East-originated exports of acetone (a part of the value-chain used to manufacture polycarbonates, solvents, adhesives and paints) to the large Indian market. Importantly, it also announced that a share of the acetone produced at the plant would be supplied to other units of Saudi Kayan to manufacture high-value polycarbonates.[30] Another example of emerging linkages between existing hubs is an agreement between the Kuwait Petroleum Corporation and the Kuwait Institute for Scientific Research to establish a Petroleum Research Center and jointly implement a number of trial applications of solar energy technologies.[31]

Higher education initiatives

Within the GCC states a series of major initiatives created centers of learning and integrated research and businesses in regional models of industry-univer-

---

[29] Steffen Hertog, *Princes, Brokers and Bureaucrats: Oil and the State in Saudi Arabia* (Ithaca, NY: Cornell University Press, 2011), pp. 100–101.

[30] "Saudi Kayan Ships First Acetone Export," *Saudi Gazette*, January 18, 2011.

[31] Personal interview, Kuwait, March 2010.

sity collaboration. These included Knowledge Village and Internet City in Dubai, Education City and the Qatar Science and Technology Park in Doha, and Knowledge Oasis Muscat. Moreover, the opening of the King Abdullah University of Science and Technology (KAUST) in Saudi Arabia and the Masdar Institute of Science and Technology (MIST) in Abu Dhabi, both in 2009, represented important steps toward enhancing indigenous institutional and educational capacity. Their enormous—by international standards—financial endowments positions them to develop into world-leading platforms for cutting-edge research into issues such as sustainable and renewable energy.[32] These multi-billion-dollar initiatives are complemented by policymakers' awareness of educational deficiencies and the adoption of reforms designed to revamp them, as, for example, in the K-12 structural and organizational reforms to the Qatari education system undertaken in collaboration with the RAND Global Policy Institute.[33] Over the past decade, the legalization and opening of private colleges added a further layer of alternatives to state-sector higher education, as evidenced in Oman, where 24 private universities opened between 1997 and 2009 to greatly broaden the provision of higher education hitherto restricted to the public Sultan Qaboos University.[34]

These myriad initiatives contributed to what one academic recently labeled an "academic revolution" in higher education in the Gulf States since the turn of the twenty-first century. This occurred as more than forty branch campuses of Western universities opened in the United Arab Emirates and Qatar alone between 2003 and 2007, while over 100 colleges and universities opened in Saudi Arabia since 2003. During this period, the GCC emerged as the major academic player in the broader MENA region as the scale of investment in higher education became clear, although its members followed very different funding models—ranging from governmental underwriting of transaction costs in Qatar to more symmetrical financial responsibility in the United Arab Emirates (UAE), where campuses were expected to cover their own costs—which led to two high-profile failures in Dubai and Ras Al-Khaimah when anticipated

---

[32] Kristian Ulrichsen, "Diversification: the Challenge of Transition," *The Gulf*, Issue 87, Vol. 3 (May 2010), p. 35.

[33] Alan S. Weber, "Web-Based Learning in Qatar and the GCC States," *CIRS Occasional Paper* No. 5, Georgetown School of Foreign Service in Qatar: Center for International and Regional Studies, 2010, p. 11.

[34] Gari Donn and Yahia Al Manthri, *Globalisation and Higher Education in the Arab Gulf States* (Oxford: Symposium Books, 2010), p. 109.

student numbers and revenues failed to materialize.[35] By 2009, a report issued by the Observatory for Borderless Higher Education (OBHE) found that forty-one international branch campuses (IBCs) out of a total of 160 worldwide were located in the United Arab Emirates, making it by far the largest single importer of branch campuses in the world.[36] Qatar's Education City opened in 1998 and now hosts branches of six prestigious American universities, one French business school and a newly-announced tie-up in University College London-Qatar (UCL-Q),[37] while the neighboring Qatar Science and Technology Park provides another example of research-business collaboration.[38]

Although the quality of education on offer does vary, the flagship initiatives in Education City, KAUST and MIST offer cutting-edge research opportunities in collaboration with leading Western academic institutions. Both the University of Cambridge and Stanford University established agreements with KAUST, while Imperial College London founded a joint research initiative with the Qatar Science and Technology Park, and Harvard University created the Dubai Initiative in connection with the Dubai School of Government. Through their publications, research and teaching these institutions have broadened and deepened the qualitative academic options available to students wishing to pursue their studies in the Middle East. The opening in 2010 of NYU Abu Dhabi constituted another landmark move, involving the transplantation of an entire research university, rather than the importation of a single faculty or school.[39] Meanwhile Qatar led the way in aligning research

[35] Romani, "Politics of Higher Education," pp. 1, 4.

[36] Jason Lane, "International Branch Campuses, Free Zones, and Quality Assurance: Policy Issues for Dubai and the UAE," *Dubai School of Government Policy Brief*, No. 20 (August 2010), p. 2.

[37] The six are the Weill Cornell Medical College in Qatar, Texas A&M University at Qatar, Virginia Commonwealth University in Qatar, Carnegie Mellon University in Qatar, the Georgetown School of Foreign Service, and Northwestern University in Qatar. In addition, Education City also hosts the Qatar Faculty of Islamic Studies and HEC Paris in Qatar, the latter a graduate school of management offering executive education programs. In October 2010, University College London announced that it would open UCL-Q in a partnership between UCL, the Qatar Foundation and the Qatar Museums Authority, offering postgraduate research-led and executive education programs.

[38] As of October 2010, companies represented included Qatar Petroleum and Q-Tel, as well as leading global companies such as Microsoft, Rolls-Royce, Tata, and GE.

[39] Melanie Swan, "NYU to Make Abu Dhabi 'Ideas Capital," *The National*, September 7, 2010.

and development with its strategic vision through the Qatar National Research Fund (established in 2006). This funds research "that meets the needs of Qatar" and strongly encourages collaboration between Qatari and internationally-recognized institutions, and between the public and private sectors.[40] The Center for Externally Funded Research and Consultancy at UAE University has been similarly successful in initiating research and development links and tangible knowledge-transfers through collaborative projects with national and international industrial partners, especially in engineering.[41]

These sites of learning and knowledge-creation can also act as agents of change in the societies within which they operate. This is particularly interesting in the case of KAUST in Saudi Arabia, as its co-educational model pushes against the social boundaries in the Kingdom concerning the role of education and women in society. Its opening is intended, according to the president of King Abdulaziz University in Jeddah, Osama Tayeb, to "accelerate scientific, technological, cultural, economic and social progress" throughout the country.[42] In this objective it has benefited from the strong support of King Abdullah bin Abdul-Aziz Al-Saud as part of his larger program of reforming Saudi Arabia's educational system. Significantly, KAUST was developed as a personal project of the King under the aegis of Saudi Aramco, rather than through the Ministry of Higher Education as in the case of the other universities opened in Saudi Arabia since 2003. It thus represents a potentially introspective instance of "enclave-twinning" in which the benefits of the linkages between two of the flagships of Saudi Arabian knowledge-creation might become largely self-contained.[43] KAUST is, and remains, a carefully-controlled social experiment in a tightly-managed enclave some eighty kilometers from the nearest large city (Jeddah). It is thus effectively sealed off from Saudi society, while the possibility of any unintended overspill of its social mixing is further diminished by the low number of Saudi students in enrollment and the controls placed on access to its campus.[44]

---

[40] Qatar National Research Fund, http://www.qnrf.org/ (accessed January 22, 2011).

[41] Imen Jeridi Bachellerie, "Knowledge Creation and Diffusion: The Role of UAE Universities," *Gulf Research Centre Report* (October 2010), pp. 21–2.

[42] "KAUST Will Serve as Bridge Between Cultures: Abdullah," *Arab News*, September 16, 2009.

[43] Zvika Krieger, "Reforms in Higher Education Raise Questions," *Arab Reform Bulletin*, December 2007.

[44] F. Gregory Gause, "Saudi Arabia: The Second Sex and the Third Rail," *Foreign Policy*, April 19, 2010.

The enclave nature of many of the new "free zones" and themed "cities" undoubtedly offers economies of scale and opportunities for research and university-business collaboration that are already being realized in sites such as Education City or Knowledge Oasis Muscat. They may also create (in the words of one recent report issued by the Dubai School of Government) "information and resource bridges between Middle Eastern host societies on the one hand, and the Western and wider world on the other."[45] Nevertheless, outside of these major enclaves the rapid expansion in institutional facilities and expenditure remains patchier in its record of transforming the quality of education. Especially in Dubai's two free zones of International Academic City and Knowledge Village, the rush to attract institutions has led to questions regarding the academic standards and integrity of some of the new arrivals.[46] Nor has the project to embed regional campuses of North American universities been an unqualified success, as evidenced by the closure of the George Mason University in Ras Al-Khaimah in 2009 or the difficulties faced by Michigan State University in Dubai, which terminated its undergraduate programs in 2010. Both campuses suffered from bad timing as their opening coincided with the global economic downturn and financial crisis that hit Dubai, while student uptake in each was far lower than expected, leading to unsustainable budgetary shortfalls.[47] Their difficulties rekindled memories of the ill-fated rush by almost forty American universities to establish branch campuses in Japan in the 1980s. By 2010, just one survived the combination of precarious financial foundations and clash of cultures that confronted the previous generation of international branch campuses.[48]

A recent study of higher education in the GCC, co-authored by a British-based academic and a former Minister for Higher Education (and current Chair of the State Council) in Oman, picked up on some of the challenges facing the implanting of foreign campuses in the Gulf. Gari Donn and Yahya

[45] Rasmus Gjedsso Bertelsen, "American- and French-Affiliated Universities in the Middle East as 'Information and Resource Bridges' to the West," *Dubai Initiative Working Paper* (2009), p. 11.

[46] Daniel Bardsley, "Dubai May Revoke University Licenses," *The National*, January 12, 2010.

[47] "George Mason Uni to Close RAK Branch," *The National*, February 26, 2009; "University Branches in Dubai are Struggling," *New York Times*, December 27, 2009.

[48] David McNeill, "Temple U. Stands Tall in Japan," *Chronicle of Higher Education*, June 23, 2010.

Al Manthri concluded pessimistically that the trend toward importing foreign, primarily American, campuses perpetuated a dependency culture in which the Gulf States remained consumers, rather than producers, of knowledge, which continued to be generated externally. The authors added that the influx of foreign institutions of higher education risked becoming "a valuable economic and political cargo for the sellers/exporters but of little educational value to purchasers/importers."[49] Further, data collected in Dubai for a study conducted by the Dubai School of Government suggested that only a minority of the students enrolled in the international branch campuses were Emirati nationals, and that the substantial majority of expatriate students expected to return to their home countries following completion of their studies in Dubai.[50] Trends in numbers of local students and the destination of graduates will be key indicators of whether the rapid expansion of higher education is producing tangible longer-term benefits for Gulf societies beyond their narrower institutional confines.[51]

For all their governments' spending on higher education over the past decade, no indigenous universities in the GCC states featured in a global ranking of the top 500 academic institutions in 2008.[52] Quick-fix solutions, such as the importing of prestigious Western universities, are at best a temporary alleviation of a deeper obstacle that will take longer to overcome. Indigenous institutions suffer from funding difficulties, problems of overcrowding and teaching-led (rather than research-led) agendas, and in many cases cannot match the imported Western branch campuses for resources. In October 2010, the vice-provost for academic and international affairs at UCL bluntly (and, some might say in view of his institution's agreement to open a branch in Qatar, insensitively) suggested that "there is no critical mass of research" in the region and claimed (provocatively) that local academics would benefit from being "part of UCL, rather than joining a university in the Arab world, most of which don't have serious research."[53] The tangible scale of investment in university campuses—imported and indigenous—over the past decade is insufficient in itself to deliver the lasting intangible benefits of a productive

[49] Donn and Al Manthri, "Globalisation and Higher Education," p. 15.

[50] Lane, "International Branch Campuses," p. 5.

[51] According to one estimate the first cohort of approximately 170 students at NYU Abu Dhabi in 2010/11 contained between four and seven UAE nationals.

[52] "Reforms Will Help Business," *Middle East Economic Digest*, July 18, 2008.

[53] John Gill, "Gulf Opens for UCL as Qatari Campus Aims to Unearth Past," *Times Higher Education*, November 4, 2010.

mentality in which educational attainment is directly linked to professional advancement. For this to happen, deeper changes must be made to primary and secondary education systems in the GCC states, and these need to be integrated into structural reforms to labor markets throughout the region. Only then can the benefits of the knowledge-creation underway in the free zones and enclaves be fully utilized in a dynamic process of mutual engagement with the wider society.

Primary and secondary education

Significant investment in long-term projects to reconfigure primary and secondary educational systems in the GCC states is needed if the changes are to become organic and underpin transformational economic diversification and labor nationalization plans. Market research by the RAND Corporation in response to a request by the Qatari leadership in 2001 to undertake a broad examination of its K-12 education uncovered numerous challenges common to all the GCC states. The initial analysis identified an overly-rigid and bureaucratic educational structure that discouraged innovation, offered teachers few opportunities for professional development, provided no Ministry of Education support to a curriculum based on out-of-date teaching material and taught through rote-learning, and had no accountability mechanisms for school or student performance.[54] A later study, undertaken in 2007, highlighted a misalignment between patterns of education and employment, especially for young Qatari males.[55] It also identified a challenge common to all of the oil-exporting states of the Arabian Peninsula: "the virtual guarantee that Qatari men with no more than a secondary school education will find secure, well-paying, and prestigious jobs in Qatar's government ministries." The report emphasized the value of a holistic strategy addressing policy reform that "coordinates the various educational institutions and considers related policy areas, especially those of employment and labor."[56] Qatar has since embarked on a thoroughgoing reform of its K-12 educational system in part-

[54] Gail L. Zellman, Louay Constant and Charles A. Goodman, "K-12 Education Reform in Qatar," *Orient: German Journal for Politics, Economics and Culture of the Middle East* Vol. 52, No. 1, 2011, p. 55.

[55] Cathleen Stasz, Eric R. Eide and Francisco Martorell, "Education in Qatar: Employer Demand, Student Choice, and Options for Policy," *RAND-Qatar Policy Institute* (2007), p. xv.

[56] Ibid., pp. xix–xx.

nership with RAND, centered around a decentralized Independent School model enjoying greater autonomy and choice in developing and implementing student learning and assessment.[57]

Other structural challenges in Gulf States' education systems include gender imbalances and social issues around the intermingling of students in coeducational classes. Research undertaken in the United Arab Emirates in 2009 highlighted a "hidden gender gap" in the country's education system: while applauding the Emirates' equality of access for women in secondary and tertiary education, it found that "men have not made the same gains as women and in some cases may be left behind." This manifested itself in Emirati boys' poorer school performance and also in figures that showed that only 27 percent of Emirati men went into higher education as opposed to 70 percent of women. Perversely, unemployment rates for men were much lower than for women, suggesting that "When public sector employment options are plentiful and education is seen to be of little relevance, it is only natural that young men will forego education past a certain point."[58] These factors tie into the difficulties identified in Qatar of incentivizing educational attainment by linking it to labor market opportunities in a highly-skewed, public-sector dominated economic setting.

In the United Arab Emirates, as elsewhere in the Gulf States, poor teacher quality, low pay and limited career advancement prospects have also been cited as obstacles to raising standards in primary and secondary education. These are intertwined as the comparatively low wage levels of teachers have made teaching unattractive to GCC nationals and led to a greater reliance on often poorly-trained Arab expatriate teachers. Improvements to recruiting standards and salaries, and linking them to performance while working to remedy the social stigmatization of teaching as a profession among citizens, are all needed to remedy this gap at the most formative level of students' interaction with the system.[59] The introduction of independent schools in Qatar, and schools such as the US Department of Defense's Bahrain School, in which Bahraini nationals represent about half the total enrolled students, will also raise standards and foster greater competition among local competitors, particularly in the medium to longer term.

---

[57] Zellman *et al.*, "Education Reform in Qatar," p. 55.

[58] Natasha Ridge, "The Hidden Gender Gap in Education in the UAE," *Dubai School of Government Policy Brief*, No. 12 (August 2009), pp. 1–4.

[59] Ridge, "Hidden Gender Gap," p. 6.

Social and religious conservatism is another factor that has hindered attempts to reform curricula and raise the standard of primary and secondary education in GCC states. Particularly in Saudi Arabia and Kuwait, schooling and curricula emerged as critical sites of contestation between regimes and Islamists, and cut to the heart of the ideological battle for the direction of change in Gulf polities. Sustained Islamist pressure in Kuwait resulted in the segregation of formerly co-educational institutions in 1996, and parliamentary deadlock over proposed measures to reform educational standards.[60] Meanwhile in Saudi Arabia, three decades of religious clerical control over the Ministry of Higher Education left a legacy of emphasis on religious instruction over liberal arts or sciences. Although the rapid opening of new universities and colleges since 2003 demonstrates the accelerating pace of change, it was nonetheless revealing that the development of KAUST bypassed the Ministry altogether.[61] Other concerns over the potential for unregulated mixed-gender interaction through internet-based e-learning programs provide further evidence of the sensitivity of reforming the education sector in GCC states.[62]

Although reforms will take years to work their way through the system, it appears that local standards in the GCC states have not improved significantly over the past decade of heavy expenditure on education. Bahrain's *Economic Vision 2030* implicitly criticized the existing educational system as it argued that reforms to education were vital to make it "relevant to the needs of Bahrain and its economy."[63] Indeed, in other countries they may even be falling behind. This was the conclusion of a World Bank report on the United Arab Emirates issued in 2007, which found that its knowledge-based sector had actually shrunk since 2005 owing, it claimed, to deteriorating standards in local education.[64] Across the Gulf States, particular weaknesses in the sciences, engineering and language skills manifest themselves in low scores in international benchmarks such as TIMSS (Trends in International Mathematical and Science Study). These translate into poor levels of knowledge genera-

[60] Michelle Dunne, "Interview With Ali Al-Rashed, National Assembly Member and Candidate," *Arab Reform Bulletin*, May 2008.

[61] Krieger, "Reforms in Higher Education."

[62] Weber, "Web-Based Learning," p. 5.

[63] "Our Vision: Economic Vision for Bahrain 2030," *Bahrain Economic Development Board*, Article 3.3.

[64] Christopher Davidson, *Abu Dhabi*, p. 150.

tion and an emerging gap in value-added wealth creation between the developed and developing worlds.[65]

This is a feature common to all the oil-exporting states in the Arabian Peninsula, but especially marked in the "extreme rentier" states of Kuwait and the United Arab Emirates. Resolving it will be critical to the success (or otherwise) of eventual transitions toward productive post-oil economies. Investment in, and reforms to, education and higher education constitute critical elements of the enabling environment that would allow knowledge economy "takeoff" but are insufficient factors in themselves. The experience of the East Asian "tigers" highlights the changing nature of the role of formal education as a source of growth and economic development. An intergenerational commitment to education at all its levels in South Korea, for example, was integral to its wider strategy of translating initial technology transfer into local competitiveness based on a comparative advantage in human capital.[66] Thus, the East Asian model demonstrates the importance of linking economic and technocratic reforms to the wider operation of the social and political system within which they operate. This raises the question of whether a genuine knowledge-based transition is fundamentally incompatible with the maintenance of rentier mechanisms of governance, for if achieved, it would involve the transformational reform of labor markets, organization of economic structures, and development of human capital.

Creating an enabling environment

The foregoing is not to suggest that an enabling environment cannot develop within the current political environment. At least in its initial stages, top-down state approaches play an important role in generating the momentum for change and the "buy-in" from key stakeholders across the state-business community. This was the case in the successful transitions underway in the East Asian economies of South Korea, Singapore, Malaysia and Taiwan. In these countries, plans were drawn up and implemented in relatively short periods of time with substantial public investment, and based on the identification of national characteristics and features around which success and expertise could be built. These specificities differed from country to country, but in

---

[65] David A. King, "The Scientific Impact of Nations: What Countries Get for Their Research Spending," *Nature*, 430, July 15, 2004, p. 314.

[66] Bachellerie, "Knowledge Creation and Diffusion," p. 10.

each case the existence of relatively strong institutional contexts, private sectors and public corporations proved critical common features and building-blocks for reform.[67]

Distinctive pathways to knowledge economy transitions reflect the wide variation in factors and variables between states. Nevertheless certain commonalities may be identified as important for (or, alternatively, obstacles to) the transition taking root. The first is the existence of an appropriate domestic institutional framework capable of both supporting innovatory projects and coordinating initiatives in a whole-of-government approach to reform. Organizations such as the Council for Economic Planning and Development in Taiwan, the Economic Development Board in Singapore, or the Research and Innovation Council in Finland have all functioned as lead agencies providing strategic direction in close cooperation with policymakers and politicians.[68] In the GCC, an early-mover in this regard was the Qatar Foundation, established in 1995 to develop human capital through education and scientific research and "making the knowledge-based society a reality," in part through the creation of Education City and the Qatar Science and Technology Park.[69]

Oman created a Research Council in 2005 in order to formulate an integrated plan for research and development in line with identified national priorities. Its objectives include supporting individual innovation and research programs and facilitating communication and collaboration between the research and industrial communities.[70] Working with Sultan Qaboos University (SQU), it aims to become a leader in knowledge generation and build a world-class infrastructure for research at SQU focusing on Solar Energy, Enhanced Oil Recovery and Nanotechnology, although this is a long-term objective not currently underpinned by adequate research capabilities.[71] In the UAE, the National Research Foundation was formed in 2008 in collaboration with the National Science Foundation in the United States, the Australian Research Council and Science Foundation Ireland. Its mandate includes the creation of a research infrastructure and internationally competitive innova-

---

[67] Brinkley *et al.*, "Kuwait and the Knowledge Economy," p. 18.

[68] Ibid., p. 28.

[69] Qatar Foundation, http://www.qf.org.qa/output/page4.asp (accessed November 3, 2010).

[70] Sultanate of Oman, The Research Council, http://www.trc.gov.om/TRCWebsite/index.htm (accessed November 3, 2010).

[71] Only two PhD holders graduated from SQU in 2010; see Donn and Al Manthri, "Globalisation and Higher Education," p. 117.

tion system and culture of entrepreneurship in the UAE, in addition to the strengthening of research linkages between universities, government and industry, but its small size is a limiting factor.[72]

Elsewhere in the GCC states, the Executive Offices and organizations being set up to implement the national visions could house the organizational infrastructure necessary to coordinate and develop the processes of transition toward knowledge economies. Such a move would integrate stakeholders such as the Ministries of Education and Higher Education with the bodies set up to drive through the economic diversification projects and prevent overlapping or cracks emerging between them. Indeed, the Blair Report on Kuwait explicitly called for the creation of a Strategy Unit within the Prime Minister's Office to "guarantee the consistency of the overall approach" and "ensure that the government program, and all major policies and investments, are aligned with the long-term vision."[73] This would overcome the obstacle of multiple and largely-uncoordinated research organizations in Kuwait that have hitherto hindered the development of a coherent approach to knowledge-creation and transfer.

For these organizations to succeed, they must be enmeshed within robust institutions that are perceived to offer an equitable and fair business and investment climate. Although institutional and regulatory reforms have reshaped the business landscape of the Gulf states over the past decade and are stronger in some countries than in others, lingering doubts remain over the presence of personalized and informal networks that undercut or bypass processes of institutionalization. In Bahrain, an internal struggle within the ruling family between Prime Minister Khalifa bin Salman Al-Khalifa and Crown Prince Salman bin Hamad Al-Khalifa diluted the impact of the Economic Development Board in driving through its reforms.[74] Meanwhile in Saudi Arabia and Dubai the corporate disputes and sudden debt restructurings in 2009 exposed weaknesses in key governance indicators (including transparency, disclosure of information, and access to information), in addition to the persistence of networks of familial political-economic alliances. These can

---

[72] UAE National Research Foundation, Director's Message, http://www.nrf.ae/directormessage.aspx (accessed November 3, 2010).

[73] *Vision Kuwait 2030*, pp. 308–310.

[74] Steven Wright, "Fixing the Kingdom: Political Evolution and Socio-Economic Challenges in Bahrain," CIRS Occasional Paper No. 3, Georgetown School of Foreign Service in Qatar: Center for International and Regional Studies, 2008, p. 3.

complicate the transition to a market economy while undermining entrepreneurship and productivity by creating and perpetuating perverse incentives and vested interests against reform.[75]

The emergence of a strong private sector capable of becoming the main engine of economic growth is a second critical element of any enabling environment. Within the GCC context, it involves stripping away layers and legacies of rent-seeking behavior and laying the groundwork for the shift to a productive, value-added economic model. The creation (and enlargement) of comparatively well-managed technocratic enclaves represent "islands of efficiency" within GCC economies.[76] They also constitute building blocks for attracting the inward flows of investment, technology and human talent that provide the core of knowledge-intensive industries and take-off. Moreover, the enclaves facilitate "industrial clustering" and technological diffusion, but the challenge facing policymakers in the Gulf States is how to expand these linkages beyond the zones and break out into the wider economy. The danger of not doing so is that knowledge-intensive hubs such as KAUST in Saudi Arabia or the free zones in the United Arab Emirates and elsewhere remain limited "parallel" sectors existing alongside, but not organically within, otherwise little-changed economic structures.

This is significant because measures to strengthen the private sector and energize it as the engine of economic growth are important elements of the wider enabling environment. They encompass support for privatization programs, small and medium-enterprises, joint ventures and foreign investment, business competitiveness and a regulatory framework that gives strategic actors adequate incentives within the host environment and can support firms that become national and regional champions.[77] Although these measures must to some extent be consistent with local norms and values to develop organic roots within society, they do face a number of obstacles and challenges in the specific context of the redistributive mechanisms of governance in the Gulf. These include the durability of public and private sector and labor market dualities in GCC states and "sticky" and persistent notions of what the Kuwaiti MP Rola Dashti terms a "culture of entitlement" among many citizens in Gulf States.[78]

---

[75] Kristian Ulrichsen, *Insecure Gulf: The End of Certainty and the Transition to the Post-Oil Era* (London: Hurst & Co., 2011), p. 104.

[76] Steffen Hertog, *Princes, Brokers, and Bureaucrats*, pp. 28–9.

[77] Brinkley *et al.*, "Kuwait and the Knowledge Economy," pp. 21–2.

[78] Interview with Rola Dashti MP, Kuwait City, March 15, 2010.

These obstacles occur to varying degrees in each of the six Gulf States, although they are most pronounced in the "extreme rentiers" of Kuwait and the United Arab Emirates. In turn, they translate into distinctive class interests and dual labor markets while maintaining deep variations in the level of political participation and its connection to economic development.[79] 92 percent of Kuwaitis in work find themselves in the public sector, for example, while 83 percent of private sector employment consists of expatriate laborers.[80] Meanwhile, in the United Arab Emirates, nationals account for roughly 85 percent of the public sector workforce but only 1 percent of the private sector, as nationals tend not to enter the latter due to the greater competition for jobs and lower salaries on offer.[81] These unique employment patterns lie at the core of the rentier system in the GCC states and the nature of the relationship between regimes and their citizenry.[82] Yet they exhibit very different models of economic development as well as markedly diverging business climates, with Kuwait lagging well behind in attracting foreign direct investment and earning a reputation as a very poor place to do business.[83] Indeed, the poor enabling environment in Kuwait is reflected in an astounding gap in inflows of foreign direct investment, which totaled a mere $58 million in 2008, as compared with $1,794 million in Bahrain, $2,928 million in Oman, $6,700 million in Qatar, $13,700 million in the United Arab Emirates, and $38,223 million in Saudi Arabia.[84]

The differing business trajectories in Kuwait and the UAE, and between "high" and "lesser" rentiers, militate against blanket "one size fits all" descriptions of the challenges facing GCC states in reformulating politico-economic

---

[79] Michael Herb, "A Nation of Bureaucrats: Political Participation and Economic Diversification in Kuwait and the United Arab Emirates," *International Journal of Middle East Studies* Vol. 41, No. 3, 2009, pp. 375–95.

[80] Ang Nga Longva, "Neither Autocracy nor Democracy but Ethnocracy: Citizens, Expatriates and the Socio-Political System in Kuwait," in Paul Dresch and James Piscatori (eds), *Monarchies and Nations: Globalisation and Identity in the Arab States of the Gulf* (London: I.B. Tauris, 2004), p. 120.

[81] Ridge, "Hidden Gender Gap," p. 4.

[82] Onn Winckler, "Labor and Liberalization: The Decline of the GCC Rentier System," in Joshua Teitelbaum (ed.), *Political Liberalization in the Persian Gulf* (London: Hurst & Co., 2009), p. 84.

[83] Herb, *Nation of Bureaucrats*, p. 377.

[84] Mahfouz Tadros, "Foreign Direct Investment in GCC Countries: The Case of Kuwait," unpublished article, p. 1.

structures and relations. This notwithstanding, some common issues across the GCC that need resolving are the legacies of "rentier mentalities" and monopoly rents nested within economic and bureaucratic structures, and the unbundling of notions of entitlement, which itself is embedded within concepts of citizenship and the very basis of the social contract as laid down in the 1960s and 1970s. The overarching theme that binds these diverse strands together is the idea of "intangible" forms of investment that complement the tangible investments in physical infrastructure or regulatory environments (for example, the economic competence and innovative quality of a workforce is as important as the new building that has just been constructed to house them). Hence, the incentivizing of work and its linkage with notions of due reward, or the erosion of risk-averse tendencies and bureaucratic immobility in public sectors that crowd out private sector initiative, are as important dimensions of the knowledge economy as the construction of "economic cities," "free zones" and importation of leading Western university branch campuses, or regulatory reforms to facilitate the opening of businesses, enforcement of contracts, and protection of investors.

Prospects for knowledge economies in the GCC

The interdependent constituents of the knowledge economy mean that efforts to support one area will be compromised if others do not function adequately, or if reforms are incomplete in scope or left unfinished or partially implemented. Actors and institutions implanted in a business environment characterized by opacity, poor transparency and regulatory compliance, limited administrative efficiency, diluted implementation and pervasive aspects of informality are extremely unlikely to develop into agents of transformative change and may even begin to reproduce these patterns of behavior in their own actions.[85] In the GCC context, the resilience of family-owned conglomerates and the ongoing utility of personal contacts to facilitate the ease of doing business represent potential stumbling-blocks to the emergence of the enabling environment described above, as do the continuing peculiarities in labor market and public-private sector imbalances. Set against this are the high levels of capital available to policymakers in the Gulf states that enables them to attract world-class research and development and to undertake expen-

---

[85] Brinkley et al., "Kuwait and the Knowledge Economy," p. 36.

sive programs of transition that would be too costly for resource-poor countries elsewhere.

The differing pathways of reform were well captured in a 2007 report on *The Gulf Cooperation Council Countries and the World* prepared by the World Economic Forum. This argued that three different scenarios lay ahead to 2025, each depending on the capacity of leaders to "implement the necessary economic and political reforms and enforce the rule of law, both in public and in private governance," in addition to maintaining domestic order and stability in a volatile regional environment. In the most negative *Sandstorm* scenario, it warned that focusing on short-term solutions at the expense of tough reforms risked a scenario in which regional events and domestic unrest contribute to "the GCC countries failing to maintain their momentum of reforms, with negative consequences for the region's economic and social development." The intermediate *Oasis* scenario projected a future of technocratic governance and top-down institutional reforms that "pays off in the form of a well-organized, cohesive and prosperous regional grouping" but in which economic growth "remains partially constrained by over-regulation and less-inclusive globalization." Meanwhile the most optimistic *The Fertile Gulf* scenario foresaw the GCC states "taking advantage of globalization" through "bold reforms at the institutional and political levels" by investing heavily in education and innovation "in order to create a healthy private sector while encouraging reforms through a bottom-up process." For this to occur, the report argued that "critical and creative thinking are central to upgrading human capital and fostering innovation."[86]

Elements of all three scenarios can be discerned in the strategies and prospects for the knowledge economy transition in the Gulf. The GCC states are indeed emerging as major global players in multiple fields, including that of higher education and research into cutting-edge renewable energy technologies. Oil revenues accumulated during the second oil price boom were put to more sustainable and longer-term use than during the first boom, while more careful fiscal policies and the emergence of an incipient private-sector less dependent on state spending indicated a maturing of GCC economies by comparison with the previous oil price boom in the 1970s.[87] Moreover, all the

[86] "The Gulf Cooperation Council Countries and the World: Scenarios to 2025," *World Economic Forum: World Scenario Series*, Geneva, 2007, pp. 6–7.
[87] Steffen Hertog, "The Current Crisis and Lessons from the 1980s," *Arab Reform Bulletin*, July 2009.

declared visions of economic diversification place human capital development at the forefront of their objectives and central to the task of transitioning toward a post-rentier political economy.

This notwithstanding, the partial and top-down technocratic nature of reforms, and the institutional stickiness of many of the challenges to embedding knowledge economies identified above, speak more to the *Oasis* scenario in which significant constraints operate to hold back attempts at change. More pessimistically, perhaps, the tough reforms necessary to restructure domestic political and economic structures—such as increasing the proportion of government revenues accruing from taxation and enhancing the efficiency and transparency of public expenditure while taking measures to diminish and overcome the structural imbalances in the economy and labor markets—were not pushed through during the era of economic boom in the 2000s, as spiking oil-based revenues provided governments with a degree of insulation from socio-economic and domestically-challenging political pressures for the long-term reforms as identified in the *Sandstorm* scenario.[88] This raises the possibility that the processes of genuine economic transformation and reformulation of the "rentier bargain" may be deferred until the imminence of resource depletion means reform can no longer be delayed, by which time it may be too late to transition toward productive post-oil economies. The case of Yemen provides an instructive, yet alarming, warning about the challenges of transition and management of depleting resources.[89]

The knowledge economy is a key component of economic transformation and should be viewed as an ongoing process of structural and intangible change rather than an acquisition-based or measurable end in itself. Policy-makers and analysts should adopt a realistic understanding of how long the transition might take and target their commitments accordingly. In the East Asian cases of Taiwan, Japan and South Korea, the shift toward knowledge economies reflects the overhaul of economic structures that began in the early 1960s and began to reach fruition in the 1980s.[90] Changing notions of educational attainment and the value ascribed to the acquisition of knowledge will similarly be

---

[88] Saif, "Oil Boom in GCC," p. 6.
[89] Kristian Ulrichsen, "Yemen: The Canary in the Coal Mine?" *Open Democracy*, November 1, 2010.
[90] Robert Wade, *Governing the Market: Economic Theory and the Role of Government in East Asian Industrialization* (Princeton, New Jersey: Princeton University Press, 2004), p. 3.

cross-generational as families with higher levels of education become role models for succeeding generations. Thus, while the Gulf states have made significant progress in creating enclaves of concentrated expertise in which research and development and university-industry collaboration can take root and flourish, embedding and expanding their share in GCC economies will be central to the task of moving from a political economy based on comparative advantage in hydrocarbons, to one based on competitive advantage in a knowledge-intensive and rapidly-globalizing environment. The challenge in coming years and decades will be to steadily widen the reach of the knowledge economy and mainstream it within sectors and professions hitherto little touched by the processes of change, while moving from top-down investments in physical capital to a more autonomous acquisition of human capital.

Yet as this occurs a profound question arises: can the concept of a knowledge economy occur within the political economy of rentierism? Put simply, is a knowledge economy incompatible with redistributive, public-sector dominated polities in which the loci of political and economic power are still confined to a relatively closed circle and implemented in a carefully-managed top-down process? If successfully carried out, the reform of economic processes inherent in any fundamental knowledge-based transition would reformulate models of governance and social and political relations in the GCC states. The rise of a productive and knowledge-intensive economy would involve systemic changes to labor markets and require the progressive stripping away of the redistributive mechanisms that have underpinned the concept of the "ruling bargain" for the past four decades.[91] Moreover, a rising highly-educated and skilled populace may emerge as agents of transformative change if they perceive limitations to their freedom to access or acquire knowledge, or utilize it autonomously from governmental oversight and control.

Linking economic transition to socio-political change demonstrates the systemic and interdependent nature of the reforms that lie ahead. Improvements to standards of education and higher education will need to be aligned with the current and future needs of labor markets in knowledge-intensive sectors. Lingering "rentier mentalities" and legacies of unproductive rent-seeking behavioral patterns have to be tackled and eventually marginalized. Any such change would be transformational in its impact on state-society relations and, inevitably, on mechanisms of political participation in decision-

---

[91] Joseph Kostiner (ed.), *Middle East Monarchies: The Challenge of Modernity* (London: Lynne Rienner, 2000), p. 9.

making processes. At first sight, it may appear counter-intuitive for GCC regimes to promote policies that could facilitate the growth of politically-engaged elements within their own polities, especially in light of developmental models based on depoliticizing and disempowering labor forces and co-opting domestic political opponents. Yet sustained and transformative processes of reform will be more likely to develop organically if they are measured and consensual, and undertaken in a spirit of partnership, rather than confrontation, between state and society. If successful, moreover, state-led efforts to promote knowledge-based economies would fit into GCC regimes' record of pragmatic strategies of survival through periods of upheaval.

This survey of knowledge economies in the Gulf has pinpointed the current state of affairs as a step in a journey, and not in relation to a fixed start- or end-point. It has brought together the critical enabling conditions that will increase the likelihood of this process of change continuing, and highlighted the obstacles and challenges that may hold it back. And while the transition toward knowledge economies is a long-term initiative, an interim assessment would venture that progress has undoubtedly been made in areas such as enclave developments and attracting institutions of higher education to the region, but would caution that many of the enabling conditions still await the politically-sensitive and systemic shift toward genuinely post-oil political economies. Buying in imported expertise and prestigious institutions may—on one reading—be seen as consistent with a pattern of throwing money at short-term solutions to longer-term problems of reformulating political and economic structures; the challenge for policymakers in this next phase of development is to link these initial achievements to reform of the wider social and political system, and strengthen the enabling conditions that would facilitate the spread of knowledge economies both horizontally across the economic spectrum and vertically into indicators of human capital development and achievement.

Part II

People, Money, and Banking
in the Persian Gulf

6

Étatisme Versus Market Driven Islamic Banking

The Experiences of Iran and the Arabian Peninsula Compared

Rodney Wilson

The world's largest Islamic banks in terms of assets are based in the Persian Gulf region, Bank Melli of Iran being first ranked with assets worth over $57 billion and Al Rajhi Bank of Saudi Arabia being second, with assets worth over $45 billion.[1] Yet these two banks operate in very different jurisdictions, with all banks being nominally Islamic in Iran, whereas on the Arab side of the Gulf Islamic banks compete with conventional banks. The aim here is to examine the contrasting approaches taken by Iran and its Gulf Arab neighbors to Islamic banking. The factors that determined these different approaches will be analyzed and their implications explored.

Measuring Islamic bank assets or deposits provides a quantitative indication of relative size, but of greater significance is the dissemination of ideas and the

[1] *The Banker*, "Top 500 Islamic Financial Institutions," *Financial Times*, November 2010.

building of international alliances. Spreading the message about the merits of Islamic finance in the Muslim World can be viewed as a facet of "soft power" in contrast to Islamist militancy, arguably a less appealing type of "hard power."[2] The outward globalist approach of Islamic bankers in the Gulf Cooperation Council (GCC) countries contrasts with the inward looking, more nationalistic approach in Iran. In particular the market-driven, competitive model of Islamic banks in the GCC is very different from the statist model of Iran, where it is the role of government which is crucial. Ultimately the future of Islamic banking in Iran will depend on the resilience of the Islamic Republic, whereas in the GCC it is arguably a bottom up phenomenon with much popular support which governments cannot ignore irrespective of political factors. In other words, in the GCC Islamic banking is primarily seen as a business, whereas in Iran politics has determined developments and will continue to do so.

Étatisme applied to Islamic banking

The concept of *étatisme* refers to the role of the state in an economy, in particular the state as the architect of structural transformation, and in the Middle East context it was applied to Turkey under Atatürk and Egypt under Nasser.[3] In the case of Iran, although the Shah professed economic liberalism, the reality was a strong state that in many respects became even more interventionist after the Islamic revolution, which was accompanied by a wave of nationalizations, including that of the banking sector.[4] The Constitution of the Islamic Republic states that the public sector should encompass all major industries, foreign trade as well as banking and insurance. There are no similar constitutional provisions on the Arab side of the Gulf.

Yet the reality in Iran has been more complex, not least because the activity of supposedly charitable foundations was expanded, and they became significant centers of economic power. For example the Pahlavi Foundation that administered many of the assets of the Shah and his family was taken over by the Foundation for the Disinherited, Bonyad-e Mostazafin. The *bonyads* are

---

[2] Clement Henry and Rodney Wilson, *The Politics of Islamic Finance* (Edinburgh: Edinburgh University Press, 2004).

[3] Nazih N. Ayubi, *Over-Stating the Arab State: Politics and Society in the Middle East* (London: I.B. Tauris, 1996).

[4] Alan Richards and John Waterbury, *A Political Economy of the Middle East*, 3rd Edition (Boulder, Colorado: Westview Press, 2007).

independent of the state but control large amounts of land and industrial enterprises and have their own financial subsidiaries, such as SINA Bank or the Bonyad Finance and Credit Company. These financing subsidiaries are outside the regulatory control of the Central Bank of Iran and are not obliged to produce audited financial statements, nor are they subject to Iran's Islamic Banking Law.

Although Islamic economics is sometimes presented as an alternative to free market capitalism and socialistic policies associated with *étatisme* and the state determination of resource distribution, in practice Islamists take many different positions on the role of the state.[5] There have been attempts to suggest that there is a single Islamic economic doctrine,[6] but in reality there is a plurality of ideas. In the case of Iran these were influenced by personality and affiliations; for example, when Ali Akbar Hashemi Rafsanjani became President in 1989, there was some rolling back in the economic role of the state, as he was associated with the *bazaari*s and consequently sympathetic to the private sector. Nevertheless, although private banking did emerge again and the state banks became more independent from government, banking policy since Mahmoud Ahmadinejad became President in 2005 has remained confused, with directives to lower the cost of financing below the rate of inflation simply adding to inflationary pressures and a property price bubble that has certainly not been helpful to the urban poor who have been the President's major source of support. It seems that *étatisme* is once again gaining ground in Iran, but without any coherent economic or financial policy.

Iran's Islamic banking law

Legal, regulatory and *Shari'a* compliance systems are very different on the Iranian and GCC sides of the Gulf. Islamic banking in Iran is governed under a law enacted in 1983, but there are no Islamic banking laws in the GCC apart from some limited and belated provision in the United Arab Emirates, and in the case of Kuwait amendments to the banking legislation with new sections introduced to cover Islamic banking. For the other GCC states it is at the regulatory level that provision is made for the particular requirements of Islamic banks.

---

[5] M. Umer Chapra, *The Future of Economics: An Islamic Perspective* (Leicester: Islamic Foundation, 2000).
[6] Muhammad Baqir Al-Sadr, *The Islamic Economic Doctrine: A Comparative Study*, trans. Kadom Jawad Shubber from *Iqtisaduna* (London: MECI, 2010).

Iran's Law on Usury (Interest) Free Banking of 1983 was only enacted four years after the Islamic Republic was declared and over eight years after the establishment of Dubai Islamic Bank, the first *Shari'a* compliant financial institution in the region. Article 1 of the law provides for the establishment of a monetary and credit system based on rightness and justice as delineated by Islamic jurisprudence.[7] The implication is that this will be free of *riba*, which the current English translation of Iran's Banking Law equates with both usury and interest, although this was ambiguous in earlier translations which only specified usury.

The main support for introducing an Islamic financial system into Iran came from Abdulhassan Banisadr, the first President of the Islamic Republic, who wrote a doctoral thesis on Islamic banking for the Sorbonne in Paris. Banisadr's presidency lasted only just over one year, however, as he soon fell out with Ayatollah Khomeini, and as a result he was impeached in June 1981, two years before the Islamic banking law was finally enacted. Despite widespread support in the *majlis*, the Iranian parliament, there was confusion about how an Islamic banking system would actually operate. It was largely the efforts of Bank Markazi, Iran's central bank, that resulted in the new law being drafted, but the staff of the commercial banks were skeptical and unenthusiastic, and although these institutions were state owned, they enjoyed considerable autonomy. It was only in 1985 that *Shari'a* compliant financing was introduced, and most deposits were not Islamized until 1987.

Iran's Islamic banking law provides for deposits on a *qard hassan* basis, the concept being that of an interest free loan by depositors to the bank, the only type of lending permitted under *Shari'a*. Those who drafted the law however recognized that depositors expect some return, especially in inflationary conditions. Hence article 6 of the law provides for non-fixed bonuses in cash or in kind. In practice prizes are given to depositors, with the lucky account holders selected through a lottery.[8] As gambling (*maisir*) is forbidden in Quranic teaching (*Sura* 2:219) it is unclear how awarding such prizes can be viewed as justified, especially as most depositors, as in any lottery, do not receive prizes.

Article 3 of Iran's Islamic Banking Law provides for term investment deposits which the banks can use for *mudaraba* financing and direct investments,

---

[7] *The Law for Usury (Interest) Free Banking*, 1983, Central Bank of the Islamic Republic of Iran.

[8] *Annual Report 2007* (Tehran: Bank Melli, 2007), p. 11.

the so-called restricted *mudaraba* which the influential Iraqi Shi'a cleric Muhammad Baqir As Sadr recommended.[9] With restricted *mudaraba* contracts the bank acts as an agent and the depositor shares in the profits from the project being financed rather than receiving interest. The contract is regarded as just, as the depositor as financier (*rabb al mal*) is sharing in the risk with the businessmen or entrepreneur (*mudarib*) undertaking the project. In practice term investment deposits rates in Iran are determined by the Bank Markazi at the macroeconomic level and are unrelated to the performance or profitability at the microeconomic level of particular projects. For 2009, for example, the term deposit rates for one year were 14.5 percent rising to 17.5 percent for five year deposits,[10] these rates largely reflecting inflationary expectations, a subject on which *fiqh* is silent.

State directed banking in Iran

In contrast to the customer driven Islamic banking in the GCC, on the Iranian side of the Gulf the policies have been dictated by the government's economic priorities. Under Article 10 of Iran's Fourth Five Year Development Plan, covering the period from 2005 to 2010, the allocation of banking facilities by sector and region was undertaken through cash subsidies which were approved at Cabinet level.[11] One quarter of bank credit was to be allocated to agriculture under the Fourth Plan, 35 percent to manufacturing and mining, 20 percent to construction and housing and 8 percent to exports. As almost half of Iran's GDP is accounted for by services, and only 10 percent by agriculture, 11 percent by industry and mining and 5 percent by construction, the financing allocations in the Fourth Plan were clearly distorted.

Article 11 of the section of the Fourth Plan dealing with credit policy states that the banks are obliged to give priority in their lending to deprived and less developed regions and technologically advanced projects. While the former may be commendable from a social perspective, the Article is contradictory, as high technology projects are unlikely to be located in such areas. Under

[9] Rodney Wilson, "The Contribution of Muhammad Baqir Al-Sadr to Contemporary Islamic Economic Thought," *Journal of Islamic Studies* Vol. 9, No. 1 (1998), pp. 46–59.

[10] *Economic Trends 2009/2010* (Tehran: Central Bank of the Islamic Republic of Iran, 2010), p. 16.

[11] *Supervisory Policy Guidelines of the Banking System in 1388* (Tehran: Central Bank of the Islamic Republic of Iran, 2010).

Article 12 housing finance is solely for construction and not for mortgages on existing properties. This is unhelpful for the development of a housing market in Iran, and limits the return that investors can expect from housing or commercial property.

Such quotas and restrictions mean that potentially profitable projects may not get undertaken while resources are channeled to sectors and areas where returns may be low. The quotas have resulted in an inefficient allocation of capital, with banks' autonomy to make financing decisions based on normal risk and return criteria severely curtailed. However, under Article 23 the Central Bank Guidelines encourage credit scoring, with banks urged to favor customers with good credit records, limiting credit to those who have not met their debt obligations by at least the amount of the outstanding debt.

Although the allocation of finance by the banks in Iran is state directed at the sector level, the economy is gradually coming under private rather than state control. The proportion of commercial bank assets accounted for by claims on the non-public sector increased from 47 percent in 2004–5 to over 54.5 percent by 2008–9.[12] Over the same period the amount allocated to public corporations declined from 5 percent to a mere 1.3 percent. Deposits with the Central Bank increased from 7.7 percent to almost 10 percent, but this was largely because banks were required to hold more liquidity against contingencies due to the uncertain economic climate.

Liberalization of banking in Iran and the role of private banks

The public sector banks in Iran appear to be becoming more autonomous in their decision making, a development welcomed by the Central Bank which appears to recognize that there are efficiency gains from liberalization. In particular the use of commercial criteria rather than political patronage is implicitly supported, although the term political patronage is not of course used in Central Bank publications. Nevertheless it is asserted that credit policies can affect sector growth rates. There was a reduction in direct controls over credit which meant that the "free" allocation increased from 35 percent in 2004 to 75 percent in 2008.[13]

---

[12] *Annual Review 2008–9* (Tehran: Central Bank of the Islamic Republic of Iran, 2009), p. 72.

[13] *Economic Report and Balance Sheet 2008* (Tehran: Central Bank of the Islamic Republic of Iran, 2008), p. 101.

Although there has been no plan to privatize Iran's major commercial banks which have been under state ownership since 1979, there is no ideological objection to private banking by the authorities in Iran. The nationalization was simply driven by expediency, as without state support in the aftermath of the revolution the banks would have become bankrupt. There was enormous capital flight in the late 1970s with a substantial run-down in bank deposits as upper and middle class Iranians, especially those influential under the Shah, left the country for a life in exile. Arguably the inefficiencies in the allocation of finance and the poor resultant returns was a result of government directives that would have applied regardless of whether the banks were under public or private ownership.

Giving the state run commercial banks more autonomy is a necessary, though not sufficient, condition to improve their performance. One issue is the banking culture, which can be categorized in Iran as relationship banking, with long-term continuity in the relationships between the banks and their clients. Relationship banking has the virtue of reducing contracting and monitoring costs, but the down side is that it can also result in cronyism and even corruption. Merely because the banks are in theory Islamic and are supposed to uphold Muslim religious values will not ensure that all employees behave honestly and responsibly, especially when effective enforcement mechanisms to reduce operational risk are absent. Bank Markazi, like other central banks, has a supervision department whose remit includes the prevention of financial crime, but its major concern is "about the fitness and propriety of the staff nominated by the banks for taking up posts of a managerial nature (assistant manager and above) in the banks' overseas branches" and not the local staff.[14] The worry is about the finance of illegal imports, evasion of taxes and money laundering by clients, and not the relationship of bank managers and clients.

In 2001, in response to lobbying by industry, there was a significant policy change in Iran permitting the establishment of private banks. Bank Eghtesad Novin (EN) was the first institution established, which is owned by a group of construction and industrial companies, including Behshahr, Behpak, and Novin, with Bank Melli, the largest state owned bank, together with the civil servants pension fund, having a minority stake. Given this ownership it is clear that the dividing line between state and private ownership is blurred in Iran. More important than the actual ownership was the ethos of EN Bank, the aim

---

[14] "Bank Supervision Department," Central Bank of Iran, 2010, http://www.cbi.ir/page/BanksSupervision_en.aspx.

being to provide more modern and innovative banking services for bank clients in line with international standards, in preference to the bureaucratic form filling approach of the state owned commercial banks. EN Bank obtained a stock market listing in 2004 and by 2008 its assets exceeded $9.4 billion.

Parsian Bank, which was also established in 2001, has experienced even more rapid growth with its total assets worth almost $22 billion by 2010, making it the largest of the six private banks in Iran. This compares with the total assets of just under $60 billion of Bank Melli, illustrating the increasing significance of the private banks, which now account for over 16 percent of total financing.[15] As on the Arab side of the Gulf, the private banks are focused on consumer finance, especially vehicle and housing funding. This contrasts with the state owned commercial banks that are mainly involved in corporate finance, particularly import finance. The private banks are aiming to gain personal customers by offering an attractive range of accounts, and encourage those with salaries to arrange direct transfers to their current accounts. In marketing terms the focus is on middle class and more affluent customers. The majority of Iranians, and virtually all of the poorer classes, do not use banks, most household payments being in cash.

The Islamic credentials of Iran's banking system

In traditional Islamic societies markets, including credit markets, were overseen by the *hisba*, a moral enforcement agency to ensure fairness and justice, usually controlled by the state. Religious guidance was provided by the *muhtasib*, a scholar versed in *fiqh*. There was no attempt to establish such an institutional framework in Iran, either during the Islamic revolution or subsequently. The Central Bank of Iran conducts monetary and supervisory policy in the same manner as any other equivalent body internationally, although the terminology used conforms to that of Islamic Finance. There is a stress on form, but in reality there is little substantial difference from conventional monetary policy.

The Monetary and Credit Council of Iran's Central Bank determines the profit rates paid for commercial bank financing, raising the rate to control inflation or reducing it to stimulate the demand for finance. As inflation has been a continuing problem in Iran, with the rate in 2009 peaking at 20.9

---

[15] *Economic Report and Balance Sheet 2008*, p. 72.

percent, monetary tightening has been the norm, partly to counteract the stimulus effects from high levels of government current spending, especially on subsidies. The other major instruments of monetary policy in Iran include credit ceilings, reserve requirements ratios, open market operations involving so-called participation papers and open deposit accounts with the Central Bank. These operate in much the same way as on the Arab side of the Gulf, the only difference being that instead of referring to interest rates, the participation papers and the open deposits pay profit rates, but as the Central Bank is a financial regulator, not a business focused on profit, it is unclear what the profit rates actually represent.

Table 6.1 shows the types of Islamic financing provided by the different categories of banks in Iran. Farsi terms are used, *gharz-al-hasaneh* being what is transliterated in Arabic as *qard hasan*, an interest free loan. Banks can levy an arrangement fee and a management charge to cover the administrative costs of such loans, but they must not earn a surplus, as this would represent *riba*. Not surprisingly little *gharz-al-hasaneh* is provided by the private banks in Iran. *Mozarebeh* (*mudaraba* in Arabic) is more widely offered by the private banks, a contract whereby the bank advances funds to a business in return for a share in its profits. Partnership contracts (*musharaka* in Arabic) are even more popular, whereby the bank and the business both invest in a new venture and share the profits according to a pre-determined ratio. Commercial banks use forward transactions (*salam*) for financing; this refers to a contract whereby the financier pays in full in advance for a commodity, usually agricultural, to be supplied at a future date. The advances can be used by farmers to

Table 6.1. Islamic Financing Facilities in Iran, %.

	Commercial banks	Specialized banks	Private banks
Gharz-al-hasaneh	4.8	2.3	0.7
Mozarebeh	4.9	0.6	18.0
Forward transactions	4.4	2.0	0.0
Partnerships	13.8	11.7	42.1
Joaleh	6.0	1.2	2.2
Installment sale	47.2	71.8	11.2
Direct investment	0.9	0.1	1.0
Other	18.0	10.3	24.8

Source: Central Bank of Iran, 2010.

cover the costs of seeds and fertilizers, as well as paying their workers. *Joaleh* (*wakala* in Arabic) is where an amount of money is advanced to an agent for a specific investment. The agent is paid a management fee but the investment and any returns remain the property of the bank. Of greater significance are installment sales (*ijara wa iqtina* in Arabic) whereby the bank purchases equipment or vehicles on behalf of a client, with the client then paying rent for its use and making repayments over a three year period after which ownership will be transferred to the client. This is the most important method of financing by the state owned banks in Iran, especially by specialized institutions such as the Bank of Industry and Mining, Bank Keshavarzi and Bank Maskan. For the private banks partnership financing appears to be more significant, possibly because the expected returns are higher, reflecting the risks involved.

The effect of sanctions on Iran's Islamic banking system

The United States has maintained sanctions on Iran since the American embassy hostage crisis in 1979 following the Islamic revolution. Initially the sanctions were on Iranian-US trade, but they were widened because of Iran's nuclear program involving uranium enrichment. In 2007 sanctions were applied to Bank Melli and Bank Saderat, and these were extended to Bank Mellat in 2009. As Bank Melli is the largest Islamic bank in the world the question arises as to how far sanctions have damaged the Islamic banking industry, primarily in Iran, but also elsewhere where the banks subject to sanctions have a significant presence.

So far the sanctions have had little impact on Iran's overseas bank branches. The current resolution on sanctions agreed with the Europeans and Russia through United Nations Security Council "calls upon states to take appropriate measures that prohibit the opening of new Iranian bank branches or offices abroad if there is reason to suspect they might be aiding Iran's nuclear or missile programs."[16] It also calls on states "to exercise vigilance over transactions involving Iranian banks, including the Central Bank of Iran, to ensure that those transactions do not aid Tehran's nuclear and missile programs." It is unlikely that this will affect the activities of Bank Melli or other Iranian banks in Europe or the GCC, not least because any financial connections with enriching uranium or missile development will be difficult to prove.

Partly as a result of pressure from the United States, the European Union has further tightened its sanctions on Iran from August 2010, with prior

[16] "Iran dismisses UN sanctions draft," *Reuters*, May 19, 2010.

authorization required for transfers of funds exceeding €40,000, and Japan introduced restrictions on dealing with fifteen Iranian banks. Russia, although a member of the quartet that aims at peaceful conflict resolution in the Middle East, has not imposed sanctions, nor has China, Iran's major trading partner.

Although it is too early to determine the impact of EU and Japanese sanctions, the impact of US sanctions on the banking system appears to be minimal. Bank deposits increased by almost 79 percent over the period from 2006 to 2010, and financing for the private sector increased even faster.[17] Admittedly some of the increase reflected inflation, which has been high in Iran, peaking at 20.9 percent in 2009 as already mentioned, but it has subsequently fallen back to 7.4 percent.

The recent financial performance of Parsian Bank, Iran's largest private bank, shown in Table 6.2, exhibits a strong upward trend in deposits and financing. As the figures are in US dollars, distortions due to inflation are less of an issue. Depositors enjoyed significant income distributions, yet there were still reasonable profits recorded which benefited shareholders. Admittedly Parsian Bank has the highest return on assets of any Iranian bank, 2.13 percent: below the 4.03 percent return of Riyadh based Al Rajhi Bank for the same period, but higher than Kuwait Finance House's 0.27 percent.[18] The latter was adversely affected by the global financial crisis, but this had much less impact on Iran's relatively closed economy, partly closed because of sanctions. In other words sanctions may actually have proved beneficial. The links between Iran and China's rapidly growing economy have been more advantageous than any links there might have been with the sluggish United States economy had sanctions been relaxed.

Table 6.2: The Financial Performance of Parsian Bank, $ Million.

	2008	2009	2010
Total assets	16,382	19,548	21,915
Financing	11,416	13,847	15,183
Deposits	14,452	17,324	19,564
Total income	2,353	2,989	3,612
Depositor income	1,751	2,275	2,655
Net profit	332	338	399

Source: Parsian Bank, *Annual Report*, Tehran, 2010, p. 16.

[17] *Supervisory Policy Guidelines.*
[18] *The Banker*, "Top 500 Islamic Financial Institutions."

Legal and regulatory developments in the Arab countries of the Gulf

Islamic banking development in the Arab countries of the Gulf has been largely ad hoc, with no comprehensive legislation attempting to Islamize financial transactions as in Iran. Within the GCC states Islamic banking is regarded as a matter of customer choice, with conventional banks competing for business in what is usually described as a dual financial system. The resilience of the GCC conventional banks is largely because they offer overdraft facilities, which give clients more flexibility in the timing of their spending. As overdrafts incur interest charges, they cannot be offered by Islamic banks; instead clients have to enter formal *Shari'a* compliant contracts which specify what is being financed and the timing of repayments. Much of the population in the GCC has a preference for banking services that are consistent with Islamic teaching, but many remain to be convinced that Islamic banking as it is currently practiced provides the best solutions, and therefore they remain content to deal with conventional banks, especially for services not provided by Islamic banks. Indeed many Islamic bank clients also maintain accounts with conventional banks without having pangs of conscience, the aim being to get the best of both worlds.

Given these popular attitudes GCC governments have not felt pressurized to introduce Islamic banking laws, but choose rather to take a pragmatic approach and introduce regulation where it is necessary. Dubai Islamic Bank, the first commercial Islamic financial institution in the world, was established in 1975, but without any specific law governing its activities when it was awarded a license by the Government of Dubai, five years prior to the Union Law Number 10 of 1980 establishing the Central Bank of the United Arab Emirates (UAE). In practice the Dubai Islamic Bank was barely regulated in its early years of operation, and it was only in 1985 that a Federal Law was enacted covering Islamic banks, financial institutions and investment companies.[19]

There are four significant provisions in the Federal Law of 1985, one regarding the rights of Islamic banks, two dealing with consequential exemptions and the final provision dealing with *Shari'a* governance. The first significant provision is under Article 3 which states that Islamic banks have the right to form companies, either on their own account or with partners, the latter presumably applying to *mudaraba* and *musharaka* partnership contracts, although these are not specifically mentioned.

[19] UAE Federal Law 6, 1985: Islamic Banks, Financial Institutions and Investment Companies.

The two exemptions are referred to Under Article 4 of the Federal Law. The first is the exemption given to Islamic banks from Article 90 Clause (a) of the earlier Union Law of 1980 which stipulates that banks should not trade in goods. As the *murabaha* contracts offered by Dubai Islamic Bank involved the bank acquiring commodities and selling them to their clients at a mark-up, this exemption retrospectively legitimized these contracts. The second exemption was from Article 96 Clause (e) of the Union Law that provided for the boards of directors of banks to determine the interest rates paid to depositors and charged to lenders. As Dubai Islamic Bank did not apply interest to any of its operations, this stipulation was clearly redundant.

Provisions for *Shari'a* governance are provided under Articles 5 and 6 of the Federal Law of 1985. Article 5 which provides for the establishment of a Higher *Shari'a* Authority attached to the Ministry of Justice and Islamic Affairs was never implemented. This provision was subject to cabinet approval, which was not given, possibly because of lobbying by supporters of Islamic banking who resisted centralized control. Instead it was Article 6 that was implemented, as this provides for each Islamic bank having its own *Shari'a* supervisory authority comprising at least three members. Article 6 provides that those nominated should be approved by the Higher *Shari'a* Authority, but as none exists, this has never happened.

An alternative approach would have been for the Central Bank of the UAE to have its own *Shari'a* board, as in Malaysia.[20] This might have been more acceptable than having a federal ministry involved, especially one with little knowledge or capacity to deal with financial matters. Another explanation for resistance to centralized control might have been that it was being exercised from Abu Dhabi whereas Dubai Islamic Bank was, as its name suggests, based in Dubai, where financial institutions, whether Islamic or conventional, sought a high degree of autonomy. However as Dubai Islamic Bank had branches in Abu Dhabi as well as other emirates, this explanation does not stand up to scrutiny. Furthermore when Abu Dhabi Islamic Bank was opened in 1997, it was subject to the same regulatory provision, demonstrating that there is a level playing field for Islamic finance throughout the UAE.

Kuwait is the only other country in the GCC to have specific legislation pertaining to Islamic banking, but in this case, there was a long lag between

[20] Rodney Wilson, "Shari'a Governance for Islamic Financial Institutions," *International Shari'a Research Academy Journal of Islamic Finance* Vol. 1, No. 1 (2009), p. 65.

the start of Islamic banking in 1977, when the Kuwait Finance House was established, and the addition in 2003 of a new section on Islamic banking to the banking law of 1968 (Section 10). The most significant provision relates to *Shari'a* governance. Under Article 93 of Section 10 each Islamic bank has to appoint an independent *Shari'a* board comprising at least three members. Where there are conflicts of opinion between *Shari'a* board members these should be referred to the Fatwa Board of the Ministry of *Awqaf* and Islamic Affairs, which is empowered to provide the definitive ruling. In practice this has never happened and the Strategic Plan of the Ministry of Awqaf and Islamic Affairs covering the 2006–2011 period contains no reference to Islamic Banking.

Qatar and Bahrain have no specific laws governing Islamic banks, but both countries have special regulations, details of which can be found in the Qatar Central Bank's *Instructions to Banks* and in the Bahrain Central Bank's *Rulebook*. In Qatar Islamic banks have invested heavily in real estate for leasing through *ijara* contracts, which poses substantial risks, although the real estate sector in Doha has suffered less severe price declines than that of Dubai. Nevertheless the *Instructions to Banks* specify that total investment by Islamic banks in real estate should not exceed 25 percent of the bank's capital and reserves and that the investment period should not exceed five years.[21] The *Instructions to Banks* in Qatar cover many areas of Islamic finance including the operations of Islamic subsidiaries of conventional banks, which have become the norm in Qatar. However the *Instructions* are not clearly presented, and there is confusion over some issues such as number of *Shari'a* scholars to be appointed to each bank, with a minimum of two stipulated, but the Accounting and Auditing Organization for Islamic Financial Institutions, whose standards are recognized in Qatar, stipulates a minimum of three scholars.

The Central Bank of Bahrain *Rulebook* contains the most comprehensive treatment of Islamic banking in the Gulf region, reflecting its status as an Islamic banking center hosting twenty-six institutions with assets worth over US$26 billion. There are detailed rules governing the capital adequacy requirements, *murabaha, salam, istisna, musharaka, mudaraba* and *sukuk*, including the treatment of credit, market and operational risk.[22] Detailed rules are also provided for profit sharing *mudaraba* investment accounts, including the treatment of profit equalization reserves that smooth the returns paid to time

---

[21] *Instructions to Banks* (Doha: Qatar Central Bank, 2008), p. 153.
[22] *Rulebook* (Manama: Central Bank of Bahrain, 2010), p. CA-3.

depositors, and investment risk reserves to mitigate possible losses. It is evident that there is much regulatory support for the Islamic banking sector in Bahrain, given its significance for the economy and employment in this small island nation. There is of course the question of whether effective regulation facilitates the growth of financial intermediation or is introduced in response to past financial crises. In the case of Bahrain's Islamic banking sector there has never been a crisis, hence the former positive proposition probably applies.

Saudi Arabia's Banking Control Law was introduced in 1966, twenty years before Al Rajhi Bank, the first Islamic bank in the Kingdom, was awarded a license. The law has never been revised to introduce provisions for Islamic banks, even though they have become of major significance, with Al Rajhi having more branches than any other bank and ranking third in terms of assets and deposits in Saudi Arabia. Under Article 10 of the Law bank involvement in wholesale or retail trade, including through imports or exports, is prohibited, yet this is the basis of most *murabaha* transactions by Islamic banks such as Al Rajhi.[23] Similarly there are minimal regulations for Islamic banking in Saudi Arabia even though the Monetary Agency ran 374 courses in the supervision and marketing of Islamic financial products attended by 6,300 people over the 2000–07 period.[24] The only mention of Islamic finance is in the Regulations for Consumer Credit, where it is stated that for Islamic products documents for the purchase and sale of goods should conform to the requirements of the bank's *Shari'a* committee[25] and that a profit rate rather than a borrowing rate applies to all credit extended under Islamic contracts.[26]

Market driven Islamic banking

The major attraction of Islamic banks from a client perspective is that they are *Shari'a* compliant, and therefore Muslim customers can undertake financial transactions with a clear conscience. Most Islamic banks in the GCC stress their Islamic ethos and values, not only in terms of avoiding *riba*, but by conveying a positive message about the *halal* nature of their financing methods. There is however a concern that they could be accused of using religion for

---

[23] Banking Control Law, 1966, Article 10.1. Riyadh, Saudi Arabia.
[24] Governor of the Saudi Arabian Monetary Agency, Speech to the Symposium on Islamic Banking Prudential Standards. Institute of Banking, Riyadh, 2007.
[25] Regulations for Consumer Credit, 2008, Article 2.3. Riyadh, Saudi Arabia.
[26] Regulations for Consumer Credit, Article 5.3.

marketing purposes, and in Saudi Arabia and Kuwait the banks offering *Shari'a* compliant financial services do not designate themselves as Islamic, hence the names Al Rajhi Bank and Kuwait Finance House (KFH). However, the term "Islamic bank" is used in Bahrain, Qatar and the UAE.

Although there has been much debate about whether modest interest receipts or charges actually constitute *riba*, or whether what is forbidden is usury, modern Islamic banks have succeeded in getting their message across that all interest transactions involve *riba*, and are therefore immoral.[27] In contrast the merits of risk sharing are stressed: bearing each other's burdens, in return for a proportion of any profits generated through a financial transaction. Hence, for example, with an investment *mudaraba* deposit a customer becomes a stakeholder and shares in the bank's profits, whereas savings accounts paying interest returns are not related to bank performance but rather to the monetary policy stance of the jurisdiction in which the deposits are placed. Furthermore if the deposits are guaranteed there is no risk for the depositor, but then arguably no justification for a return.

The first modern Islamic financial institutions in Pakistan and Egypt in the 1960s were organized as non-profit making credit unions which provided finance for rural communities with low incomes, but in contrast the emergence of Islamic banking in the GCC accompanied the oil boom of the 1970s, with the main focus on providing financial services for affluent personal and business clients. The underlying philosophy was that Muslims who wished to use *Shari'a* compliant financial services would want to have the same types of financial services as clients of commercial banks. In other words the purposes for which the finance was used was the same, only the methods of financing were to be different. Hence Dubai Islamic Bank was established as a limited liability company, initially privately owned, but later to become a listed company on the Dubai Financial Market with the aim of paying dividends to its shareholders and producing capital gains on their investments.

Initially institutions providing Islamic finance in the GCC focused on commercial banking, especially import finance with *murabaha* whereby the bank would purchase goods from a foreign exporter and then sell them to a local distributor who would repay in installments, including a profit mark-up for the bank. In recent years the use of *murabaha* has been widened to include consumer finance for retail clients, especially for the purchase of vehicles.

[27] Abdulkader Thomas (ed.), *Interest in Islamic Economics: Understanding Riba* (London: Routledge, 2006), pp. 125–34.

Some Islamic banks such as KFH even have their own vehicle showrooms where customers can come and choose from a variety of makes. By bulk buying KFH can save on purchase costs and pass on some of the discounts to its clients.

The marketing of retail financial products by Islamic banks in the GCC has become very professional and often is more focused than that of their conventional competitors. Dubai Islamic Bank for example offers an attractive range of tiered investment accounts for those with a minimum of $ 3,000 to deposit. For one month deposits the profit rate paid was 2.78 percent during the fourth quarter of 2010, rising to 3.03 percent for one year deposits. For those with only $1,000 to deposit Dubai Islamic Bank offers savings accounts paying a profit rate of 1.5 percent. These accounts are of course designated as Islamic but neither the bank publicity nor the bank's financial statements specify what Islamic contract governs the deposit, whether *wakala* or *mudaraba*. It seems that clients are not concerned with such detail, and simply take the bank's *Shari'a* assurance on trust.

Much of the emphasis in retail financial product development has been on branding, with, for example, Dubai Islamic Bank offering Wajaha private banking services to clients of high net worth. These services include personalized asset management services and private facilities in selected branches for conducting financial transactions, including stock exchange dealings. Johara banking is provided exclusively for women at ten branches of Dubai Islamic Bank with incentives to use these services including shopping vouchers and health club discounts. Al Rajhi Bank has branded its web-based service Al Mubasher, and clients can use this to check account balances and make transfers and payments on-line.

Islamic banking facilities in the GCC

The methods of funding used by Islamic banks in the GCC are similar to those used in Iran, although there is considerable variation between institutions and it would be incorrect to generalize about the GCC or even within particular countries. For Al Rajhi, the largest Islamic bank in the GCC and the largest in the world with a stock market listing, installment sales are even more significant than with the state owned banks in Iran, accounting for 63 percent of total financing in the quarter ending September 30, 2010. *Mutajara* refers to commodity *murabaha*, a facility that enables the client to receive a cash advance. Under this type of financing the bank purchases a commodity on behalf of a client and resells it to the client who repays by deferred install-ments, including a premium, as with *murabaha* trading transactions. The bank appoints an agent to purchase the commodity from the client, the proceeds from the sale being deposited in the client's account. The client and indeed the bank never take physical delivery of the commodity, but they have temporary legal title to make the transaction *Shari'a* compliant. Many *Shari'a* scholars object to such transactions, and the *Fiqh* Academy of the Organization of the Islamic Conference issued a *fatwa* condemning the practice at a meeting in Sharjah in May 2009, but it still continues.

Table 6.3: Al Rajhi Bank Financing.

	September 2009 SR million	September 2010 SR million	September 2009 %	September 2010 %
Mutajara	33,039	29,977	29	25
Installment sale	64,662	75,595	57	63
Istisnaa	1,000	585	1	1
Murabaha	13,988	12,449	12	10
Visa credit cards	508	672	1	1
Total	113,197	119,278	100	100

Source: Al Rajhi Bank, *Interim Consolidated Financial Statement*, Riyadh, Septem-ber 30, 2010.

An analysis of the financing facilities provided by Kuwait Finance House (KFH), the second largest Islamic bank in the GCC, is provided in Table 6.4. The receivables, which accounted for over 45 percent of total financing in 2009, refer to the installments on *murabaha* financing which can extend to over one year. Leasing accounts for 11.4 percent of total financing, which in the case of KFH does not involve installment sale, as the equipment or other assets remain the property of the bank until sold to a third party at the end of the period. KFH has over KWD 1 billion of investments in traded and private equity as well as in *sukuk* securities, and in addition a property portfolio and investments in affiliates. Such exposure to market risk raises regulatory issues, but the assets are sufficiently diversified not to cause major concern.

The overseas expansion of Islamic banks

Islamic banking has become a global industry with its hub in the Gulf. Rather than being a destination for foreign investment in financial services, within

Table 6.4: Kuwait Finance House Asset Maturity, KD Million.

	3 months	3–6 months	6–12 months	Over 1 year	Total
Cash and bank balances	440	5	–	–	445
International *murabaha*	1,257	–	–	–	1,257
Trading properties	29	39	4	55	126
Leasing	269	236	272	510	1,288
Investments	67	39	55	882	1,042
Investment in associates	–	–	–	411	411
Property investment	–	–	–	506	506
Other assets	94	72	122	234	522
Premises	–	–	–	602	602
Total	3,376	1,447	1,400	5,068	11,291

Source: Kuwait Finance House, *Annual Report*, December 2009.

the *Shari'a* compliant segment, the Gulf has become a source of investment. What seems to have arisen is a new phenomenon, an Islamic mode of capital formation, that presents an alternative to the Western interest based system. It is becoming possible to delineate an Islamic form of capitalism with its own unique characteristics, where spiritual rather than material values determine the agenda.[28] Capitalism arguably best thrives under competition, meaning not only competition between Islamic capitalism and other forms such as Anglo-Saxon, Russian or even Chinese capitalism, but also between different strands within the Islamic World, especially between the ideas and concepts emanating from Iran and those coming from the countries of the GCC. Of course Iran is the center for Shi'a Islam which has its own Jafari School of Islamic jurisprudence, whereas the GCC, and Saudi Arabia in particular, is the center for Sunni Islam, including the Hanbali school of *fiqh*.

It would be mistaken nevertheless to view the overseas expansion of Islamic banking as part of a struggle for worldwide influence and supremacy of Shi'a versus Sunni Islam. Firstly, in Islamic finance there are no distinctive Shi'a and Sunni approaches, indeed insofar as there are differences they are most pronounced between the Shafii, a Sunni school which predominates in South East Asia, and the other three Sunni schools. In particular the Shafii School permits trading in debt instruments, whereas this is not allowed in the GCC,

[28] Rodney Wilson, "Islam et Capitalisme Reconsidérés," *Maghreb-Machrek* No. 187 (2006), pp. 29–44.

or indeed in Iran. The differences between the GCC and Iran in the way Islamic finance is organized and regulated largely reflect historical factors and perceptions of the role of the state.

Furthermore, and most importantly, the aims of overseas banking expansion are very different for Iran and the GCC. Bank Melli has had two branches in London since 1967, long before the Islamic Revolution, one being in the City, its business mainly involving trade finance, whereas the other branch is in Kensington, its remit being to serve affluent Iranians visiting or semi-permanently resident in London—including, during the reign of the Shah, many of his entourage. Bank Melli's most significant overseas operations in recent years have been in the UAE, where it has seven branches, its local headquarters being in Deira in Dubai. As much of Iran's imports pass through Dubai, the major business is trade finance, especially of supplies coming from Asia. In other words the rationale for the presence of Iranian banks overseas is primarily to serve the country's internal business requirements and is unrelated to the Islamic credentials of the banks.

On the GCC side of the Gulf the expansion of Islamic banking overseas has been prompted by three factors. Firstly, the limited size of the domestic markets has meant that further branch expansion and the attraction of more business have become increasingly challenging. Secondly, the successful Islamic retail banking model can be exported to other countries where there are significant Muslim populations potentially receptive to the services offered. Thirdly, there is a demand for asset management and treasury services that can best be provided from international financial centers such as London. Furthermore, by operating in such markets Islamic financial institutions can acquire investment banking skills which they currently lack, such as the ability to arrange initial public offerings and advise on mergers and acquisitions.

KFH was the first GCC based Islamic Bank to expand abroad, when it established in 1989 the Kuveyt Türk Participation Bank, of which it owns 62 percent, a further 9 percent being owned by the Kuwait Social Security Fund; the remaining minority stake is held by the Islamic Development Bank and Turkish investors. Over the last two decades the bank has expanded throughout Turkey with a network of a hundred and thirteen branches compared with thirty-four in Kuwait. Kuveyt Türk provides a full range of Islamic deposit and financing facilities for personal and small business clients, but it also has the capacity to provide larger-scale finance including aircraft leasing to Turkish Airlines. More recently KFH has expanded into Malaysia where it has nine branches and the Kuala Lumpur regional office also oversees new ventures by the bank in Singapore and Australia.

Al Rajhi Bank has an even greater presence in Malaysia with nineteen branches. Like KFH it replicates the range of services it provides in its home location. Pragmatism has governed its *Shari'a* approval processes, as the *Shari'a* board in Kuala Lumpur comprises one Saudi scholar who serves on the home *Shari'a* board in Riyadh and three Malaysians, two of whom studied in Saudi Arabia. A similar *Shari'a* governance system has been adopted for Dubai Islamic Bank's operation in Pakistan, which already has fourteen branches with a further twenty openings planned. Operating since 2006, it has attracted business from many Pakistanis working in Dubai, who are already clients of the bank and want to use its facilities in their home country.

Qatar Islamic Bank has adopted a different strategy, as rather than establishing retail networks overseas it has opened three investment banking operations, European Finance House in London, Arab Finance House in Beirut and Asia Finance House in Kuala Lumpur. It already has an investment banking subsidiary in Doha, QInvest, which is regulated by the Qatar Financial Centre. The major focus to date has been on asset management, including private equity and real estate investment. Services are provided for Qatari citizens of high net worth and Doha based corporate clients, rather than retail services for the British Muslim community. European Finance House is the largest of the four Islamic investment banks in London, all of which are owned by GCC based institutions. Islamic Bank of Britain, the retail institution that has attracted over 50,000 British Muslims to open accounts, is part Qatari owned.

Conclusions

In terms of spreading the message about Islamic finance GCC based institutions appear to have been much more successful than their Iranian counterparts. In the GCC Islamic finance is viewed as a business opportunity rather than being politically driven, and the aim increasingly is to reach a global market rather than being inwardly focused. The GCC based Islamic banks have attracted considerable media coverage, most of it favorable, whereas in the case of Iran much of the press coverage has been concerned with the effects, or possible effects, of sanctions. Islamic banking is one non-energy-related activity where the GCC has a comparative and increasingly a competitive advantage. The future looks promising, as links with the West and other parts of the Muslim World have developed. In contrast the prospects for Islamic finance in Iran seem much more uncertain, and will be inevitably tied to political developments and the sustainability of the Islamic revolution in its present form, which many question.

7

Population and Human Capital in the Persian Gulf

Djavad Salehi-Isfahani

The most salient feature of the economies of the Persian Gulf—their hydrocarbon wealth—has a profound impact on their demography and human resource development. In this chapter I review these developments in the Gulf Cooperation Council (GCC) and Iran, noting the specificities of the region's experience, especially as it relates to its oil and gas wealth. Besides the obvious effect of this wealth on the inflow of large numbers of foreign workers who now dominate the working population of several GCC countries, there are less obvious effects on fertility transition and accumulation of human capital in the region.

As the hero in Fitzgerald's story *The Rich Boy* knows, the rich are different from the rest of us, and the difference is more than just having more money. In terms of demographic behavior, not only being rich makes a difference, the source of riches—whether from rent or higher productivity—matters greatly. Oil and gas rents create a large gap—in some cases a very large gap—between personal incomes and individual productivity that influences individual decisions, such as the number of children and the level and type of investment in child education, that affect long run economic growth in fundamental ways. To varying degrees, families in the region enjoy a higher standard of living thanks to income from oil. In most cases the money is not a straightforward transfer, as in the form of a check from the government, but rather comes in exchange for work or supply of some factor of production, physical or financial capital or land. All government expenditures (such as direct transfers, subsidies, public sector wage and salaries, and infrastructure investment) that are not financed by taxes on individuals and corporations help raise the standard of living above productivity.

The influence of rent income is evident in key aspects of human resource development of the oil- and gas-rich countries of the Persian Gulf that I examine in this chapter: delayed fertility transition, high youth unemployment and low productivity of human capital investments.

The integrating theme in my discussion of human resource development in the GCC and Iran is growth of human capital. Development literature recognizes that growth of modern economies increasingly depends on the accumulation of human capital. Seminal works by Becker, Murphy and Tamura and by Lucas argue that families play a critical role in the transition from population-expanding economic growth to economic growth that augments per capita income.[1] As they show, the critical variable in this transformation is the rate of return to human capital, which provides the incentive for families to become smaller and to invest more in child education. They distinguish between two types of exogenous technological shocks. The first type, which was predominant before the Industrial Revolution, promotes population growth rather than investment in human capital; it increases fertility but not returns to human capital. Shocks of this type thus tend to dissipate in time into a larger population without much benefit in terms of greater individual welfare. The history of pre-modern economic growth is full of technological advances, many associated with agriculture, that expanded economies and populations but failed to increase per capita income. The second type, associated with industrial revolution, encourages investment in human capital, lowers fertility, and raises per capita incomes. The crucial characteristic of these types of technological improvements is that they increase the benefits of investment in children relative to having a larger family.

[1] See Gary S. Becker, Kevin M. Murphy, and Robert Tamura, "Human Capital, Fertility, and Economic Growth," *Journal of Political Economy*, October 1990, Part 2: S12-S37; R.E. Lucas, *Lectures on Economic Growth* (Cambridge, Mass.: Harvard University Press, 2002).

In the case of the Persian Gulf countries drawing this distinction between two types of positive technological change is particularly fruitful. The large inflows of oil and gas revenues of the last three decades can be seen as positive shocks to incomes that potentially can increase the size of the population of the countries involved or raise the standard of living of their people, or both. The interesting distinction that arises in the case of oil-rich countries is that because oil revenues form a large part of the unearned family incomes, these positive shocks tend to increase rather than decrease fertility.[2] The reason why higher incomes are in general associated with lower fertility is that, in the absence of rents, income is closely correlated with higher productivity, which is itself associated with the opportunity cost of time spent in raising children. This may be one reason why the fertility response to growth of incomes has been delayed in some GCC countries.

This is not to say that, properly spent, oil incomes cannot increase the returns to education and therefore cause a substitution away from the number of children in favor of child quality, thus promoting investment in human capital and productivity. Government policy determines to a large extent the extent to which the inflow of vast amounts of oil income can play the role that they did in the "Industrial Revolutions" of the nineteenth century in Europe and the twentieth century in East Asia—increasing returns to human capital. Unfortunately, economic policy analysis in the oil rich countries, where such has been taken seriously, has been largely based on the Dutch disease model,[3] which has little to say about the impact of oil revenues on human capital accumulation. The thrust of the Dutch disease model is to warn against the danger to tradable sectors (agriculture and manufacturing) and against lop-sided economic growth with flourishing non-tradable service sectors. The logic of the model is easy to understand and is therefore compelling: oil exports overwhelm all productive tradable sectors because they cause the local currency to appreciate, preventing these sectors from competing globally, and thus shifting productive resources from tradable to non-tradable sectors. This model has been a useful way to think about industrial policy in oil rich countries in the past, but as the level and quality of human capital in these coun-

---

[2] T.P. Schultz, "Human Capital, Family Planning and their Effects on Population Control," *American Economic Review Proceedings* Vol. 84, No. 2 (1994), pp. 255–60.

[3] W.M. Corden, "Booming Sector and Dutch Disease Economics: Survey and Consolidation," *Oxford Economic Papers*, New Series, Vol. 36, No. 3 (November, 1984), pp. 359–80.

tries have increasingly come to determine comparative advantage, and thus who wins and who loses in global competition, the division of the economy into sectors with more or less tradability has lost its relevance. Unless one can argue that tradable and non-tradable sectors have different capacities for promoting human capital—as in the learning-by-doing model of Lucas,[4] where one sector (manufacturing) has a higher potential for learning by doing than primary sectors—there is no obvious advantage to viewing the economy in terms of tradability. But with the growth of human-capital intensive services, such as finance and insurance, the assumption that tradable sectors are good for human capital accumulation, while services are not, is no longer valid.

From the point of view of the Becker-Lucas approach to economic development what matters most is not how oil income affects the balance between tradable and non-tradable sectors, but whether it raises the returns to human capital sufficiently to trigger change in family behavior. Government policy may not be able to fight the strong winds of change brought about by the inflow of oil revenues that shift resources from tradable to non-tradable sectors, but it may influence how oil incomes affect incentives for human capital accumulation. From this point of view, the relationship between demographic and human resource development in these countries takes a greater significance for understanding the long term growth potential of these countries. In the remainder of this chapter I examine the principal trends of these variables for Persian Gulf countries and discuss what these trends imply about the future of human capital growth for the region.

Demographic transition

The countries of the Persian Gulf lead the rest of the Middle East and North Africa (MENA) in the pace of mortality decline,[5] but, with the important exceptions of Iran and the United Arab Emirates (UAE), they lag behind MENA in fertility transition. Figures 7.1a and 7.1b show the path of fertility transition for two groups of countries using the total fertility rate (TFR). Until about 1970, most of the Persian Gulf countries had higher fertility rates relative to the average for MENA. One group of countries—Bahrain, Kuwait,

---

[4] Robert E. Lucas, Jr. "On the Mechanics of Economic Development," *Journal of Monetary Economics* Vol. 22, No. 1 (1988), pp. 3–42.

[5] The UAE registers the lowest infant mortality rate in the Middle East, at 11 per 1000, compared to 28 in Iran and 39 in Egypt (World Bank, *World Development Indicators*, 2010).

Figure 7.1a: Total Fertility in Early Transition Countries.

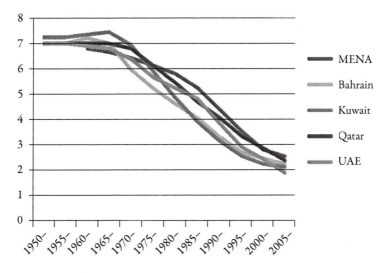

Figure 7.1b: Total Fertility in Late Transition Countries.

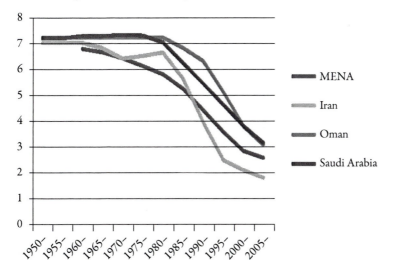

Qatar and UAE—started their transition around 1970, while fertility in Iran, Oman, and Saudi Arabia remained high for another ten years before beginning to fall. Iran's TFR fell sharply but in the latter two countries it declined more gradually and remains still high by world standards.

To get a better idea of the comparison with world standards, in figure 7.2 I plot the TFR for the Persian Gulf countries against the predicted TFR from a regression of TFR on log GDP per capita (2005 PPP). The line represents the well-established negative relationship between income and fertility. With the exception of Iran, Lebanon, Tunisia and Turkey, all MENA countries lie above this line, indicating that their fertility is higher than the world average given their income per capita. Farthest away from the line are the GCC countries. In other words, the higher the importance of oil revenues in personal incomes, the greater the gap between personal incomes and productivity and the greater the disconnect between fertility behavior and the standard of living.

Finally, consider how the Persian Gulf countries have performed relative to other countries in terms of average household behavior with respect to fertility and investment in children. Figure 7.3 shows the transformation of average family behavior in the Persian Gulf compared to a line representing average "international" behavior. This line represents the regression of TFR on years of schooling for the age group 15–19 (and years-of-schooling squared) for a sample of countries for the period 1980–2005. The negative slope of this line, and the fact that most countries fall into one of two quadrants—the upper left for the less developed and the bottom right for the developed—and that income per capita increases as we slide down the transformation curve, conforms to the Becker-Lucas view of development as described above. Economic development, as measured by income per capita, is well represented by the change in family behavior from a focus on procreation to investment in human capital. As we move from 1980 onwards, countries of the world move in one direction only—downward, some faster than others. The delay in the demographic transition of the Persian Gulf countries is noticeable, especially between 1980 and 1990 when rising incomes helped raise their years of education without much effect on fertility—a movement to the right but not down, as other growing developing countries experienced. However, in the following fifteen years, 1990–2005, with the notable exception of Saudi Arabia, all the countries in the sample have moved to the bottom right quadrant, where all the advanced countries of the world had moved decades ago. In 2005, the upper left quadrant, in which most of the Sub-Saharan African countries were to be found, still included a few MENA countries (Djibouti, Sudan, and Yemen).

Figure 7.2: Total Fertility Rates Conditional on Log GDP per Capita, 2005.

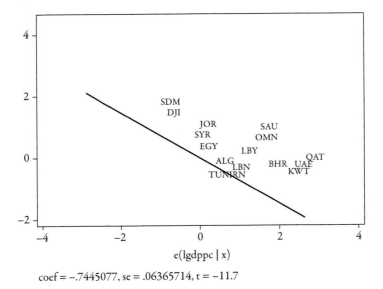

coef = −.7445077, se = .06365714, t = −11.7

Source: Author's calculations using the World Bank World Development Indicators Database.

Labor force

The main determinants of labor force growth in the GCC are demographic transition and importation of foreign labor. As demographic transition advances, the contribution of the local national labor force to total workforce will decline, but with a lag. In Iran, where the transition completed over a decade ago, the labor force is still growing at 3.7 percent per year, more than twice the rate of population growth. For the GCC countries that are still in the middle of their fertility transition, the national labor force will continue to grow by nearly 4 percent per year for at least the next two decades.

Import of labor has been by far the larger of the two factors in determining labor force growth in the GCC states. During the oil boom of the 1970s their labor force grew at annual rates ranging from 7 to 10 percent, which are historically unprecedented, raising the proportion of the non-national workers in the labor force from 39 percent in 1975 to 67 percent in 1985 (World Bank 2004). The latest oil boom saw increases in the labor force of equal magni-

Figure 7.3 (a to d): The Transformation of Family Behavior 1980–2005 (years of schooling for 15–19 year olds and the total fertility rate).

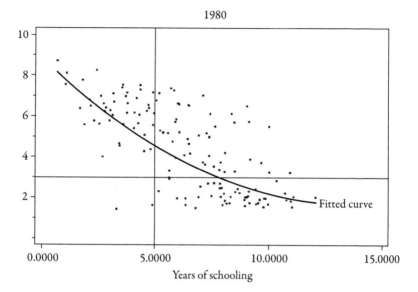

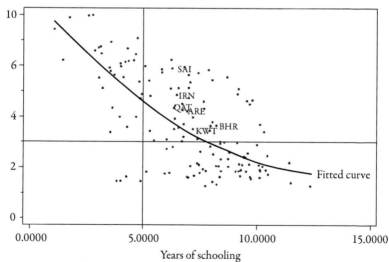

POPULATION AND HUMAN CAPITAL IN THE PERSIAN GULF

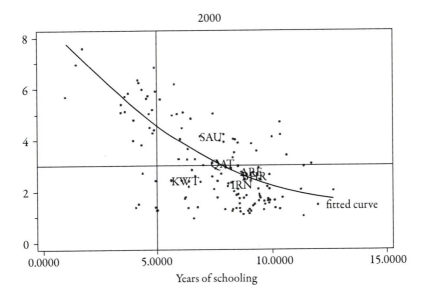

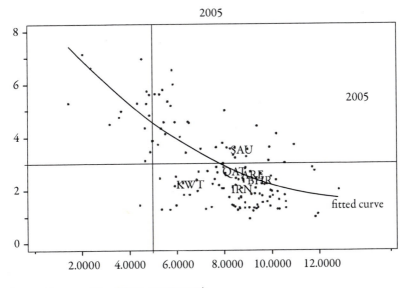

Source: Barro and Lee (2010, WDI 2009)

tudes. In Qatar and the UAE the proportion of the non-national labor force now exceeds 80 percent.

The labor force of the region is well educated relative to the rest of MENA. The United Arab Emirates and Bahrain had over nine years of schooling, whereas Iran, Kuwait, and Saudi Arabia had six to seven years (see Table 7.3).[6] The data on the education level of the labor force by national origin is not available for most countries. Table 7.1 shows the share of the population living in Qatar in 2009 with university education or above. Qatari men are more than twice as likely to be university educated compared to their non-Qatari counterparts in the 30–54 age group, whereas Qatari women are more similar to non-Qatari women, except in ages above 50. Older female foreign workers are much more educated than Qatari women because university education for women is a more recent innovation in Qatar.

Table 7.1: The Share of Population with University Education by Age, Qatar 2009.

	Qatari		Non Qatari	
	Men	Women	Men	Women
20–24	7.83	13.27	7.28	21.22
25–29	18.26	39.77	12.31	34.82
30–34	28.76	41.19	14.17	35.65
35–39	35.87	49.13	15.86	38.53
40–44	37.93	44.24	18.92	39.35
45–49	35.77	35.45	17.46	32.23
50–54	36.21	22.28	17.82	29.46
55–59	29.09	7.38	18.37	35.68
Total	25.00	32.23	14.20	33.83

Source: Qatar Labor Force Survey, 2009.

The role of women in the Persian Gulf labor force is still relatively small despite the fact that they outnumber men in universities. In Qatar, in 2009, 25 percent of men and 32 percent of women aged 25–59 had university education or above (Table 7.1). In Saudi Arabia, Kuwait, and UAE, too, women outnumber men in universities. In Iran, in the highly coveted public universi-

[6] See also Robert J. Barro and Jong-Wha Lee, "A New Data Set of Educational Attainment in the World, 1950–2010," NBER Working Paper 15902, 2010.

ties for the last several years women have outnumbered men two to one in the entering class, prompting the Iranian parliament to consider ways to introduce affirmative action for men.[7]

Youth: Potentials and pitfalls

High levels of past fertility create age structure effects that can last for decades. The most important of these is a rapidly growing youth population. Two measures of age structure have important implications for economic development, and I will focus on those here. The first is the ratio of youth (15–29) to adult (30–64) population, which is related to the more familiar "youth bulge," and is an indicator of the labor market pressures from the large cohorts of youth born in previous decades. Individuals belonging to a large cohort, the youth, face challenging circumstances when they enter the labor market, which is dominated by the adults. As Easterlin has extensively studied in the case of the US (which had its baby boom after the Second World War), an increase in the supply of labor of specific age and skills depresses that group's wages and makes it hard for its members to find employment.[8] These difficulties are exacerbated by high reservation wages and labor market rigidities in the Persian Gulf countries and together explain a large part of rising youth unemployment. The second measure is the ratio of adults to children (0–14), which increases following the youth bulge and is the result of decline in fertility. This ratio measures the human resources available in a society for the education of its next generation and represents a one-time benefit from the country's fertility transition.[9]

Figure 7.4 compares the trend in youth-adult ratios (ratio of youth 15–29 to adults 30–64 years old) in the US and Korea, two countries with past histories of gyrations in this ratio, with the two largest countries in the region, Iran and Saudi Arabia.[10] This ratio shows the significance of the labor market

---

[7] See Salehi-Isfahani, "Are Iranian Women Overeducated?" Brookings Institution, March 2008.

[8] R.A. Easterlin, *Birth and Fortune: The Impact of Numbers on Personal Welfare*, 2nd Edition (Chicago, IL: University of Chicago Press, 1987).

[9] See D.E. Bloom, D. Canning, and P. Malaney, "Demographic Change and Economic Growth in Asia," *Population and Development Review* Vol. 26 (2000), pp. 257–90; D. Salehi-Isfahani, "Population, Human Capital, and Economic Growth in Iran," in Ismail Sirageldin (ed.), *Human Capital: Population Economics in the Middle East* (London: I.B. Tauris, 2002).

[10] Age structure data by national origin are not available. For Iran and Saudi Arabia,

entrant to those who currently hold most of the existing jobs. The baby boom of the 1960s in the US, which was central to Easterlin's analysis, seems here muted, with the youth to adult ratio varying between 0.5 and 0.7, compared to the variation in Korea, where the ratio fell from nearly 1 in the 1980s to about 0.4 in 2010, following its rapid fertility decline in the 1960s. In Iran the youth ratio has been in excess of 1 for a long time, but is expected to fall sharply in the next ten years, from 1.1 to 0.4, following a similar path to Korea. Saudi Arabia will also experience a decline in its youth ratio, falling from 0.8 to 0.6 in the coming decade. In Qatar, in 2009, this ratio was 0.75 for the Qatari population and 0.64 for non-Qataris. The Qatari ratio will decline, in line with falling fertility; the ration for non-Qatari does not follow the same logic as the composition of the immigrant population changes according to demand for labor rather than past fertility.

The literature on the demographic gift emphasizes the benefits of the rising numbers of young people relative to old, and often refer to Korea as a particularly good example of a country that was able to cash in on this gift.[11] How-

Figure 7.4: The Ratio of Youth to Adult Population in Selected Countries.

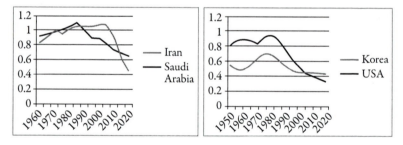

Source: United Nations, Population Prospects and author's own projections.

because they are large, their age structures are not significantly altered by the presence of foreign workers.

[11] See R. Barlow. "Population Growth and Economic Growth: Some More Correlations," *Population and Development Review* Vol. 20, No. 1 (1994), pp. 153–65; D.E. Bloom and J. Williamson, "Demographic Transitions and Economic Miracles in Emerging Asia," *World Bank Economic Review* Vol. 12, No. 3 (1998), pp. 419–56; Bloom, Canning, and Malaney, "Demographic Change"; Robert Fogel, "123,000,000,000,000," *Foreign Policy* (Jan/Feb 2010), pp. 70–75.

ever, the outlook for MENA countries is much less bright because of distortions in their education and labor markets. As Salehi-Isfahani[12] and Salehi-Isfahani and Dhillon[13] have argued, the strong role of the state in regulating private sector employment, which increases the attachment of older workers to their jobs, making it harder for young workers to find employment. In addition, because in the past education was a way to seek government jobs, state hiring and compensation policies promoted credentialism—seeking degrees—rather than skills acquisition. As a result, educated young workers were less desirable to private employers and ended up joining long queues for public sector jobs. For most of the MENA region these constraints have turned a demographic gift into a liability.[14]

The experience of the GCC economies in taking advantage of rising youth ratios is likely to be different from those of non-oil exporting MENA countries studied in Dhillon and Yousef because of the large entry of foreign labor, which complicates the absorption of their own young workers into the labor market.[15] As noted earlier, in the UAE and Qatar foreign workers account for as much as three-fourths of the population, more of the labor force. In Iran, the main source of foreign labor has been refugees from Afghanistan who generally take unskilled positions, mainly in the construction sector, and the proportions are much lower than in the GCC (less than 5 percent of the workforce). Despite its small proportion, the availability of low skilled foreign labor has driven unskilled wages down, encouraging youth to stay in school longer and, upon graduation, to search longer for a job that matches their education. By contrast, the GCC draws on foreign labor with a much broader range of skills, making it difficult even for the educated youth to compete. While foreign labor has been tremendously helpful in enabling these countries to turn their oil wealth into physical capital, it has probably not hurt human capital accumulation.

[12] Djavad Salehi-Isfahani, "Microeconomics of Growth in MENA: The Role of Households," in J. Nugent and M.H. Pesaran (eds), *Explaining Growth in Middle East and North Africa* (Amsterdam: Elsevier, 2006).

[13] D. Salehi-Isfahani and N. Dhillon, "Stalled Youth Transitions in the Middle East: A Framework for Policy Reform," Wolfensohn Center for Development Working Paper, The Brookings Institution, 2008.

[14] See also the studies in N. Dhillon and T. Yousef (eds), *Generation in Waiting: The Unfulfilled Promise of Young People in the Middle East* (Washington, DC: Brookings Institution Press, 2009).

[15] Dhillon and Yousef, *Generation in Waiting*.

This is evident in the high rates of youth unemployment in the GCC and Iran, despite robust economic growth in the past decade, shown in Table 7.2. Bahrain, Iran, and Saudi Arabia have high rates of youth unemployment, comparable to the average for MENA and all middle-income countries. Qatar and the UAE have low rates of unemployment, but these rates include foreign workers and therefore do not reflect the difficulties faced by the local youth population.

Table 7.2: Youth Unemployment in Selected Countries, Ages 15–29.

	Youth	Overall	Youth/Overall
Bahrain	20.1	5.50	3.65
Iran	23.0	11.27	2.04
Kuwait	5.3	1.12	4.73
Qatar	5.4	3.90	1.38
Saudi Arabia	16.3	5.25	3.10
UAE	7.6	2.71	2.80
MENA	25.9	11.14	2.32
Low income	9.9	4.88	2.03
Middle income	19.6	6.58	2.98
High income	13.6	6.68	2.04

Notes: The classification of countries is based on GDP per capita in 2005 PPP US dollars: Low income: less than $3000; middle income: $3000–$15000; high income: greater than $15000.
Source: Country groups are from WDI (ages 15–24), average 2000–07; MENA countries from Brookings, MEYI website.

Human capital

Unlike physical capital, whose rate of accumulation can be directly enhanced by oil income, accumulation of human capital requires more than financial resources. Human capital is embodied in people, so its accumulation requires the willing participation of every individual. Physical capital, like large infrastructure projects, can be built with minimal participation of the local population, as long the resources to import the machinery and workers to put things together are available. But with human capital the incentive of the local population to acquire skills is the key. Furthermore, a large part of the accumulation is transfer of knowledge and skills from one generation to the next, again requiring popular participation.

Persian Gulf governments have contributed relatively generously to education. Table 7.3 shows the share of overall expenditures on education (public and private) in Gross National Income, and Table 7.4 shows the share of public spending (in GDP). These tables show that Persian Gulf countries follow the general norm of developing countries in spending on education, which is about 5 percent. The share of spending in the richer countries is lower because the denominator includes mostly oil income, which is independent of education. Except for Iran, which has reduced its spending on education relative to its pre-revolution days, other countries for which we have data for the entire period have either maintained their spending or increased it (Saudi Arabia). A comparison of the two tables shows that, except in Saudi Arabia, public resources provide the lion's share of total spending on education. Most of these governments devote about 20 percent of their expenditures to education, but Oman and UAE devote about 30 percent.

Table 7.3: Investing in Education: Expenditures on Education as Percentage of Gross National Income.

	1970	1980	1990	2000	2008
Bahrain	4.93	4.93	4.73	4.36	4.36
Iran	6.60	6.60	3.39	4.01	4.15
Iraq	4.69	2.98			
Kuwait	4.07	2.25	3.46	5.00	3.02
Oman	3.65	3.65	3.23	3.96	3.89
Qatar	2.99				
Saudi Arabia	2.59	2.59	5.70	7.19	7.19

Source: World Development Indicators, 2010.

Table 7.4: Government Expenditures in Education (as Percentage of GDP).

	1970	1980	1990	2000	2008
Bahrain	na	2.81			2.93
Iran	na			4.38	4.79
Iraq	na	2.69	5.11		
Kuwait	na	2.79			3.76
Oman	na	1.85		3.14	4.02
Qatar	na	2.53			3.28
Saudi Arabia	na	4.33		5.94	5.71
UAE	na	1.33		1.98	0.90

Source: World Development Indicators, 2010.

A key determinant of productivity of these resources is their distribution by level of education. Although from the viewpoint of individuals expenditures on higher education are the hallmark of government commitment to education, in reality expenditures at primary level are more productive, in part because higher levels of education are much more expensive per pupil, and the amount of learning that can take place at higher levels depends on the quality of education at the primary and even the pre-primary level.[16] Table 7.5 shows expenditures per pupil in 2005 Purchasing Power Parity (PPP) dollars for Persian Gulf countries over the last decade. The values range widely, from about $1,000 for primary expenditures per pupil in Iran in 2004, to over $50,000 for tertiary expenditures for Kuwait. Per pupil expenditures are generally higher for tertiary compared to secondary and primary. For example, in Iran, where data are more uniformly available, on average the government has paid about twice as much for university education than for primary education, and one-third more for secondary education. From an equity point of view, the government is more under obligation to provide its citizens with quality free public education at the lower levels than at the tertiary level, where the benefits are more likely to go to upper income families.

Besides money, the production of human capital requires transfer of knowledge and skills from one generation to the next. Thus the human capital of the younger generation depends on the level of knowledge of the older generation, which represents the pool of knowledge that can be transferred, and on the ratio of potential teachers to pupils, which is a consequence of demography. It is true that sizeable financial resources can to some extent reduce the importance of this intergenerational link because knowledgeable teachers can be imported from abroad, as they have been in the GCC, but this is not possible for certain types of skills that families specialize in providing. In Iran the education of the young depends almost entirely on domestic resources, whereas in Qatar and UAE import of education services is quite significant. The literature on human capital stresses the importance of the family in production of education, so parents play a role both in teaching and in providing the incentives for students to learn.

As in the case of youth unemployment, age structure data are once again useful in explaining economic phenomena, this time human capital accumulation. A good measure of resources available for training the next generation is

[16] World Bank, *The Road Not Traveled: Education Reform in the Middle East and North Africa* (Washington, DC: The World Bank, 2007).

Table 7.5: Expenditures per Pupil by Education Level (in 2005 PPP$).

	2000	2001	2002	2003	2004	2005	2006	2007	2008	2009
Primary										
Bahrain			3771					1597	1408	
Iran		713	916	956	938	920	1326			
Kuwait		6313	6225	6972	6403	4964	4276			
Oman		2169	3045		3115	3077				
Qatar										
Saudi Arabia	3521	3402	2914	3327	3057	2653	2529	3921		
UAE										2549
Secondary										
Bahrain			4218							
Iran		772	971	1031	1122	1144	1808	2305	2121	2205
Kuwait			7436	7855	7225	7389	6527			
Oman		3745	3335		2965	2584				
Qatar										
Saudi Arabia								3907		3517
UAE		4472	5039	4215	3983	3715	3538			
Tertiary										
Bahrain	–	–		–	–	–	–	–	–	
Iran		2720	3124	2767	2363	2163	2917	2868	2164	2327
Kuwait			44585	54643	50816					
Oman			5684		4450	2850				
Qatar						23086				
Saudi Arabia	18475	15237	11946	12071					–	
UAE	–			–				–	7652	–

Note: Expenditures per pupil are reported in 2005 PPP dollars, obtained by multiplying the shares of GDP per capita as reported by the United Nations with the PPP values of GDP per capita in 2005 international dollars, as reported by the World Bank. As such, these numbers are generally higher than the local currency equivalents of the actual expenditures, but reflect fairly accurately the values of these expenditures in comparable international dollars.
Source: United Nations data bank for expenditures as share of GDP per capita, and GDP per capita from the World Bank, WDI 2010.

the ratio of adults (30–64) to children (0–14), which, combined with the years of schooling of adults (the human capital to be used in that training), gives us a good picture of the potential for investment in human capital.

Figure 7.5 shows adult child ratios for Persian Gulf countries. As before, I begin with a comparison of the US and the Republic of Korea on the one hand, and Iran and Saudi Arabia on the other. The demographic potential for human capital accumulation is highest in Iran, where this ratio shoots up from less than 1 to 2 by 2020, one adult per each child, increasing threefold the resources for human capital accumulation. In Saudi Arabia, this number reaches 1.5 by 2020, doubling the resource base. In Korea, where education has grown faster than in any other country and average length of schooling matches that of the US (with twice the per capita income), this ratio has been increasing for the last three decades, from about 0.7 in 1970 to about 3.2 in 2010, and is projected to reach 4 by 2020. The US has enjoyed a ratio of more than 2 for the last two decades as well.

Figure 7.5: The Potential for Human Capital Growth, the Ratio of Adults to Children.

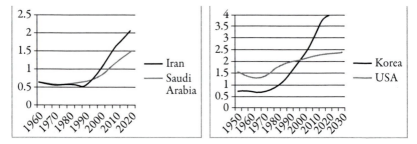

Source: United Nations.

Unlike economic projections, projections of the age structure are highly accurate, for the only sources of prediction error are also demographic: fertility, outmigration, and mortality. All three seem to follow rather predictable courses. Historically, wherever fertility has started to decline it has eventually fallen to replacement level and not reversed its course; out-migration and mortality are unlikely to change in such a way as to affect substantially the course of the adult child ratios. But it is important to remember that these projections show the potential for human capital growth but do not actually predict it. There is much uncertainty in how this potential may be realized.

As noted earlier, families are changing their fertility and child education strategies across the region. In Iran, where fertility has been at or below replacement for a decade, adults already outnumber children by more than 50 percent; in other countries with delayed transition, such as Saudi Arabia, this will happen in the next ten years. For greater resources for education to result in actual productive human capital three things need to happen. First, the parents (and the adults in general) must be educated and willing to apply their enhanced resources to educate their children; second, the education system should provide access on a wide basis to all children, and not only to those who can afford it; and, third, the labor market rewards should be for productive skills and not merely for degrees and diplomas.

We know that the first requirement is satisfied in the case of the Persian Gulf countries (as well as for most MENA countries) because enrollment rates at young ages are everywhere quite high.[17] Table 7.6 lists the enrollment rates for primary, secondary and tertiary levels for the Persian Gulf and the average for MENA and for middle-income countries.[18] Except in oman (and to a lesser extent Saudi Arabia and Kuwait) the enrollment rates are high and comparable to MENA averages.[19] On average, Persian Gulf countries have higher enrollment rates in secondary (but not tertiary) compared to MENA countries. The average length of schooling of the adult population (15+ years), shown in Table 7.6, is also relatively high, especially compared to the average for MENA.

The second requirement is partially met because there is access to free public education at the lower levels but not at the tertiary. In most of these countries there are private universities but tuition limits access by the low-income families. Even where free public universities are available, such as in Iran, the competition to enter them favors those who can spend money on private classes and tutoring.

The third requirement, that labor markets guide productive investment in human capital, is sadly missing in most MENA countries. The evidence for this is high unemployment rates for educated youth, even those with univer-

---

[17] World Bank, *The Road Not Traveled*, p. 10.

[18] Djavad Salehi-Isfahani, "Human Development in the Middle East and North Africa," UNHDR 2010 background report, UNDP, http://hdr.undp.org/en/reports/global/hdr2010/papers/HDRP_2010_26.pdf.

[19] The lower enrollment rates are for both sexes and not caused by lower female enrollments.

Table 7.6: Enrollment Rates, 2005.

Country	Primary	Secondary	Tertiary
Bahrain	98.2	92.90	32.6
Iran	95.4	77.30	27.4
Kuwait	86.1	78.20	18.2
Oman	74.3	77.20	23.1
Qatar	94.2	90.10	17.7
Saudi Arabia	83.8	70.30	29.7
UAE	88.2	79.60	22.9
MENA	92.5	74.75	30.4

Source: World Bank, WDI data files.

Table 7.7: Average Years of Schooling for the Population 25 Years and Older.

Country	1985	1990	1995	2000	2005	2010
Bahrain	5.2	6.0	7.2	8.3	9.0	9.4
Iran	2.8	3.7	4.4	5.1	6.1	7.3
Kuwait	5.3	5.5	5.7	6.1	6.0	6.1
Saudi Arabia	4.8	5.5	6.0	6.6	7.2	7.8
UAE	3.6	4.3	5.6	6.9	8.4	9.3
MENA	3.0	3.7	4.3	5.0	5.8	6.5

Source: Barro-Lee data files 2010.

sity degrees, which is often blamed on a mismatch of skills.[20] What explains the mismatch is that for decades, in MENA at large, the prospect of public sector employment has been the path to social and economic mobility, generating huge investments in schooling. But, with time, the ability of the public sector to absorb the increasing numbers of labor market entrants has decreased and it is no longer able to reward everyone who has followed that path.[21] Most MENA countries entered this game earlier than Persian Gulf countries, with Egypt and Morocco promising anyone with a high school diploma (later a

[20] See World Bank, *The Road Not Traveled*, p. 239; Salehi-Isfahani and Dhillon, "Stalled Youth Transitions."

[21] R. Assaad, "The Effects of Public Sector Hiring and Compensation Policies on the Egyptian Labor Market," *World Bank Economic Review* Vol. 11 (1997), pp. 85–118.

university degree) a government job. In Egypt, the promise resulted in lop-sided investments in education, such that the proportion of university edu-cated male workers aged 20–54 is 29 percent compared to 11 percent in Turkey, which has a more robust and productive economy.[22] Overall, enroll-ment rates in universities are higher in MENA than the average for middle income countries, 30 percent versus 28 percent.[23]

The ability of the public sector to absorb university graduates has declined sharply, in MENA and in the Persian Gulf, but its lure continues to influence skill formation in the region's schools and universities. Public sector jobs are desirable because they offer *de facto* tenure.[24] However, the downside for skill formation is that low turnover forces employers, public or private, to focus on a person's *ex ante* signals of productivity or credentials—the level of education, test scores, the type of university attended—rather than his or her potential for productivity on the job. In Qatar, according to the 2001 Labor Force Sur-vey, the unemployment rate for previously employed workers is only 1 percent, about one-tenth of the rate for first time jobs seekers.[25] Public sector pay is often higher than private sector pay, as in Saudi Arabia,[26] but even where it is lower the promise of tenure and superior benefits seems to adequately com-pensate for lower pay. This is probably the reason why in Iran, as in many MENA countries, more than two-thirds of university-educated youth find employment in government.[27]

The lure of public sector jobs also influences the choice of subject and fields of study. Because the government defines employability on the basis of a per-son's credentials more than his or her actual skills, those aiming for public sector jobs often enter non-technical fields, such as the humanities. The prob-lems of public sector-induced investment in education also manifest them-selves in the content of MENA education. Testing by centralized multiple-

[22] D. Salehi-Isfahani, I. Tunali, and R. Assaad, "A Comparative Study of Returns to Education in Egypt, Iran and Turkey," *Middle East Development Journal* Vol. 1, No. 2 (December 2009), pp. 145–87.

[23] Salehi-Isfahani, "Human Development in the Middle East and North Africa," p. 46.

[24] Salehi-Isfahani, "Microeconomics of Growth in MENA," p. 186.

[25] Claude Berrebi, F. Martorell and J.C. Tanner, "An Overview of the Qatari Labor Market," *The Middle East Journal* Vol. 63, No. 3 (2009).

[26] Steffan Hertog, *Princes, Brokers, and Bureaucrats: Oil and the State in Saudi Arabia* (Ithaca, NY: Cornell University Press, 2010).

[27] Djavad Salehi-Isfahani, "Human Resources in Iran: Potentials and Challenges," *Iranian Studies* Vol. 38, No. 1 (2005), pp. 117–47.

choice exams, and teaching to these tests, encourages rote memorization rather than learning problem-solving skills, increasing the mismatch between the content of MENA education and skills needed by employers. This is as much the fault of public sector hiring practices as of the weak influence of private employers—who need productive skills—in determining the content of public education.

The role of the private sector in education and employment is different in the oil-rich GCC from that in Iran or the rest of MENA. In the GCC, unlike in MENA, private employment trumps government employment in terms of numbers, and private employers resist the hiring of nationals, preferring to satisfy their labor needs from abroad, mainly South Asia. In the UAE only 1.5 percent of private sector employees are Emirati nationals. For their part the nationals, especially the educated, prefer to queue for public sector jobs than to compete with foreign labor, whose reservation wages are considerably lower.[28] Relative to productivity, local workers cost more than foreign labor and are able to stay on queues for jobs much longer. In Iran, where private employers cannot import foreign workers, high reservation wages cut off middle class youth from private employment. As a result, about one in four high school and university educated youth are unemployed in Iran.[29]

The high reservation wage is also reflected in the low labor force participation rates of women in the region.[30] Women's participation in market work is

[28] Razzaz and Iqbal (2008) make a similar point in the case of Jordan, where oil money indirectly raises reservation wages above productivity. See also Tarek Yousef and Paul Dyer, "Will the Current Oil Boom Solve the Employment Crisis in the Middle East," in Margareta Drzeniek Hanouz, Sherif El Diwany, and Tarik Yousef (eds), *The Arab World Competitiveness Report* (Geneva: World Economic Forum, 2007), pp. 31–9.

[29] See Djavad Salehi-Isfahani, "Iranian Youth in Times of Economic Crisis" (Working Paper No. 3, Dubai Initiative, Harvard Kennedy School, 2010), http://belfercenter. ksg.harvard.edu/publication/20414/iranian_youth_in_times_of_economic_crisis. html; Djavad Salehi-Isfahani and D. Egel, "Beyond Statism: Toward a New Social Contract for Iranian Youth," in N. Dhillon and T. Yousef (eds), *Generation in Waiting: The Unfulfilled Promise of Young People in the Middle East* (Washington, DC: Brookings Institution Press, 2009); D. Egel and Djavad Salehi-Isfahani, "Youth Transitions to Employment and Marriage in Iran: Evidence from the School to Work Transition Survey," *Middle East Development Journal* Vol. 2, No. 1 (2010), pp. 1–32.

[30] Masood Karshenas, "Economic Liberalization, Competitiveness and Women's Employment in the Middle East and North Africa," in Djavad Salehi-Isfahani (ed.),

Figure 7.6 Participation of Women in the Labor Force.

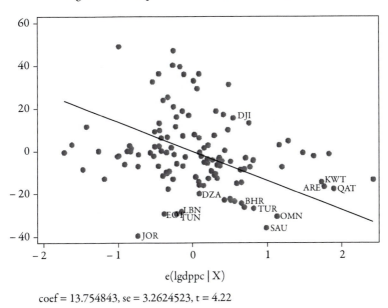

$$e(lgdppc \mid X)$$

coef = 13.754843, se = 3.2624523, t = 4.22

Source: Author's calculations using WDI data files.

influenced by several factors, including their reservation wage, which is heavily influenced by government transfers and subsidies from oil income. Figure 7.6 shows the labor force participation rates of women predicted conditional on incomes per head and female education. The relationship is negative, indicating that, given education, higher incomes mean lower participation. Even with this effect included, with the exception of Kuwait and UAE, all other Persian Gulf countries are below the line representing average participation rates.

Conclusions

In this chapter I have approached the demographic and human resource developments in the GCC and Iran from two angles: one that takes into

---

Labor and Human Capital in the Middle East: Studies of Labor Markets and Household Behavior (Reading: Ithaca Press, 2001).

account the abundance of oil and gas incomes, and the other offered by the Becker-Lucas analysis of long run growth. I have argued that while hydrocarbon wealth has financed an impressive increase in infrastructure and education it has failed to increase productivity in line with rising reservation wages, the result being unemployment of the educated workforce. As in other MENA countries, the failure of education to increase productivity is a consequence of the much greater influence of the public sector compared to the private sector in shaping incentives to learn. The reasons for the lack of influence of private employers in human capital accumulation in the GCC are different from what has been observed in Iran or the rest of the MENA countries. The difference is, as I argued, due to the abundance of hydrocarbon income and access of private employers to foreign labor and human capital. This wealth has raised the reservation wages of the educated workers without giving them the incentive to learn global skills so that they can successfully compete with educated foreign workers for private sector jobs. For most of these countries, hydrocarbon wealth has also delayed their demographic transition, though it is now completed in all of the countries except Oman and Saudi Arabia. This has delayed the change in family behavior, from emphasis on the number of children to quality of upbringing, keeping population growth rates high well into the 1990s.

The age structure effects of past population growth are potentially favorable once fertility declines, resulting in rising ratios of adults to children, which, along with the oil wealth, could result in high levels of investment in human capital. However, the oil wealth also presents these countries with a serious challenge in finding useful employment for the new wave of educated nationals with high reservation wages. Oil revenues have expanded public sector employment, which has been good for education because public sector jobs require university education. However, the resulting encouragement has been more for degrees than for the acquisition of global skills, credentialism instead of skills formation. This situation has affected the rising young cohorts particularly hard. As the initial boom in the public sector has come to an inevitable end, youth equipped with only formal education must turn to the private sector, where they face stiff competition from foreign workers. In short, the employment crisis in the GCC, and to a large extent in Iran, can be explained by a rise in the proportion of the national labor force with tertiary education, declining ability of the government to absorb them into the public sector, and unwillingness of private employers to fill the gap in demand because of the high oil-induced reservation wages of the educated nationals.

In the long run, the only way for educated labor with access to oil rent to compete globally is to raise its productivity, in step with rising reservation wages. The current economic development strategy in the region—using the hydrocarbon wealth to facilitate the accumulation of physical capital by easy importation of skilled workers—is good for accumulation of physical capital, but not for the accumulation of productive human capital. Success in global competition depends increasingly on a nation's quality of human rather than physical capital. The solution for the region must therefore include the use of the oil wealth to raise the productivity of educated nationals high enough for them to compete with cheaper labor from East and South Asia. To do so, the region needs greater investment in human capital, guided by incentives that encourage the seeking of global skills, rather than degrees and certificates. Unfortunately, for this strategy there are no ready models to emulate or recipes to follow. The current strategy of building "knowledge economies" (see Ulrichsen in Chapter 5), is in the right direction in so far as it emphasizes high quality global human capital, but it falls short in tackling the adverse incentive structure that currently drives youth to focus on the value of the credentials offered by famous US universities, rather than on the formation of skills for which they are indeed famous. In the end, for this strategy to succeed, and for these universities to have the same effect on the GCC economies that they have in their own countries, the GCC states need to import more than educational institutions. They need also to import the institutional environment in which these universities operate, in which families and youth invest in skills that private employers are willing to reward. For that the region needs a more comprehensive agenda for the overhaul of its education and employment policies.

8

The Gulf Cooperation Council Monetary Union

Alexis Antoniades

January 2010 was the targeted date for countries of the Gulf Cooperation Council (GCC) to launch the Gulf Monetary Union (GMU). The move by the six oil-rich Gulf countries to adopt a single currency would be the final and most far-reaching aim of the Unified Economic Agreement that was signed by the GCC countries about thirty years ago, making it an unprecedented event. GCC countries account for 45 percent of the world's proven oil reserves and 17 percent of the proven natural gas reserves.[1] The stability of the global economy depends on the ability of these countries to maintain a smooth supply of oil at a fair price. At the same time, any decision of the countries to move away from pegging to the US dollar can exacerbate global imbalances by adversely affecting the value of the US currency.

Had these countries succeeded, the GMU would have been the biggest monetary union outside of Europe. With an area almost half the size of the Eurozone, the GMU economy would have matched Germany's. But the

---

[1] IMF data and author's calculations.

launch of the GMU has been postponed for now. Some of the factors that have contributed to this delay were the impact of the global financial crisis and the slow progress made by the member states toward fulfilling some of the accession criteria and toward harmonizing their economies, as well as the decision of Oman and the United Arab Emirates to drop out of the negotiations in 2006 and 2009 respectively. Whether the union will be established later or not remains unclear. It is also unclear whether the Gulf countries are any closer now to establishing the GMU than they were five years ago. In fact, there does not appear to be any tangible progress toward a monetary union.

The decision to establish the Gulf Monetary Union is a political one, driven by a single goal: to maintain and enhance political stability in the Gulf through the added political and economic unity that a successful monetary union can bring. By establishing a bigger political constituency, the GCC countries, as a block, increase their bargaining power and can overcome external threats, especially from Iran and Iraq. Moreover, moving to a single currency makes the expectation of a move away from the US dollar more credible and gives the block more leverage at the negotiating table.

Since the GMU is driven by political considerations, we must recognize that the decision to postpone or even abandon the launch will not depend on the economic advantages and disadvantages. Instead, it will reflect the political environment within the GCC countries and the political will of their rulers.

The key political cost of the GMU, if it comes to pass, will be the surrendering of policy autonomy at the national level. How big the cost is for the member states depends on their ability to maintain national unity and avoid internal conflicts while pursuing a common external policy at the block level. While the other GCC states endorsed the US efforts in 2003, Saudi Arabia refrained from openly supporting the war on Iraq in order to maintain national unity. Had the Gulf Monetary Union been in place, it would have been more difficult for the Saudis to deviate from the consensus, for such an act would have damaged the credibility of the GMU. At the same time, Saudi Arabia would have faced the risk of internal conflict.[2]

The magnitude of the political cost associated with the surrendering of policy autonomy at the national level also depends on whether decisions are dictated by Saudi Arabia or taken by consensus in a democratic environment among the GCC states. That is not to say that Saudi Arabia should not have

---

[2] Many Saudis cite internal conflict as the cause for the demise of the first and second Saudi states in the nineteenth century—a history they would rather not repeat.

more voting power; after all, Saudi Arabia accounts for 67 percent of the national population and 83 percent of the total territory of the whole of the GCC. Nonetheless, the decision makers must ensure that the views of all member states are taken into consideration and that the policies promote the interest and wellbeing of the GMU as a whole, and not the interests of individual countries. The timing of the United Arab Emirates' exit from the GMU was not random. It came after it was announced that the regional Central Bank would be located in Riyadh and not in Abu Dhabi. Clearly, if the interests of other member states are not taken into account, the political costs may outweigh the political gains.

As for the economic impact, the GMU will have a positive, yet limited effect in the short term. Abandoning the local currencies in favor of a single currency lowers transaction costs, eliminates nominal exchange rate risk, and increases trade among the GMU members. It is unclear how sizeable the increase in trade will be. Evidence suggests, in fact, that it will not be significant. In the case of the European Monetary Union (EMU), trade at the bilateral level within the EMU increased by 5 percent to 15 percent, although not all of the increase can be attributed purely to the EMU's formation. In the case of the GMU, the increase in trade will be smaller since there is already less bilateral trade among the GCC countries than there was among pre-EMU countries.

Nevertheless, the two main economic disadvantages of monetary unions—loss of monetary autonomy and loss of the ability to use exchange rates as an automatic stabilizer—are not a major concern for the GMU countries. For all intents and purposes, the countries gave up monetary autonomy and the ability to use exchange rates as automatic stabilizers when they pegged their currencies to the US dollar.[3] Actually, moving to a single currency could eventually help them gain back some monetary autonomy and control over their currency.

The biggest gains from the GMU will neither be political nor economic but rather institutional. Thus a successful monetary union requires discipline, transparency, accountability, institutional independence, well-developed analytical capabilities, coordination and communication. It also requires that each

---

[3] Kuwait is an exception. The country chose to move away from the dollar peg in May 2007. It now pegs the Kuwaiti dinar to a basket of currencies, although it is widely believed that the US dollar dominates the basket; as a result, the currency does not fluctuate much with respect to the US dollar.

country expands its research capacity and improves the quantity and quality of data that it produces.

Whether and when the GMU is established is not that important. What is most significant is the progress the countries make on the technical requirements along the transition path. If they succeed in fulfilling those requirements, the quality of institutions in each country will be much improved and a stronger institutional framework will bring long-term growth, improved welfare, and enhanced stability regardless of the GMU's success. Only then would the countries participating in the Gulf Monetary Union fully benefit from the provisions of a monetary union.

This chapter starts with an outline of the historical timeline on the establishment of the GCC and the GMU process. By examining the political, economic, and institutional aspects of the GMU, the chapter chronicles the various obstacles that have so far hampered substantive moves aimed at monetary union despite the substantial economic—and no doubt political—benefits that could be gained if such a union were to take place.

The timeline

The first shot at a Gulf monetary union was made in 1975–78 by Bahrain, Kuwait, the United Arab Emirates (UAE), and Qatar. An attempt was made to reach monetary coordination and issue a single currency, the Gulf Dinar. Though met with initial enthusiasm, the idea ultimately did not translate into reality. Without Saudi Arabia's involvement, the effort did not gain much momentum. Furthermore, border disputes between Qatar and Bahrain strained the negotiations.[4]

By the late 1970s and the early 1980s, the Persian Gulf states found themselves confronting regional crises that demanded immediate attention and derailed many of their longer-term goals. The Islamic revolution in Iran in 1978–79, the Soviet invasion of Afghanistan in 1979, the takeover of the Grand Mosque in Mecca by Saudi Muslim extremists the same year, and the Iraqi invasion of Iran in 1980 all confronted the regional states with immediate threats that needed addressing. With heightened threat perceptions, local state leaders turned their focus to regime security and efforts to contain the spread of Iran's revolutionary impulses across the region.[5] Faced with the mili-

---

[4] Beatrice Maalouf, "The GCC: A Union to Be Reckoned With," Presented at the Congress of the Czech Political Science Society (2009).
[5] Ibid.

tary and ideological threats to their very existence, the states in the Persian Gulf recognized the need to unite and to establish a more cohesive, collective identity. This time, Saudi Arabia and Oman were on board.

On May 25, 1981, Qatar, Bahrain, Oman, United Arab Emirates, Saudi Arabia, and Kuwait formed the Cooperation Council for the Arab States of the Gulf, commonly known as the Gulf Cooperation Council (GCC). The Charter, signed in Abu Dhabi by the leaders of these countries, encouraged member states to coordinate their policy, intergrate their economies, and foster unity with one another.

A few months later, on November 11, 1981, the second Supreme Council meeting of the GCC took place in Riyadh. There, the Unified Economic Agreement was ratified. The Agreement encouraged coordination and standardization of economic, financial, and monetary policies, and set the stage for full economic integration. Article 22 of the Agreement specified the need for economic convergence criteria: "Member States shall seek to coordinate their financial, monetary, and banking policies and enhance cooperation between monetary agencies and Central Banks, including the endeavor to establish a joint currency in order to further their desired economic integration." To be implemented in three stages, the Agreement called for the sequential establishment of a free trade area, a customs union, and a common market and economic union.[6]

Consequently, the Central Bank Governors and Monetary Agencies Committee and the Committee on Financial and Economic Cooperation of the GCC were founded. These two bodies later joined to form the GCC Technical Committee for Monetary Union. Its mission was to provide a blueprint for implementation of Article 22 of the Agreement on issues such as inflation, interest rates, exchange rates, and fiscal coordination. In 2009, the Committee concluded its work and passed on the recommendations to the newly established Monetary Council, a body that includes the governors of the regional central Banks. Muhammad Al Jasser, the Governor of the Saudi Arabian Central Bank, was elected as the first Chair of the Council, a position with a one-year term limit.

---

[6] A free trade area calls for the elimination of all tariffs and not-tariff-barriers (NTBs) in most traded goods and services between the participating countries. A customs union calls for a common external tariff between the free-trade area and its trading partner. Finally, a common market calls for freedom of movement of labor and capital, and the elimination of all physical, technical, and fiscal barriers across the member countries.

The free trade area was established in 1983 and the customs union in 2003. The common market that provides the GCC residents with equal treatment and equal rights was launched on January 1, 2008. However, the actual provisions of the common market have not yet been fully implemented, as they require coordination and unified procedures and mechanisms across all six GCC states. The process is underway, but progress has been slow.[7]

The final and most far-reaching part of the Unified Economic Agreement is the establishment of an economic union, the GMU. As part of the agreement, the GCC states will have to abandon their local currencies and adopt a unified one instead. Monetary sovereignty will be transferred to the regional Central Bank, and a single monetary policy will apply to the entire GCC bloc.

An important milestone in the process toward the monetary union was reached at the Muscat Summit in 2001. There, the Supreme Council ordered all members to adopt the US dollar as the common peg no later than January 2003.[8] The Council also set January 2010 as the deadline for the introduction of a single GCC currency. In a 2005 report, the IMF welcomed and supported the decision and viewed the 2010 deadline as reasonable.[9]

A major setback to the establishment of the GMU was the withdrawal of Oman and the United Arab Emirates. In 2006, Oman announced that it was officially out of the GMU because it found the 2010 launch target to be too optimistic.[10] The country expressed its willingness to reconsider joining after the GMU is established. In 2009, the United Arab Emirates, a front-runner for hosting the Gulf Central Bank, exited a few days after the decision to position the Bank in Riyadh.

The political context

In establishing the Gulf Monetary Union, the leaders of the GCC states saw a clear political advantage. If they form a common market and adopt a single

---

[7] See the IMF's *GCC Monetary Union—Choice of Exchange Rate Regime* (Washington, DC: IMF, 2008).

[8] Khalid Al-Bassam, "The Gulf Cooperation Council Monetary Union: A Bahraini Perspective," *BIS Papers* No 17 (2003), pp. 105–107.

[9] See International Monetary Fund, Roberto De Rato, *Press Release*, No 05/231 (October 2005).

[10] Willem H. Buiter, "Economic, Political, and Institutional Prerequisites for Monetary Union Among the Members of the Gulf Cooperation Council," *Open Economies Review* Vol. 19, No. 5 (Spring 2005), pp. 579–612.

currency, the GCC states will achieve a greater degree of integration, sending a stronger message of unity and enhancing political stability. At the regional level, the states will gain bargaining power by creating a larger and more substantive, regional political constituency. The direct benefit will be that any policy communicated at the supranational level carries more weight than policies communicated at the national level.

There is also an indirect benefit. Managing a single currency would give GCC states added leverage at the negotiating table. For some time now, the GCC states have been contemplating a possible move away from the US dollar. For various political, economic, and institutional reasons, with the exception of Kuwait, the countries have chosen to maintain their pegs to the dollar.[11] The introduction of a single currency, however, will be combined with a discussion on the exchange rate regime for the new currency, rendering more credible a possible move away from the dollar. This move would have an adverse impact on the value of the US dollar, raising exchange rate volatility globally, and most certainly exacerbating global imbalances.[12] Therefore, how and when the GMU chooses to alter the exchange rate regime of the new currency becomes a policy instrument that provides the bloc with added leverage.

However, the increase in bargaining power at the supranational level will come at a cost. The countries will have to surrender policy autonomy at the national level. That is, while each country will have the right to vote on every decision and policy, financial and economic integration requires that a large number of decisions be taken at the supranational instead. That is not to say that all decisions need to be taken collectively. Nevertheless, the greater the degree of national sovereignty the countries are willing to surrender, the higher will be the gains at the bloc level.

The loss of policy autonomy at the national level will be costly as it will raise tensions internally for some countries. It will also increase conflicts across the GCC states. At the macro-level, the GCC region seems relatively homogenous. In fact, the countries share borders, their people speak the same language, they share the same culture and ethnic background, and they observe the same religion. But at the micro-level, there are substantial differences across these states. There are variations in levels of income, modernization,

---

[11] Bassema Momani, "Gulf Cooperation Council Oil Exporters and the Future of the Dollar," *New Political Economy* Vol. 13, No. 3 (September 2008), p. 293.

[12] The US dollar will be negatively affected by a potential move of the GCC countries away from the peg because the markets may perceive the de-peg as the first step of a process that will lead to a non-dollar pricing of oil and oil derivatives.

conservatism, sectarian sensitivities, receptivity to radical movements and ideologies, and expectations about the future cultural and developmental directions. These differences make some constituencies less receptive to change than others. They also make some people less willing to accept policies devised at the supranational level, for they fear that such policies do not reflect their best interests but are instead driven by the interests of specific member states. As a result, maintaining national unity and avoiding internal conflicts, while pursuing policies at the supranational level, can be more challenging for some states than others. These are the states for which the cost of giving up policy autonomy will be higher.

The importance of maintaining national policy autonomy can be illustrated from the positions the GCC states took with regard to the US invasion of Iraq in 2003. At the Sharm El Sheikh Arab League summit held just before the invasion, the UAE's Sheikh Zayed called for Saddam's resignation and supported the US effort to change the regime in Iraq by force if needed. Qatar, Kuwait, and Bahrain endorsed Sheikh Zayed's call, while Saudi Arabia, the biggest US ally in the region, maintained an ambiguous front, not openly backing the US effort, so as to minimize the risk of upsetting local groups. Saudi society remains very conservative and the state's battles with radicalism and terrorism are ongoing. Had the Saudis endorsed Sheikh Zayed's call, they would have certainly faced rising tensions at home.

The cost of surrendering national autonomy is further exacerbated by the dominance of Saudi Arabia. Saudi Arabia accounts for 83 percent of the total GCC land, 67 percent of the population, 49 percent of total market capitalization of listed companies, and 46 percent of the aggregate GDP (see Figure 8.1). The smaller GCC states remain concerned that decisions at the bloc level reflect the interests of the GMU as whole and not Saudi interests alone. Saudi Arabia's failure to gain the trust of the smaller states will continue to give rise to tensions across a whole range of political and economic issues. While the European Monetary Union benefitted from France's and Germany's dualism preventing the dominance of any one country, the dynamics in the GMU are different, making it extremely difficult for the smaller states to ensure that their voices are heard. The UAE's clear dissatisfaction with the decision to locate the Gulf Central Bank (GCB) in Riyadh, and its subsequent withdrawal from the GMU negotiations altogether, is a lesson of what is to come if the Gulf states cannot strike a balance between Saudi Arabia's weight on the one hand and the fairness of policy-making at the bloc level on the other.[13]

[13] The GMU countries must recognize that where the GCB is located and who gets to

Figure 8.1 Population, GDP, Land, and Market Capitalization across the GCC.

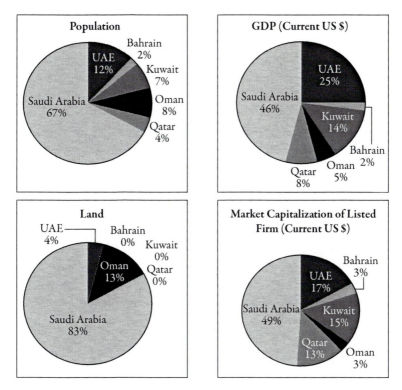

Source: World Development Indicators 2009.
*2007 data used for GDP.

Overall, the GCC states see the Gulf Monetary Union as a political liability. The cost of surrendering policy autonomy at the national level will outweigh the benefit of increased bargaining power at the bloc level. Of course, Saudi Arabia has every incentive to want the GMU to be implemented. As it is the largest regional economy and the region's self-ascribed superpower, hav-

---

run it are two separate issues. Kuwait, Qatar, and Bahrain can argue that since the GCB is in Riyadh, the governor should be a national of their countries in order to maintain a balance. In Europe, tensions were created when both France and Germany fought over the location of the ECB. The tensions subsided when Germany got the location, and France the presidency.

ing a single voice representing the GCC on economic and foreign policy issues is more likely to reflect Saudi Arabia's interests and policy preferences.

But what do the smaller states gain from a potential monetary union? Kuwait's involvement in the GMU stems largely from security considerations. Being part of the GMU enables Kuwait to rely more on the GCC states for support and protection, and less on the US against potential threats from the outside. For Bahrain, while security considerations are not unimportant, economic reasons are the primary drivers for wanting to join the GMU. Given Bahrain's comparative economic underdevelopment, the GMU will enable its nationals to seek employment opportunities in the region's other oil and gas rich GCC countries. Furthermore, not being part of the GMU can have serious adverse effects on Bahrain's financial sector, as many firms would exit Bahrain and relocate to another state within the monetary union.

For Qatar, the benefits of a potential GMU are less obvious. Since 1995, Qatar has taken a more active role on foreign policy issues, and it has become a regional conflict mediator, to the surprise—and perhaps irritation—of its neighbor Saudi Arabia. In 2008, Qatar initiated and led a mediation effort to solve the Lebanese conflict behind closed doors, preventing a renewed civil war in the country. Qatar has also been involved in mediation efforts in the Sudan and Yemen, and in border disputes between Eritrea and Djibouti. By entering the GMU, Qatar may have to scale back its role as a regional mediator, and the country will have to work with Saudi and the rest of its neighbors to promote policies that reflect the consensus of all GMU members. Whether or not Qatar will benefit politically from the GMU remains to be seen. In large measure, this will depend on the extent to which the GMU will allow Qatar to continue to high-profile diplomacy both across the region and beyond.

The economic context

If the Gulf Monetary Union is established, the union members will be sacrificing their local currencies in favor of a single, common currency. The move to a single currency will promote trade as transaction costs will fall, nominal exchange rate volatility will disappear, and price transparency will increase.[14]

The gains from trade will be positive, but not substantial. The economist Andy Rose has estimated that currency unions triple trade among their

---

[14] Exchange rate volatility is not a major concern for intra-industry trade in the Gulf, as all currencies, with the exception of the Kuwaiti dinar, are pegged to the US dollar.

members.[15] However, subsequent research has shown this estimate to be too optimistic. Empirical studies on the Eurozone find that the introduction of the euro contributed to anywhere from a 5 to a 15 percent increase in trade within the Eurozone.[16] But these studies also argue that not all gains can be attributed to the euro, as trade with non-Eurozone members, such as the United Kingdom, Sweden, and Denmark, increased by roughly the same amount. Taking into account the lessons from the Eurozone, and the fact that there is less intra-industry trade within the GCC than within the Eurozone, the increase in trade that may arise from the GMU is likely to be limited. At the same time, the potential gains will not come entirely from trade creation, but rather from trade diversion. The single currency will encourage GMU members to trade more with each other and less with other, non-GMU partners.

The key disadvantages of monetary unions are that by giving up the local currencies, the countries lose monetary autonomy and the ability to use exchange rates as automatic stabilizers. Monetary autonomy enables the Central Banks to pursue expansionary policies when output is low and contractionary policies when the economy is overheating and expected inflation rises beyond a tolerable level. Exchange rates can also help stabilize the economy. Under floating exchange rates, an adverse demand shock that lowers output will also cause a depreciation of the local currency. The depreciation makes domestic goods cheaper abroad and foreign demand for the goods rises. An export-led recovery then takes place as domestic firms increase their exports. Similarly, an increase in inflation, which can occur if there is strong domestic growth, will cause an appreciation of the exchange rate. The appreciation makes it harder for the domestic firms to export, as the goods then become more expensive abroad. The resulting drop in exports slows down the economy and the inflationary pressure subsides.

By entering a monetary union, the state has to concede its local currency. Without a local currency, state leaders no longer have the ability to use mon-

---

[15] Anthony Rose, "One Money, One Market: The Effect of Common Currencies on Trade," *Economic Policy* No. 30 (2000), pp. 9–45.

[16] For evidence on the effect that the euro had on trade in Europe, see J. Frankel, "The Estimated Effects of the Euro on Trade: Why are they Below Historical Evidence of the Effects of Monetary Unions Among Smaller Countries?" in Alberto Alesina and Francesco Giavazzi (eds), *Europe and the Euro* (Chicago, IL: University of Chicago Press, 2009), R. Baldwin and D. Taglioni, "Trade Effects of the Euro: A Comparison of Estimates," *Journal of Economic Integration* Vol. 22, No. 4 (2007), and A. Micco, E. Stein, and G. Ordonez, "The Currency Union Effect on Trade: Early Evidence from EMU," *Economic Policy* Vol. 18, No. 37 (2003), pp. 315–56.

etary policy or the exchange rate to stabilize the economy. Not surprisingly, entering the union and adopting a single currency comes at a high cost to the individual state.

In a series of influential papers published before the EMU was launched, the economist Martin Feldstein, one of the biggest opponents of the euro, argued that because the cost of giving up the local currencies would be too high for some European economies, especially the small ones, the EMU would be an economic liability. For Feldstein, the EMU made political, but not economic sense.[17]

In the case of the GMU, however, getting rid of the local currencies entails no such costs. Since 2003, the GCC countries, with the exception of Kuwait, have pegged their currencies to the US dollar. With the currencies pegged, the exchange rates no longer act as automatic stabilizers.

Furthermore, by and large the GCC states have already given up monetary autonomy. Under the fixed exchange rate regime, and with the relatively free flow of capital across the GCC, the real mandate of the GCC Central Banks is to maintain exchange rate stability by shadowing the policies of the US Federal Reserve, and not to pursue price stability or high output. For example, if the Fed implements an expansionary monetary policy through lower interest rates because of a slow-down in the US economy, the Gulf countries have to lower interest rates as well, regardless of whether or not the GCC economies are also experiencing a slowdown. Similarly, if the Fed raises interest rates in order to prevent inflation from building up in the US economy, interest rates in the GCC will also need to rise in lockstep in order to maintain the peg.

Because the GMU members do not have monetary autonomy and cannot use the exchange rate as an automatic stabilizer, they will not need to worry about the cost of giving up the local currencies once the GMU is established. Therefore, they will not have to incur the typical and important costs associated with the introduction of a single currency.[18]

---

[17] See Martin Feldstein, "The Case Against EMU," *The Economist*, June 13, 1992, pp. 12–19; Martin Feldstein, "Why Maastricht Will (Still) Fail," *The National Interest* No. 32 (2003), pp. 19–22; Martin Feldstein "The Political Economy of the European Economic and Monetary Union: Political Sources of an Economic Liability," *The Journal of Economic Perspectives* No. 4 (1997), pp. 23–42; and Martin Feldstein, "EMU and International Conflict," *Foreign Affairs* Vol. 76, No. 4 (1997), pp. 60–73.

[18] Of course, an absence of tangible economic costs does not mitigate attendant political costs; whether or not the political costs of giving up of local currencies can be easily absorbed by the GCC states remains unclear.

Several studies conducted on the GMU miss this very important point. Most observers question whether the GCC is an Optimum Currency Area (OCA).[19] An OCA is characterized by low inflation and the free movement of labor, capital, and all other factors of production, as well as economic convergence through business cycles synchronization. Using a range of methodologies, some scholars conclude that the GMU will be an economic liability because the OCA criteria are not met.[20] Others are of the opinion that the OCA criteria are indeed met, emphasizing the economic advantage a GMU would have.[21] As I demonstrate below, GCC states do not in fact satisfy the OCA criteria.

The economic evaluation of monetary unions is a straightforward cost-benefit analysis. The benefits come from the increase in trade between the union members, and the costs come from the loss of monetary autonomy and the ability to use exchange rates as automatic stabilizers. To assess the benefits we must estimate how big the increase in trade will be, while assessing the costs requires that we must estimate how difficult it will be for a country to give up its local currency.

If the OCA criteria are not met and the economies of the union members do not converge, giving up the local currency will be painful. On the other hand, if the OCA criteria are met and the economies converge, giving up the local currency will not be economically difficult. Moreover, meeting OCA criteria will lead to a smooth transition because policies at the bloc level will closely match the preferred policies at the national level.

[19] For the original discussion on Optimum Currency Areas see R.A. Mundell. "A Theory of Optimum Currency Areas," *American Economic Review* (September 1961), pp. 657–65.

[20] See for example B. Laabas and I. Limam, "Are GCC Countries Ready for Currency Union?," Arab Planning Institute, Kuwait (2005) and K. Shams and M. Shotar, "Economic Policies and the Possibilities of Unified GCC Currency," *Studies in Business and Economics* Vol. 12, No. 12 (2006), pp. 81–9.

[21] See for example Khalid AlKhater, ""The GCC Monetary Union and the Potential Strategic Gains: Aspirations and Challenges," Working Paper submitted at a seminar held at the GCC General Secretariat, March 6, 2010, Riyadh, E. Jadresic, "On a Common Currency for the GCC Countries," IMF Policy Discussion Paper 02/12 (Washington: International Monetary Fund, 2002); A. Darrat and F. Al-Shamsi, "On the Path to Integration in the Gulf Region: Are the Gulf Economies Sufficiently Compatible?" 10th Annual Conference of Economic Research Forum, Marrakesh, Morocco (2003); A. AlKholifey and A. Alreshan, "GCC Monetary Union" (Riyadh: Saudi Arabian Monetary Agency, 2009).

If countries have to bear a cost for giving up their local currencies, then the OCA and convergence analysis reveals how big the associated cost is. But in the case of the GMU, union members do not have to incur this cost for the reasons explained above. Therefore, measuring how big the cost would be, if it existed, is not very informative for assessing the economic impact of a potential GMU.

This is not to say that establishing whether the GCC countries form an OCA, and analyzing whether their economies converge, is unimportant. The answer to both questions is central to understanding the dynamics of the GMU. But we must first make sure that we ask the right question. If the choice presented to the GMU potential member states were between maintaining their local currencies and moving to a flexible exchange rate regime and adopting a single currency and a common monetary policy, then we would like to know whether the potential members of the GMU satisfy the OCA criteria.[22]

But even if we ask the right question, we must be very cautious when performing cross-country comparisons across the GCC. The methodologies used to calculate the data in each country differ substantially. Take inflation, for example. To compare inflation measures across the GCC countries, it is essential that the methodologies used to calculate inflation in each country be harmonized. Furthermore, measures need to be taken to ensure that this common methodology is the most appropriate.

However, the states of the Persian Gulf have far to go before achieving harmonization or appropriate measurement methods. To begin with, there is an absolute lack of transparency on the methodologies used by each of the GCC states. Moreover, these methodologies do not measure inflation accurately because the formulas used are based on fixed baskets of goods that do not change dynamically over time. This is a problem because the rate at which new products are introduced in the market is massive. Recent empirical evidence reveals that on average 40 percent of the retail items available today were not available two years ago, and 30 percent of the items that existed two years ago have disappeared today.[23] Simply put, pick a basket of goods in 2006

---

[22] We would also need to be able to evaluate whether monetary autonomy and a flexible exchange rate would be a blessing or a curse. Independence of the Central Bank, transparency, accountability and credible commitment to fight inflation are some of the attributes required for the former to happen.

[23] The evidence, which is part of ongoing work by the author, is based on monthly or bi-monthly scanner level retail data for each of the GCC countries going back five years.

and try to measure how the price of that basket changes over time. If you look at the basket in 2011 it will seem as if there were a big hole in the basket, for now the basket is half-empty. So we end up measuring the price of the remaining goods, readjusting the weights, and ignoring all the new goods that appear in the economy. Currently, the GCC states are taking substantial steps to improve the quality of their data. While their hard work and commitment will have an impact on the quality of the data in the future, nothing can be done to improve the quality of the historical data. Therefore, in the absence of harmonized methodologies and quality data, we must not attribute too much weight to cross-country comparisons.

Most central, however, is the fact that these cross-country comparisons reveal nothing about the future. Great efforts are taken at huge cost to diversify the economies away from the hydrocarbon sector. Every country invests heavily in education, research, technology, and in promoting industries that are not linked to the oil and gas sector (see Kristian Coates Ulrichsen's contribution in this volume). Under their corresponding National Visions, all countries have set their own roadmaps and set of strategies for how to become advanced economies in the next ten to twenty years. While some countries will be more successful than others, the sure thing is that the future structure of the economies will be different. There is absolutely nothing we can learn from historical data today about how the countries may look ten years from now. Even today, the UAE and Qatar bear little resemblance to the countries they were ten years ago.

I conclude this section with a brief discussion of two ingredients that are extremely important for a functioning and successful monetary union: price stability mandate and fiscal coordination mechanisms. Price stability results in high levels of output, low unemployment, financial stability, exchange rate stability, and low inflation. Economists and policy-makers alike agree that the most important, if not the only, mandate of a Central Bank should be price stability. Most of the macroeconomic gains associated with the EMU are attributed to the European Central Bank's commitment to fight inflation, a credible commitment inherited from the Bundesbank. In the case of the GMU, setting price stability as the mandate of the Gulf Central Bank is purely symbolic as long as the single currency remains pegged to the dollar. With a pegged currency, maintaining exchange rate stability will be, by default, the only true mandate.

A future change in the exchange rate regime that will see the single currency float will enable the Gulf Central Bank to adopt price stability as its mandate.

When this happens, developing a mechanism for fiscal coordination in the GMU will be critical. Strong fiscal coordination ensures that the burden of country-specific shocks is not borne entirely by a single country. Without fiscal coordination and restrictions on borrowing, independent national fiscal policies that are favorable to bailouts raise the risk of moral hazard. Furthermore, in the absence of coordination, high pro-cyclical fiscal spending that is linked to substantial oil revenues will undermine the goal of price stability set forward by the Gulf Central Bank.

Institution-building

A monetary union is not simply formed when a group of countries adopt a single currency and common monetary policy. Equally essential are institutional building blocks, from which participating countries tend to draw the most benefit. Identifying and understanding these factors, which are often overlooked, is the most important element in discussing the potential benefits that the process of developing the Gulf Monetary Union may bring to the candidate states.

Much of the GMU doctrine is based on the paradigm of the EMU. The institutional structure of the EMU is replicable, and its legal and regulatory frameworks are indeed adoptable. But the GMU would not operate in the same manner as the EMU. Their contexts and circumstances—in fact, their very DNA—are very different.

A true monetary union requires discipline, collaboration, communication, transparency, accountability, central banks' independence, expanded research capabilities, and broad availability of data to guide policy-making. Quite contrary to the case of the EMU, when it comes to the Persian Gulf most of these ingredients are conspicuously absent.

As mentioned earlier, much work needs to be done in strengthening the institutional framework of each GMU member, particularly insofar as the collection and processing of statistical data are concerned. GCC states must work on the quality, timeliness, dissemination, and coverage of macroeconomic and financial statistics. Furthermore, the methodologies used in each case must be harmonized. Better data will improve the quantity and quality of research, leading to enhanced and better-informed policymaking. Preliminary discussions on the establishment of the GMU helped some of the GCC states to recognize the need to strengthen the statistical frameworks of their central banks. Recently, Bahrain and Qatar joined the IMF's General Data Dissemination System, and Saudi Arabia asked the Fund for technical assistance to improve its statistical framework.

Another requirement for a successful union is that the regional central banks and the Gulf Central Bank become truly independent. Independence will help the countries maintain inflation at low levels. In the 1970s and the 1980s, several countries faced high inflation rates because the central banks had set high employment targets above natural levels. These central banks were subject to political influence that looked at the short-term political gains associated with lower unemployment, and ignored the long-term economic costs of high inflation. Central Bank independence helps resolve this time-inconsistency problem. For the rapidly expanding Gulf countries, especially Qatar, maintaining low inflation is a challenge. Failure to control inflation can have a serious adverse effect on the long-term growth potential of the region.

Independence of the Gulf Central Bank is a necessary, but not sufficient, condition for successful monetary policies by the Gulf Central Bank. Both the GCB and the regional central banks must be accountable for their actions so that independence is used appropriately. They also need to be transparent regarding the economic, procedural, policy, and operational aspects of their operations.[24] Accountability and transparency will boost the GCB's credibility, protect its independence, and enhance the understanding and effectiveness of monetary policy. The importance of these three pillars of central bank governance—independence, accountability, and transparency—is well understood and implemented in Europe and in other advanced economies. For the time being, they are not commonplace among central banks in the Persian Gulf.

Another challenge the GCC states face is the need to improve communication and collaboration. Currently, insofar as monetary policy is concerned, there is little collaboration across countries, across departments, and even within departments. This lack of collaboration among central banks arises

---

[24] Economic transparency in a central bank is reached when all the information used to make assessments is made available to the public. Procedural transparency is when the information on the process used (such as publication of minutes) is made available. Policy transparency is when there is immediate and timely announcement of monetary policy decisions, and operational transparency is when the central bank provides information on the implementation of monetary policy, as well as evaluations of past policies. A recent book, J-F. Segalotto, M. Arnone and L. Bernard (eds), *Central Bank Independence, Accountability, and Transparency: A Global Perspective*, New York: Palgrave Macmillan, 2009, is an excellent reference on central banks governance.

primarily from a lack of well-developed intellectual property rights, preventing policymakers and bankers from sharing information for fear of compromising information they consider privileged. In Europe, such "technical requirements" were in place before the creation of the EMU. Across the GCC, instead, much focus is placed on evaluating the OCA criteria, on testing the convergence of the economies, and on examining whether the candidates satisfy the accession criteria that were set in Maastricht for the EMU candidates. The resulting neglect of necessary technical requirements does not serve the long-term financial and banking interests of the GCC states.

Even if a Gulf Monetary Union is not established, preparatory steps toward enhancing monetary coordination across the GCC are likely to have long-term economic benefits for the future member states. With attention to appropriate areas of development, the GMU process is likely to provide guidelines and incentives for macroeconomic stability, long-term growth, and low inflation at the state level.

Conclusion

For the past three decades, the six countries of the Gulf Cooperation Council have been discussing the possibility of instituting a Gulf Monetary Union. The establishment and early success of the European Monetary Union, along with the strong growth of Persian Gulf economies, accelerated the GMU discussions. By 2003 all GCC states pegged their currencies to the US dollar, and 2010 was set as the target data for the launch of a single currency.

Beginning in the second half of the decade, the process was derailed and the launch of the single currency was postponed. Several factors have accounted for this slowdown. These include, most notably, the withdrawal of Oman and the United Arab Emirates from the discussions toward establishing the GMU, the impact of the global financial crisis on the regional economies, the slow progress that the GCC states have made toward more meaningful integration and cross-border collaboration, and, perhaps, second thoughts by some states on the actual benefits that the GMU will bring them.

Politically, the GMU is likely to be a liability. While it will increase bargaining power at the supranational level, it will also bring tensions both across and within countries. Economically, the GMU will bring some gains to the GCC through an increase in trade, but the gains will be small.

The institutional benefits of the GMU, on the other hand, are likely to be significant. The GMU process, if implemented correctly, will expedite the speed at which the Central Banks can achieve meaningful independence, transparency, and accountability. Furthermore, the process will require the countries to expand their research capabilities and strengthen their statistical frameworks. Finally, it will demand more discipline, collaboration, coordination, and sharing among the policy-makers and academics across and also within countries.

By meeting these requirements for the benefit of the Union, the GCC states are likely to increase economic efficiency in their countries and facilitate further macroeconomic stability, enhanced policy-making, low inflation, and long-term growth. These gains are likely to be realized even if the GMU's establishment continues to be delayed.

A successfully established monetary union will have two additional and substantial benefits. First, the introduction of the single currency will act as a precursor to a possible change in the exchange rate regime and a move away from the US dollar peg. Moving away from a fixed exchange rate regime and closer to a floating one will give back monetary autonomy to the GCC and the ability to use the exchange rate as an automatic stabilizer.

Second, it will encourage other non-GCC Middle Eastern states to aspire toward becoming a part of the GMU by achieving political and economic stability. One of the major benefits of the EMU is to provide non-EMU countries with model legal and regulatory frameworks and to encourage them to improve their socioeconomic and political environments for possible membership. By giving non-GCC states tangible institutional and policy goals to strive toward, a strong GMU has the potential to export stability in the Middle East and lower the vulnerability of the GCC economies to exogenous shocks.

For the time being, the GCC's delay in launching the single currency appears to be a prudent course of action given a lack of insufficient infrastructural requisites. Among the most urgent initial steps that need to be taken two stand out. First, all of the countries involved must move further along in their economic diversification efforts. Second, Oman and the UAE must come back to the negotiating table before the GMU is established. If the discussions and preparations should continue, the discussion and implementation committees must recognize the need for additional and more fundamental requirements for establishing a successful monetary union.

The author thanks Khalid Al Khater, Nicola Zaniboni, and Mark Farha and participants at the CIRS Working Group on the Political Economy of the Persian Gulf for very helpful comments. Fatima Mussa and Lamia Adi provided excellent research assistance.

Part III

Case Studies

9

The Dubai Model

Diversification and Slowdown

Christopher Davidson

Since 2008 the economic development model employed by the United Arab Emirates' second wealthiest and historically most autonomous Emirate of Dubai has gone from being an exemplar of post-oil diversification for the region to being a warning on the perils of over-reliance on foreign direct investment and credit-fueled growth. The world's leading newspapers posted dozens of articles—with varying degrees of accuracy—detailing Dubai's perceived collapse.[1] This chapter provides more substance and perspective to these accounts, arguing that Dubai's current economic crisis is not only a product of the global credit crunch, but a direct consequence of the new economic sectors that were introduced in the 1990s, the speed with which they were developed in the 2000s, and the debts incurred in the process.

With this aim, an overview of the "Dubai model" is provided, explaining the motivation and rationale behind the various diversification strategies pur-

---

[1] See for example *New York Times*, February 11, 2009; *Daily Telegraph*, November 25, 2009.

sued by "Dubai Incorporated" or "Dubai Inc."—the business-oriented government of Sheikh Mohammed bin Rashid Al-Maktoum, Dubai's hereditary ruler. In particular, the chapter focuses on Dubai's recognized need for reducing dependency on oil and gas exports and its early role as a free port, before turning to its building of advanced commercial infrastructure and manufacturing and agricultural sectors. The setting up of giant export processing and investment "free zones" to harbor foreign companies is then examined, along with the Emirate's establishment of luxury tourist and real estate industries and the necessary economic liberalization required by these sectors. The impact of the global credit crunch on Dubai is then considered, especially the Emirate's inability to re-service debts and its reliance on bailout packages from its fellow United Arab Emirates (UAE) member, Abu Dhabi. Finally, the chapter questions the level of autonomous control Dubai Inc. can still have over its economy in the wake of such substantial assistance from oil-rich Abu Dhabi.

Oil dependency

Throughout the 1980s the Dubai Petroleum Company's volume of oil exports increased greatly, and in 1991 Dubai reached a production peak of about 420,000 barrels per day, with proven reserves of over four billion barrels— around $1.5 million per capita value of oil reserves for Dubai nationals.[2] With such abundant resources Dubai was able to harness its comparative advantage of cheap energy and had already begun to set up heavy industries capable of producing metals, plastics, gases, and other hydrocarbon-dependent goods that could be profitably exported. Dubai Aluminium (DUBAL) was opened, quickly becoming the centerpiece of Dubai's industrialization program. This was followed by a liquid natural gas plant (DUGAS) so that gas could be captured from oil drills, and in 1992 the Dubai Cabling Company (DUCAB) also began exporting.[3] All were successful, with DUBAL at one point accounting for over 60 percent of Dubai's non-oil exports,[4] and since then a number of other energy-reliant companies have been established in the Emir-

---

[2] Hendrik Van Der Meulen, "The Role of Tribal and Kinship Ties in the Politics of the United Arab Emirates" (PhD thesis, The Fletcher School of Law and Diplomacy, 1997), p. 268.

[3] Graeme Wilson, *Rashid's Legacy: The Genesis of the Maktoum Family and the History of Dubai* (Dubai: Media Prima, 2006), pp. 374–5.

[4] Economist Intelligence Unit, January 2000.

ate, including Arabian Liquid Chemicals, the Gulf Metal Foundry, Gulf Engineering Industry, and Foseco Minsep (producing chemicals and water-proofing compounds).[5]

In tandem with this strategy, much of the wealth generated by oil and these related industries was placed overseas, so that interest payments on such investments could be used as a buffer should Dubai's domestic economy falter. By the mid-1990s most of these investments were being handled by Sheikh Mohammed's Dubai Holdings group and its various subsidiaries, most prominently Dubai International Capital, the Dubai Investment Group, and Jumeirah International. By the mid-2000s Dubai Holdings and its subsidiaries were thought to control over $15 billion of overseas assets[6] and were believed to be generating around $2 billion in revenue per annum. Significantly, while many of the group's investments were in short-term instruments such as US Treasury bills and in blue chip companies such as DaimlerChrysler,[7] EADS (the Airbus parent company),[8] and the Doncasters Group,[9] a number of its overseas acquisitions were also connected to hotels, sports facilities, and often glamorous or prestigious projects. Examples included the Carlton Tower and Lowndes hotels in central London, a fashionable art deco hotel in Manhattan,[10] a share in Arsenal Football Club's new stadium, and, most conspicuously, the London Eye ferris wheel and the Madame Tussauds waxworks center.[11] In late 2006 Dubai International Capital even attempted to purchase Liverpool Football Club, only to be defeated by a massive bid from an American consortium.

Despite such promising returns, it was nevertheless accepted that such oil-backed strategies would never be enough on their own to allow Dubai to maintain its status as the Persian Gulf's business capital and its relative autonomy within the UAE federation. Moreover, while it was acknowledged that heavy industries and overseas investments should remain an important component of Dubai's economic plan, it was also recognized that they would never provide the Emirate with a future of post-oil self-sustainability. With

---

[5] Easa Saleh Al-Gurg, *The Wells of Memory* (London: John Murray, 1998), pp. 186–7.

[6] Author's estimates, based on a figure of 55 billion dirhams for 2006.

[7] A $1 billion investment made in 2005.

[8] In the summer of 2007 Dubai International Capital acquired a 31 percent stake in EADS. *Gulf Today*, July 25, 2007.

[9] Purchased for around $1.4 billion from the Royal Bank of Scotland in 2005.

[10] The Essex Hotel.

[11] The latter of which was acquired in 2006 for $800 million.

Abu Dhabi just an hour's drive away, there was always a keen awareness of Dubai's limitations, given the massive oil reserves and the much greater potential for oil-related development enjoyed by its more resource-rich UAE neighbor. Indeed, with Abu Dhabi commanding around ten percent of the world's proven hydrocarbon deposits by the mid-1990s and accounting for over 90 percent of the UAE's oil exports, Abu Dhabi was always able to dwarf the capabilities of the DPC and Dubai Holdings. Its overseas investments now outrank those of even the much longer established Kuwaiti Investment Authority (KIA), and similarly enormous are Abu Dhabi's oil-associated heavy industries, many of which are internationally competitive, prominent examples including the Abu Dhabi Polymers Company (also known as Borouge), the Abu Dhabi National Oil Company's partner chemicals firm Borealis,[12] and the Abu Dhabi Shipbuilding Company.[13]

Clearly unable to compete over the long term with Abu Dhabi or other regional rivals as an oil focused emirate, Dubai's planners felt that pursuing such externally-oriented strategies would eventually place the Emirate's economy at greater risk from "dependent circumstances."[14] Following a series of oil price slumps in the 1980s,[15] and a number of oil industry security scares during the Iran-Iraq War and the invasion of Kuwait,[16] it became increasingly apparent that Dubai's economy was fragile. Furthermore, it was felt that even with the DPC's balanced multinational concessions, Dubai's economy still remained in the hands of a select group of foreign companies and oil-consuming nations. Such companies were believed to be the greatest beneficiaries from Dubai's oil given their insistence on purchasing only crude products, thereby preventing any refining or value addition to the commodity in Dubai.[17] It was estimated at one point that the concession holders were mak-

---

[12] Oxford Business Group, "Emerging Emirates" (London, 2001), pp. 90–91.

[13] *Gulf News*, 2 August 2005.

[14] Personal interviews, Dubai, January 2007.

[15] Caused by OPEC-related oversupplying.

[16] During this war a stray Iranian missile hit and damaged an Abu Dhabi offshore terminal.

[17] Al-Gurg, *The Wells of Memory*, p. 162. And in 2001 a former Egyptian Oil Minister visited Dubai and stated that "the real benefits of oil as a support for the industry were being gained by the West who refused our repeated attempts to sell them refined oil and insisted on buying it from us as a crude product. We were not making enough profit from oil as far as selling it for a good price as well as refining it and manufacturing its products are concerned."

ing more than four times as much revenue from each barrel as the DPC, which further promoted the view that the Emirate had become dependent and that, in the words of a veteran Dubai national, "...the western powers had left the region through the front door, but were coming back in again through the window."[18] It was also feared that having such a narrow economic base would eventually expose Dubai to the dual threats of unemployment, due to a lack of meaningful job opportunities outside of the oil and public sectors, and increased money supply and possible hyperinflation, given that the economy would not be able to absorb any surplus liquidity generated by oil revenues. By the early 1990s, oil-related strategies again came into question following changing energy consumption patterns in the consuming nations. Dubai's oil exports began to decline to around 300,000 barrels per day,[19] and this was partly blamed on a combination of stronger antipollution legislation in the West and new oil-producing regions in Central Asia and Latin America beginning to come on-stream.[20]

Early diversification and commercial infrastructure

In the mid-1980s, following a particularly bad month of interruptions to oil exports during the Iran-Iraq War, Dubai's Crown Prince at the time, Sheikh Maktoum bin Rashid Al-Maktoum, together with his younger brothers Hamdan and Mohammed met to discuss the Emirate's future direction. At a time when other governments in the Persian Gulf were reacting to the conflict by increasing their overseas investments in the West, the Al-Maktoum family decided the best solution was to buck the trend by making a commitment to invest in their own domestic infrastructure so that Dubai would be able to support and enhance its existing re-export-oriented commercial sector while also facilitating broader diversification away from oil in the future.[21]

Even during the height of the oil boom in the 1970s Dubai had continued to build trade-related infrastructure, providing the Emirate with strong foundations for such non-oil activity. In 1972 a second and even larger deep water port began to be built, and by 1979 the facility opened with a massive sixty-six berths,[22] making the new Port Jebel Ali nearly twice the size of Dubai's origi-

[18] Al-Gurg, *The Wells of Memory*, p. 162.
[19] By 1995 production had dropped to around 300,000 barrels per day.
[20] Personal interviews, Dubai, January 2007.
[21] Wilson, *Rashid's Legacy*, p. 476.
[22] Ibid., pp. 368–70.

nal port and one of the largest ports in the world. Soon after, Dubai opened a new dry dock compound. As Dubai's most expensive project at that time, many believed it to be a mistake, especially given that Bahrain was also building a dry dock and therefore would provide strong regional competition. However, Dubai correctly predicted the subsequent increase in Persian Gulf traffic, and the resulting rise in demand for ship repair facilities ensured that the dry dock was soon fully booked.[23] Most symbolically, in 1979 the Dubai World Trade Centre was completed and ceremonially opened by Britain's Queen Elizabeth II.[24] Although the Centre was soon overtaken by even taller buildings, its trade-related title, distinctive architecture, and prominent location close to Dubai's arterial highway succeeded in conveying a message to visitors that Dubai was not just about oil.

Over the following two decades investment in physical infrastructure continued unabated with at times an estimated 25 percent of GDP being spent on building and improving Dubai's network of seaports and roads.[25] Recently Dubai also began constructing a metro system, some lines of which are now open, and which will eventually give the Emirate one of the most advanced mass transit systems in the developing world. Although Dubai's maritime facilities have not developed quite so dramatically as this inland infrastructure, they have nevertheless benefited from substantial reorganization. With the recent merger of the Dubai Ports Authority and Dubai Ports International, the new Dubai Ports World Company assumed responsibility for both Port Rashid and Port Jebel Ali, and, in an apparent dovetailing with the Emirate's overseas investments strategies, it began to acquire operations in other countries. As a result the Dubai Ports World Company is now the fourth biggest ports operator in the world, controlling fifteen complexes across the Middle East, Asia, Europe, Latin America, and Australasia. Notably, it has made major investments in Jeddah, Djibouti, Gwadar in Pakistan and Constanţa in Romania, and in the Indian port of Visakhapatnam. Although it spectacularly failed to assume control over the Peninsula and Oriental Steam Company's (P&O) American operations in early 2006, due to an outpouring of xenophobia and anti-Arab sentiment in the US Congress, the Dubai Ports World Company nevertheless quietly acquired P&O's Brit-

---

[23] Al-Gurg, *The Wells of Memory*, p. 109.

[24] Donald Hawley, *The Emirates: Witness to a Metamorphosis* (Norwich: Michael Russell, 2007), p. 18.

[25] Personal interviews, Dubai, June 2006.

ish facilities and the US-based CSX International, bringing its net worth to some $8 billion.[26]

Equally remarkable has been Dubai's commitment to building up air infrastructure. Dubai International Airport (DXB) had already been established in 1960, complete with a terminal building and the region's first duty free shop. But as it was realized that Dubai needed to go even further and create a truly international airport so that its "open skies" policy could attract airlines and businessmen from further flung destinations, a new steering committee was set up in the early 1980s under Sheikh Mohammed.[27] Millions of dollars were invested in expanding the airport and by the mid-1980s the gamble on infrastructure once again appeared to have paid off, with over forty airlines visiting DXB at least once a week.[28] In late 1985 Mohammed was provided with over $10 million in seed money to lease a number of Pakistan International Airlines Boeing 737s,[29] and he appointed his uncle, Sheikh Ahmed bin Said Al-Maktoum, to launch Emirates, a completely new, Dubai-based airline.

Ahmed's new team recommended that for Emirates to survive, Dubai's open skies policy would have to be dropped or at least curtailed, with some small degree of protection permitted. Mohammed intervened and rejected the proposal on the grounds that it was against everything Dubai stood for, and demanded that the airline post profits from the very beginning so as to prove that it did not receive subsidies. The airline soon lived up to these great expectations, and has since turned a profit every year, even in the troubled 2001.[30] Much of Emirates' success can be attributed to the extensive upgrades and additions to DXB, which encouraged the airline to accommodate more passengers and, in 1999, allowed DXB to overtake the Mecca-servicing King Abdul-Aziz Airport in Jeddah to become the busiest hub in the region. In the near future Dubai's air infrastructure will expand further to include a second airport on the western side of the city, close to Jebel Ali. Although construction has been delayed,[31] it is estimated that upon its completion in 2017 the new "Dubai World Central Airport" (JXB) will be the fourth largest airport in the world: boasting six runways and three terminals, it will be able to handle in excess of 120 million passengers per annum.

[26] Personal Interviews, Dubai, February 2006; *Daily Telegraph*, October 31, 2005.
[27] Wilson, *Rashid's Legacy*, p. 425–7.
[28] Personal interviews, Dubai, January 2007.
[29] Wilson, *Rashid's Legacy*, p. 484.
[30] Ibid., pp. 482–3.
[31] *Middle East Economic Digest*, September 22, 2010.

Also of note, in terms of commercial infrastructure, has been the massive growth in the number and size of Dubai's shopping malls since the late 1990s. Many of the largest are run by major government-backed parastatals, most notably the giant Dubai Mall,[32] or are owned by the most powerful of the old merchant families, such as Mall of the Emirates. With protectionism largely prohibited, competition is fierce but healthy, and encourages the latest malls to offer novelties such as giant aquariums, ice rinks, and snowy ski slopes in order to attract customers. Dubai has actively encouraged these megaprojects by making it easier for individuals or investors to buy adjacent plots of land to house their malls. Tellingly, in Abu Dhabi, where such governmental backing has been absent until recently, there is a considerable contrast given that only a handful of malls currently exist, and only very powerful businessmen who are part of or are closely connected to the ruling family can really attempt such projects.

Alongside these physical improvements, Dubai has boosted its commercial sector by building up its regulatory environment and non-physical supporting infrastructure. In 1989 a Department of Commerce Marketing was established in order to "contribute to economic diversification by promoting non-oil development; and creating new opportunities for the Dubai business community by attracting trade and investment."[33] In practice, the department has complemented the existing Dubai Chamber of Commerce and Industry and has more aggressively promoted the Emirate's reputation as a trade entrepôt to overseas delegations. Furthermore, it also set up offices in several regional and international capitals including London and Paris. With regard to financial regulations, since 1980 the Dubai business community benefited from the establishment of a UAE Central Bank (originally the UAE Currency Board): although this new institution introduced protectionist measures (notably the limiting of foreign banks to having just one main branch in each emirate), it is nonetheless credited with helping confidence in the sector.[34] Also supportive, especially for Dubai's entrepreneurs, has been the Emirates Industrial Bank (EIB). Since its launch in 1982 this semi-government-backed[35] bank has provided low-interest "soft loans" in excess of $350 million

[32] Built by Emaar Properties.

[33] Dubai Department of Economic Development, *Statistical Book* (Dubai: 1999), p. 247.

[34] Al-Gurg, *The Wells of Memory*, p. 156.

[35] Abdulkhaleq Abdulla, "Political Dependency: The Case of the United Arab Emirates" (PhD thesis, Georgetown University, 1985), p. 250; personal interviews,

to various new business projects, especially those unrelated to the oil sector.[36] In parallel to these state run developments Dubai has continued to attract more foreign banks, including branches of most multinationals, and is widely considered to offer a conducive environment for locally-chartered banks.

Diversification into manufacturing and agriculture

With the aims of complementing the commercial sector, establishing additional non-oil-related activities, and reducing the value of imports into the Emirate, Dubai also began to build up both its light manufacturing and agricultural processing sectors. A new industrial law was introduced in 1979, the first Article of which stated that "the government must prepare a productive base capable of allowing manufacturing industries to thrive and thereby reduce the reliance on oil."[37] The Emirate duly focused on relatively simple manufacturing plants that rarely required expensive foreign technology and were not dependent on cheap energy to offer a competitive advantage in the same way as the heavier, oil-dependent industries. In the 1980s several such plants, most of which produced construction materials such as cement and piping that would have been costly and inefficient to import, were established and by the 1990s these were joined by many more low cost "import substitution industries" manufacturing goods such as plastic water bottles, ice cream, and workers' uniforms. At one stage Dubai's import costs were held in check,[38] and much of that brief success was attributed to this sector.

Dubai's agricultural sector enjoyed modest growth during this period of early diversification, with attempts to increase both productivity and total cultivable area of land meeting with some success. Substantial government investment in rural infrastructure, farming equipment, and the development of new, desert-hardy crop strains allowed many farms and agricultural businesses to flourish. Output increased, with vegetable production tripling during

---

Dubai, February 2006. EIB is 51 percent owned by the Abu Dhabi government and 49 percent by a consortium of local banks.

[36] Oxford Business Group, "Emerging Emirates," p. 88; personal interviews, Dubai, June 2006.

[37] Christopher M. Davidson, *The United Arab Emirates: A Study in Survival* (Boulder: Lynne Rienner, 2005), p. 123.

[38] During the late 1980s the cost of imports was held at around $5.5 billion. See Dubai Department of Economic Development, *Statistical Book* (Dubai, 2001), p. 110.

the 1990s, dairy production rising a hundredfold over a twenty-year period,[39] and the Emirate beginning to enjoy one of the highest per capita agricultural productivity rates in the Persian Gulf.[40] An afforestation program facilitated a doubling of cultivable hectares in Dubai between 1987 and 2007.[41] But perhaps most importantly, there was an improvement in food security, with Dubai becoming over 80 percent self-sufficient in several foodstuffs.[42]

Establishing Free Zones

Dubai's strategy of attracting foreign, non-oil related investment by setting up export processing zones specifically for foreign companies has been more complex. Unlike the relatively straightforward commercial, manufacturing, and agricultural sectors, the free zones required controversial reforms in order to overcome existing legislation. Since the mid-1980s federal directives emanating from Abu Dhabi, most notably the 1984 Commercial Companies Law, had required all of the UAE's constituent emirates to adhere to a local sponsorship or *kafil* system under which all registered companies had to be at least 51 percent owned by a UAE national. These protectionist rules were increasingly viewed as inappropriate given that they impeded further investment and diversification while also undermining Dubai's reputation as a laissez-faire free port.

The Dubai planners decided that the best course of action was to circumvent federal laws by creating special authorities to manage zones within the Emirate that would technically fall outside of UAE jurisdiction. It was decided that the first "free zone" project would be set up alongside the new port at Jebel Ali so as to allow foreign companies easy access to unloading facilities and also to keep the new authority on the periphery of the city and as something of an "enclave." Launched in 1985 by the Dubai Department of Industry, the Jebel Ali Free Zone Authority guaranteed 100 percent foreign ownership and "supplied the zone with all the necessary administration,

[39] Dubai Department of Economic Development, 2001, p. 75.

[40] Crown Prince Court Department of Research and Studies, *Statistical Book* (Abu Dhabi: 1996), pp. 31, 76.

[41] Dubai Department of Economic Development 2001, p. 17; personal interviews, Dubai, February 2008.

[42] Most notably over 80 percent in vegetables and dairy products, although only about 25 percent in meat and 20 percent in poultry. Personal interviews, Dubai, June 2008.

engineering, and utility services required by its clients."[43] In practice this meant that foreign companies could move into ready-made "lease office buildings" and would benefit from streamlined visa processing for their employees, cheap energy, and good transportation infrastructure. As with the dry docks development, the timing was perfect as many merchants disadvantaged by the Iran-Iraq War and the Lebanese civil war—most of whom had previously been wary of investing in Dubai due to the 1984 *kafil* system and their reluctance to take on a local "sleeping partner"—now found that they had a suitable alternative. The zone duly enjoyed rapid growth, and was soon home to around 300 companies including textile manufacturers, chocolate factories, and farm machinery exporters. By 2002 the zone had expanded to accommodate over 2,000 companies, and by 2008 it was employing over 40,000 workers and had generated over $6 billion in investments.[44] Jebel Ali has also proved popular with multinationals intent on establishing a Middle Eastern headquarters, and in some cases has even begun to host companies intent on total relocation, notably Halliburton which moved to Dubai in 2007.

Pushing the boundaries further, Dubai has since created other, more specialized free zones to attract and accommodate new sectors that have specific infrastructural requirements. In 1999 two new "cities" were set up, one for internet companies and one for media companies, and in 2000 new emirate-level enabling legislation was introduced that built upon the experience of Jebel Ali and added new articles in support of such new foreign firms. The resulting Dubai Technology, Electronic Commerce, and Media Free Zone Law promised that establishments would be excluded from any UAE restrictions placed on the repatriation and transfer of capital, would never be nationalized, and would be free to choose employees of any nationality (except Israelis).[45] By late 2000 Dubai Internet City was ready to open its doors, providing IT infrastructure (including a dedicated submarine Internet cable) to over 100 companies that had been waiting to move in. Incredibly, by 2008 the City had expanded to house nearly 850 companies employing some 10,000 workers, and soon hosted the regional headquarters of leading technology firms including Microsoft, Hewlett-Packard, Dell, and Canon. Situated on an adjacent site,

---

[43] Dubai Department of Economic Development, 1999, p. 241.

[44] Dubai Department of Economic Development, *Statistical Book* (Dubai: 2002), p. 245.

[45] See Articles 15, 16, and 17 of the Dubai Technology, Electronic Commerce, and Media Free Zone Law Number 1 of 2000. Free zone companies are not allowed to hire nationals of "boycotted countries," most notably Israel.

Dubai Media City was launched at the same time and is operated by a new Media Free Zone Authority. Much like the Internet City, the Media City also grew to around 800 companies, including many leading regional and international brands such as Al-Jazeera, CNN, the BBC, and Reuters.

More recently, several other zones have been established around Dubai, so many in fact that about one third of the city's land area is now believed to be controlled by free zone authorities. These have included the Dubai Airport Free Zone, located close to Terminal 2 of Dubai International Airport and providing facilities geared toward international cargo companies such as Federal Express and DHL. Also notable are Dubai Healthcare City, which serves as a base for foreign medical companies and services;[46] and Dubai Knowledge Village, which, since its launch in 2003, now houses branches of several international universities. Although there have been some failures in the Knowledge Village,[47] most universities have generated considerable revenues from their operations given the many young professionals who now live in Dubai or are willing to travel there in order to gain Western-accredited MSc or MBA degrees.

Most significant among the new free zones has been the Dubai International Financial Centre (DIFC) and its constituent Dubai International Financial Exchange (DIFX). This zone was conceived not only to advance further and complement the commercial sector's existing financial infrastructure, but also to provide a means of absorbing the surplus liquidity generated by neighboring oil and gas exporting economies. Dubai's planners hoped to create a zone unencumbered by local legislation and, in an effort to boost investor confidence, created a dollar-denominated environment and based the DIFC's regulatory framework on English law.[48] An impressive headquarters building opened in 2004 and within months this "gateway" complex was home to international financial institutions including KPMG, Swiss Private, Swiss International Legal, Merrill Lynch, and Credit Suisse.[49]

Diversification into luxury tourism

Attracting more foreign investment and boosting the domestic non-oil economy further has been Dubai's commitment to building up a luxury interna-

---

[46] Wilson, *Rashid's Legacy*, p. 581.
[47] Notably the University of Southern Queensland and, most recently, Michigan State University.
[48] *Gulf News*, September 22, 2004; personal interviews, Dubai, June 2006.
[49] *Khaleej Times*, October 2, 2004.

tional tourist industry. By 1990 some 600,000 visitors per annum were staying in Dubai's seventy or so hotels, with most utilizing the twenty-five four and five star business hotels.[50] From 1992 onwards the sector mushroomed, with a newly established Dubai Tourism Promotion Board (later integrated into the Dubai Department of Commerce Marketing) concentrating on international promotions and positioning Dubai as not just a commercial hub, but also as a resort destination. With offices set up in Britain, France, the US, India, and South Africa,[51] the new "Destination Dubai" initiative was judged to be highly successful, with the number of visitors doubling to over 1.3 million per annum by 1995, the majority being sun-seeking tourists staying in Dubai's forty-five new resort hotels.[52]

In the late 1990s Dubai entered the international high-end tourist market by investing in some of the world's most luxurious hotel projects. Following the establishment of the Jumeirah International group in 1997, work was completed on the iconic Jumeirah Beach Hotel to the west of Dubai, and in 1999 its sister hotel, the seven star Burj al-Arab, was opened. Alongside these beachfront properties Jumeirah International also committed to managing the Emirates Towers Hotel, housed in the second of two new 300 meter towers that had been constructed in downtown Dubai. These constructions became highly symbolic of Dubai's strategy; while Abu Dhabi's tallest building were oil-related,[53] Dubai's tallest skyscrapers were housing hotel bedrooms and commercial offices.

By 2000, 3.4 million tourists were visiting Dubai each year,[54] a testimony to these pioneering developments, and in more recent years Jumeirah International added to its portfolio by converting the Al-Maktoum family's former winter camping ground into the Al-Maha Desert Resort, by building the new Fairmont Hotel close to Sheikh Zayed Road, and by redeveloping the beachfront to the west of the Burj al-Arab in order to accommodate two large hotels (Al-Qasr and Mina As-Salam) and an adjoining shopping mall, the Madinat Jumeirah. In mid-2007 another Dubai entity purchased the Cunard line's most famous cruise ship, the QE2, which was intended to serve as a luxurious

---

[50] Personal interviews, Dubai, January 2007.

[51] Wilson, *Rashid's Legacy*, p. 486.

[52] Personal interviews, Dubai, June 2006.

[53] The headquarters of the Abu Dhabi Investments Authority, Abu Dhabi's largest sovereign wealth manager.

[54] Data supplied by the Dubai Department of Tourism and Commerce Marketing.

floating hotel.[55] It is estimated that in the mid-2000s over 10 percent of Dubai's GDP was invested in these Jumeirah and other government-backed tourism projects.[56] Similarly ambitious were the foreign chains, with both the Sheraton and Hilton groups expanding their number of properties, and many other leading companies choosing to build flagship hotels in Dubai. Most notably the Thai Dusit and the Chinese Shangri-La chains constructed large tower block hotels, while the Hyatt group built a second complex, and Le Meridien constructed several hotels and furnished apartment towers all around the city. Together, it is thought that these predominately luxury hotels, most of which were enjoying much higher occupancy rates than the lower class hotels, were accounting for nearly two thirds of Dubai's tourism in 2007, which may have been as high as 6.5 million per annum.[57]

Dubai's tourist industry has not relied on hotels and beaches alone, as planners were keenly aware that Dubai had to provide additional incentives to draw people to the Emirate and to fend off competition from other destinations. With this purpose in mind, several leisure and recreation-oriented initiatives were launched to make Dubai not only the region's commercial capital, but also its entertainment hub. Also successful in attracting tourists (and further complementing the commercial sector) was Dubai's investment in promoting and running an annual shopping festival. First staged in 1996, the new Dubai Shopping Festival was the largest event to ever take place in the UAE: with promotions in hundreds of hotels, restaurants, and shops, and with dozens of street entertainment events, it was estimated that over $1 billion was generated by the festival in its first year.[58] It has been a perennial success and only had to be cancelled on one occasion, following the unexpected death of Sheikh Maktoum in early 2006. To support the festival, and to provide similar activities during other seasons, Dubai also created a giant "Global Village" to house country-specific, mini-compounds selling goods and performing traditional dances; and in 2001 the Dubai Summer Surprises festival was launched to promote regional tourism in the traditionally slow summer months.

---

[55] *The Guardian*, June 18, 2007. The QE2 was purchased by Istithmar, the investment arm of the Dubai Ports World Company.

[56] Personal interviews, Dubai, January 2007.

[57] Data supplied by the Dubai Department of Tourism and Commerce Marketing. In 2007 there were officially 6.4 million visitors to Dubai.

[58] Wilson, *Rashid's Legacy*, p. 532.

Further in support of tourism was Dubai's commitment to live music and the performing arts, with a new theater in Madinat Jumeirah hosting several major touring companies each year, and with the Dubai International Film Festival showcasing new releases and attracting many leading Hollywood names to the Emirate. Similarly successful have been the well attended annual Dubai International Jazz Festival staged in Media City and the Dubai Desert Rock festival. Since 2001 other large venues such as the Dubai Aviation Club, the Dubai Country Club, and the Nad Al-Sheba racetrack have brought stadium-filling artists to the city, with most of these events bringing thousands of tourists to Dubai from across the region and many parts of Asia, just to see their favorite performers.

Exhibition tourism has also been extremely profitable for Dubai, many business hotels having been filled to capacity during off peak periods due to an increasing number of professional and industrial exhibitions. In particular, Dubai's annual GITEX event, staged in an annex of the World Trade Centre, grew to become the third largest IT-related international event since its launch in 1998, and in 2008 was drawing around 130,000 visitors from over 3,000 companies. Similarly well attended have been Dubai's Arabian Travel Market exhibition, which hosts delegations from over 100 of the Middle East's tourist companies and attracts about 25,000 visitors, and the bi-annual Dubai Air Show, which since its launch in 1989 has expanded to feature nearly 100 aircraft marketed by over 500 companies.[59]

A real estate industry

Also encouraging foreign investment, from both companies and individuals, and closely associated with the tourist sector and its associated "entertainment infrastructure" has been Dubai's diversification into freehold real estate. With the multiple aims of converting impressed tourists into holiday home or buy-to-let purchasers and, perhaps more realistically, persuading nationals of less stable parts of the developing world to make a safe investment and create a new residence for their families, the real estate sector also managed to circumvent and modify existing restrictive legislation much like the free zone developments, and soon accounted for another sizeable slice of Dubai's non-oil-related GDP.

As late as the mid-1990s there was no property market as such in Dubai, most of the developed land around the city having been donated by the ruling

[59] Personal correspondence, May 2007.

family to other national families so as to build new homes for themselves or to build residential and commercial blocks to lease out to expatriates and businesses. In 1997, however, this began to change following an announcement that the new $200 million "Emirates Hills" residential complex near to the Emirates Golf Club would offer luxury villas to selected foreigners.[60] This project was managed by Emaar Properties, a company that had been set up in the early 1990s by Mohammed Ali Al-Abbar, the first director of Dubai's Department of Economic Development. Up until the launch of Emirates Hills, Emaar had confined itself to building fairly nondescript condominiums on land provided by the ruler, with the intention of offering the same sort of short-term leases common everywhere else in the UAE. However, following work experience in Singapore, where he had recognized the potential of a vibrant real estate sector, Al-Abbar returned to Dubai and encouraged the ruling family to press ahead with reforms that would enable the Emirate to create such a sector.

In much the same way that the pioneering Jebel Ali Free Zone circumvented the federal laws regarding foreign business ownership during the 1980s, the marketing of the Emirates Hills villas to foreigners was also technically illegal, as only UAE nationals were permitted to own property in the UAE. Although Al-Abbar sought to work around the federal law by offering ninety-nine year leases to foreigners with the promise of renewal following a nominal payment of just $1, there is little doubt that in the early days of Dubai's real estate market, Emaar entered a legal minefield. Certainly, the federal government could in theory revoke all ownership rights from investors,[61] and this rendered the sector reliant on an unwritten promise from Dubai's ruling family that there would be future enabling legislation.[62]

Nevertheless, this royal assurance was enough to kick-start the largest property boom in the Middle East, with Emaar selling out all of its available plots within days of the official launch, and with several other projects receiving equally enthusiastic receptions. Most notably, the Westside Marina development (later renamed Dubai Marina) proposed to cut a man-made canal inland from the sea and construct a number of high specification residential towers with marina and coastal views; the "Greens" complex began to advertise quiet

---

[60] Davidson, *The United Arab Emirates*, p. 230.
[61] Personal interviews, Dubai, February 2006. For a journalist's interpretation see *Daily Telegraph*, January 15, 2005.
[62] Personal interviews, Dubai, January 2007.

poolside three-storey blocks complete with integrated amenities such as supermarkets, gyms, and social clubs; and the Emaar Towers offered city center living in large apartments with balconies overlooking Dubai's creek. In addition, several large villa complexes (The Springs, The Meadows, and Arabian Ranches) were launched in the hinterland, most of which were completed within just a few years. Following in Emaar's footsteps was Dubai Properties, a group under the umbrella of Dubai Holdings, which began work on the enormous thirty-six tower Jumeirah Beach Residence on the beachfront of Emaar's new marina. Believed to be the largest single phase residential project in the world, it cost over $1.6 billion and was originally intended to house over 25,000 residents upon completion. Perhaps most significant among Emaar's stable mates has been Nakheel. As a property company dating back to 1990, it sought to emulate the success of Emaar's Emirates Hills by seeking backing from the government together with a personal commitment from Sheikh Mohammed. With this in place, it embarked on several of Dubai's most memorable real estate developments. Most famously, Nakheel constructed two separate "Palm Islands" off the coast of Jumeirah and Jebel Ali, the first of which now features villas, apartments and—in cooperation with international chains—several five star hotels. As giant patches of reclaimed land the islands sought to expand Dubai's waterfront from about 70 km to over 500 km, given that each "palm" was to have several fronds and a number of additional, more exclusive mini-islands in the shape of Arabic lettering to represent one of Sheikh Mohammed's best known poems. In 2004, with both palms being sold out off-plan, Sheikh Mohammed instructed Nakheel to launch a third palm off the eastern coast of Dubai,[63] and a further archipelago of islands further out at sea. While the eastern palm island quickly stalled, the archipelago project, entitled "The World," attracted enormous international media attention given that its 300 or so islands were each to represent a separate country, while several high profile investors had supposedly committed to purchasing various islands.

By early 2006, with several of the major projects completed, the three big developers were thought to have provided in excess of 30,000 new homes, most of which were sold to expatriates. As the newly installed ruler of Dubai and vice president of the UAE federation following his eldest brother's death, Sheikh Mohammed was in a strong enough position to press ahead with more comprehensive emirate-specific legislation to safeguard the nascent real estate

---

[63] *WAM* (UAE National News Agency), October 6, 2004.

sector. By this stage, with Dubai home to over $50 billion in committed property-related projects,[64] the federal government was presented with something of a fait accompli, and there is evidence that for quite some time before, Abu Dhabi had come to terms with Dubai's strategy.[65] Thus, by the spring of 2006 Sheikh Mohammed unilaterally announced the Dubai Property Law. This included articles stipulating that foreigners were entitled to own real estate in "some parts of Dubai, as designated by the ruler," and would be entitled to receive residency visas from the Dubai government (previously residency visas were only issued to foreigners subject to proof of employment). Moreover, to settle investors' minds further, the law called for the establishment of a Lands Department that would provide a centralized land registry capable of issuing deeds upon purchase.[66]

With the new legislation in place, demand for Dubai's announced projects soared further, and additional developments were launched. In some cases, demand was so high that prospective customers for new off-plan villas and apartments had to arrive at sales centers on the morning of the launch in order to queue for lottery-like tickets that would entitle them to make a purchase. In particular, Emaar, which became a 67 percent publicly owned company following its flotation on the DIFX,[67] pressed ahead with its magnificent Burj Dubai. As a mixed residential, commercial, and hotel complex that was to total some 165 or more storeys it was to be built with a dynamic design to ensure that upon its completion it would be the world's tallest structure. Complementing the Burj was the "Old Town" district which was to feature more traditional architecture and was to form a boulevard at the skyscraper's base. Next door to the Burj, Dubai Properties began constructing an enormous Venetian-style downtown area of smaller skyscrapers that was to be connected by small canals fed from a larger waterway that was to extend all the way into the creek. At one point this "Business Bay" project was thought to be employing nearly 10 percent of the world's cranes, and by 2008 it was visibly transforming Dubai's skyline into something of a Middle Eastern Manhattan.

Similarly ambitious, and also incredibly popular with off plan investors, was Nakheel's follow-up scheme: envisaging a coastal city larger than downtown

---

[64] Merchant International Group, "Strategic Research and Corporate Intelligence: Instant Analysis on Dubai" (London, 2005).

[65] Personal interviews, Abu Dhabi, 2002.

[66] See Law Number 7 of 2006: The Dubai Property Law.

[67] Following allegations of insider trading, the Dubai government chose to retain 33 percent of the shares.

Beirut, the $13-billion Dubai Waterfront was to stretch out far beyond Palm Jebel Ali and to feature the confusingly titled Al-Burj, intended to become Dubai's second tallest building, as its centerpiece. Also noteworthy were the attempts of some developers to provide investment opportunities for lower income households, especially the Emirate's large middle class South Asian community. Nakheel's oddly titled Jumeirah Village, sandwiched between the city's two main arterial highways, and its International City, located on the periphery of the desert, were joined by other low-end developments from new property companies, including Sama's Lagoons, close to the creek. Together, these developments enjoyed some success, albeit not on a par with the high-end projects—the deeds of which were being sold and re-sold, or "flipped" for significant profits long before any units were close to completion.

Superficial success

Together, Dubai's various diversification strategies appeared to have greatly reduced the Emirate's former reliance on oil exports and oil-related strategies such as energy dependent heavy industries and oil-financed overseas investments. By the mid-1990s Dubai's non-oil sectors were already contributing 82 percent of the Emirate's GDP,[68] and by the summer of 2008 the figure may have been as high as 95 percent.[69] In comparison, the non-oil contribution to the UAE's overall GDP was only 63 percent at this time,[70] and it is believed that in 2007, close to the height of its boom, Dubai was responsible for the vast bulk of the UAE's total foreign direct investment inflows of about $3 billion per annum (compared to $2.1 billion in 2003 and $0.5 billion in 1995).[71] This figure of $3 billion placed Dubai and the UAE far ahead of peers such as Kuwait (which was managing only $0.5 billion per annum),[72] and among the top Middle Eastern countries for such investment, despite having a much smaller population. International reports published by the United Nations Conference on Trade and Development (UNCTAD) even compared Dubai's foreign direct investment potential with that of Geneva, New Delhi, Tokyo, and even New York, and ranked the Emirate seventeenth out of over

[68] Data supplied by the Ministry of Planning.
[69] Data supplied by the Ministry of Economy.
[70] Ibid.
[71] Personal interviews, Dubai, March 2007; data from the Inter-Arab Investment Guarantee Corporation.
[72] Personal interviews, Dubai, February 2006.

100 surveyed countries with respect to foreign investment attractiveness.[73] Thus, on paper at least, Dubai had escaped from its former situation, with Dubai Inc. giving a strong impression that it had succeeded in creating a self-sustaining, multi-component economy capable of generating vast wealth independently of the old oil industry.

The credit crunch reaches Dubai

By September 2008, with the global credit crunch entering its second year, Dubai appeared to have decoupled from the toxicity spreading throughout the developed economies, as there were few visible signs that the Emirate was being affected by international recession. In November 2008, in an article entitled "Escape to Dubai," *New York Magazine* claimed Wall Street bankers were decamping in their dozens to a new "city of gold" and, if anything, Dubai was growing faster than before.[74] Delegates in Kuwait's quasi-democratic parliament were complaining that even without oil Dubai was doing better than their economy. And on a personal level, Sheikh Mohammed was hailed as a captain of industry and a visionary ruler across the Arab world, and in some cases far beyond. From Dubai's side the message was equally loud and clear: Dubai was different from other developed economies and as such was circumventing the global tsunami.

To underline the Emirate's optimism, in early October 2008 at Cityscape, Dubai's premier real estate convention, plans for a one kilometer-tall tower were announced, even as Emaar's Burj Dubai stood unfinished. Moreover, Jumeirah Gardens, a real estate project the size of metropolitan Hong Kong, was being aggressively promoted. And most dramatically, in November 2008, as perhaps the ultimate Bonfire of the Vanities, a $15 million party was staged at the new Atlantis Hotel, which had just opened on the first of the palm islands. With hours of firework displays and guest appearances from A-list Hollywood celebrities, the launching of the $800 a night resort was a clear signal that Dubai was bucking the global trend, and doing so with considerable panache.[75]

Behind the glamour and bluster, however, Dubai was already experiencing problems, with so much of its "new economy" being reliant on foreign direct

---

[73] *Gulf News*, September 23, 2004.
[74] *New York Magazine*, November 16, 2008.
[75] See for example *The Times*, November 21, 2008.

investment and tourism. Interest in real estate was declining markedly as for-eign investors retreated to problems in their domestic markets, and Dubai-based realtors admitted that transactions had slowed to a trickle. Hotel occupancies also began to falter as tourists from countries in recession turned to cheaper destinations. Most seriously, Dubai's banks and mortgage lenders were struggling to find credit on the international market. Loans dried up, speculators began to disappear, and the first major wave of resale properties began to hit the classifieds as nervous expatriates sought to cut their losses and run. The confidence bubble was pricked, and the Dubai stock markets went into freefall, with share prices for erstwhile government-backed "blue-chips" such as Emaar Properties shedding over 80 percent of their value by the end of 2008. The first major redundancies were announced, in their thousands, and the Emirate's two biggest mortgage lenders, Tamweel and Amlak, had to be merged under a new federal authority.[76]

Facing political pressure from investors and other stakeholders in the new economy, the Dubai Inc. planners began a strenuous chorus of defense and denial in an effort to keep the Emirate's brand alive. The defense was led by the ruler himself and he was joined by individual expatriates who had put their entire life savings into real estate. Wrong-footed academics, think tank profes-sionals, bloggers, and UAE-based newspaper editors—few of whom had predicted the crash and very few of whom had identified any shortcomings of the Dubai model—joined in, and a stream of articles and opinion editorials were published in government-backed newspapers, notably *Gulf News*, most of which claimed the Emirate's fundamentals were perfectly sound while some, even as late as November 2008, stated that Dubai was "the safest place to anchor in the global crisis."[77]

But as the weeks went by, the negative indicators increased. By the end of 2008 hundreds of cranes stood motionless over incomplete projects, fewer lights were shining from the windows of tower blocks at night, and—refresh-ingly for some—Dubai's infamous traffic jams were easing up. More employ-ees were being fired, especially from property companies, and a large number of expatriate laborers were sitting idle in their camps. A string of high profile suspensions and cancellations were tersely announced, including the short-lived Jumeirah Gardens and even Dubailand, a planned theme park that was

---

[76] Tamweel and Amlak were merged in November 2008. *Gulf News*, November 22, 2008.

[77] See for example *Gulf News*, November 1, 2008.

to be even larger than Florida's Disneyland. In an effort to appease investors and creditors, a decision was taken by the Dubai Executive Council—the formal institution representing Dubai Inc.—to reveal publicly the size of the Emirate's sovereign debt mountain. An official claim was made that the total debt did not exceed $80 billion, and that overseas assets could cover this. However, it was admitted that most of the debt was short-term and was due for re-servicing over the next few years, and most of it had been accumulated by the state or the various state-affiliated property companies.[78]

The major ratings agencies, led by Moodys, responded by downgrading Dubai's banks, and by February 2009 the Emirate's credit default swaps—that is, the cost of insuring debt sold by Dubai companies—were much the same as Iceland's, in the wake of its banking collapse.[79] Exacerbating the situation, a large number of expatriates who either had already lost their jobs or were fearing imminent redundancy decided to abandon Dubai, leading to reports of abandoned vehicles and credit cards. Thousands of exit visas were being processed each day and a landlord and hotel price war began, with rental contracts and room rates being slashed by over 70 percent. Newspapers, bulletin boards, and blogs groaned under the weight of hastily produced property adverts—some of which threw in all furniture and fittings—and for those laborers whose employers were still in business, hundreds were being rounded up each evening and bussed to the airport.

As Dubai's economic crisis unfolded, the Emirate's long history as a laissez-faire free port appeared to be coming unstuck, with revelations of rampant corruption—especially in the real estate industry—increasing authoritarianism, and intensifying protectionism. With investors seeking their money back, pyramid schemes that had been building up unchecked over the years were being exposed. Foreign investigative journalists began to report on expatriate real estate developers who were being held without charge and claimed to have been tortured, and even companies backed by senior members of the ruling family were coming under scrutiny.[80] Column space in domestic newspapers began to be handed over to the Dubai chief of police who briefly become the government's primary spokesperson for economic matters. Over the course of 2009 he publicly blamed the crisis on greed (rather than a lack of regulatory

---

[78] *Al-Arabiya*, November 24, 2008.

[79] *Bloomberg*, February 5, 2009.

[80] See for example the case of Zack Shahin, former CEO of Deyaar Properties. *Maktoob*, February 4, 2010.

infrastructure or sound economic planning). He also appeared regularly on the record to refute the claims of foreign journalists, and publicly warned employers not to make any UAE national employees redundant.[81] Other government spokespeople went on the record to claim that there existed an international conspiracy to undermine Dubai's economic success.

In what was perhaps the most irrecoverable setback, new legislation was quickly ushered through at the federal level, seemingly at Dubai's behest, in order to formalize the protection of nationals in their jobs. It was ruled that they could only be released from their duties if the employer could prove they had violated the law.[82] This was primarily because Dubai Inc. feared discontent among Dubai's national population if redundancies began to affect nationals as well as expatriates. This measure, together with the well-timed circulation of a draft of a new media law that prohibited criticism of the economy (and allowed journalists to be fined up to $270,000 for violations) and thereby encouraged self censorship,[83] effectively sent out a fresh wave of signals that Dubai's laissez-faire attitudes were eroding.

What next—loss of autonomy?

By the end of February 2009 Dubai Inc. was effectively bankrupt, as it struggled to service even the first of the year's major debt renewals. Borse Dubai, which had earlier taken out loans to buy the Norwegian stock exchange, OMX, needed to refinance 3.8 billion of debt. A last minute deal was reported in the domestic press as proof that Dubai could keep going, but it soon became apparent that only $2.5 billion of credit had been acquired on international markets, and that other Dubai entities had had to step in and make up for the shortfall.[84] Rumors resurfaced that the Emirate would have no option but to seek assistance from its oil-rich neighboring Emirate, Abu Dhabi, no matter how unpalatable such a move might be. Up until this point Abu Dhabi had remained aloof from Dubai's problems, having injected just $19 billion of liquidity into federal entities in November 2008, and having only gone so far as to guarantee banks in Abu Dhabi, rather than across the whole of the UAE.[85]

---

[81] *The National*, March 4, 2010.
[82] *Gulf News*, February 18, 2009.
[83] *Gulf News*, April 13, 2009.
[84] *New York Times*, February 20, 2009.
[85] *The National*, October 12, 2008.

On February 25, 2009 a brief notice was posted by a Dubai government department that the UAE Central Bank—of which Abu Dhabi is in effect the major stakeholder—had issued a $10 billion, five year bond for Dubai. With interest rates set at 4 percent, this was a lifeline for Dubai, as the Emirate had been unable to acquire sufficient credit elsewhere.[86] Although it was not technically a bailout, given that Abu Dhabi sought no equity from Dubai and this was a bond rather than a gift, Abu Dhabi had nonetheless devised an unsubtle means of channeling aid to its beleaguered neighbor and thereby avoiding, or at least delaying, a complete meltdown of the Dubai economy. But by the end of 2009 it became apparent that this initial assistance was not going to be enough for Dubai to maintain its economic autonomy within the UAE. On November 25, 2009, seemingly cast adrift by Dubai Inc. and apparently disowned by the ruling family, the debt-ridden Dubai World company released a terse statement to the effect that it would need to restructure massive debts that were due for financing. These totaled $23 billion and included debts accrued by its constituent property company Nakheel, the aforementioned developer responsible for the palm islands.[87] The news was released under the cover of the Eid al-Adha festival and the coinciding US Thanksgiving holiday, which most analysts regarded as an attempt to disguise sensitive news and buy breathing space for the Emirate's government. International investors with interests in Dubai were alarmed and interpreted the announcement as a sovereign default, given the centrality of Dubai World to the Emirate's economy, and the company's close relationship to the government. Global markets panicked and fears were raised of a wave of such defaults, not only in Dubai but also in other emerging markets.

In many ways the biggest shock in the wake of the announcement was the apparent indifference of Abu Dhabi, even though Sheikh Mohammed had been repeatedly hinting it would automatically lend further support if need be. On November 9, 2009 he addressed foreign journalists and investors in Dubai, stating that there were no tensions between the two Emirates and that doubters should "shut up."[88] Similarly, his son and Crown Prince, Sheikh Hamdan bin Mohammed Al-Maktoum, addressed the World Economic Forum in Dubai on November 20, 2009, telling observers that Dubai's economy was "humming again."[89] International observers had wrongly assumed that Abu

---

[86] *Wall Street Journal*, February 23, 2009.
[87] *Guardian*, November 25, 2009.
[88] *New York Times*, November 29, 2009.
[89] *Gulf News*, November 21, 2009.

Dhabi's oil revenues and sovereign wealth funds would be immediately deployed to shore up Dubai's economy and reputation. While an additional bailout was provided, most analysts agreed that its limited nature represented the end of Dubai's economic autonomy within the UAE, as Abu Dhabi was able to assume the position of ultimate creditor to its struggling neighbor. This shift of economic primacy to Abu Dhabi was perhaps underscored in early January 2010, when the opening ceremony for the Burj Dubai skyscraper involved the unexpected renaming of the tower as *Burj Khalifa*—in honor of Abu Dhabi's ruler, Sheikh Khalifa bin Zayed Al-Nahyan.[90] Tellingly, no senior member of the Abu Dhabi ruling family was present at the ceremony, and the Dubai authorities were unprepared for the name change, not having had the opportunity to register a new Internet City address for the tower, rename the corresponding metro station, or even rebrand the merchandise.

Conclusion

Without sizeable hydrocarbon reserves, Dubai's economic development has had to focus on more urgent diversification from oil exports and oil-backed investments than Abu Dhabi's. Although Dubai's manufacturing sector grew in the 1970s and 1980s, most of the activity was on a fairly small scale. The main emphasis was placed on reinforcing the Emirate's historic role as a regional trade hub by building up transport and communications infrastructure. From the mid-1980s Dubai also began to seek foreign direct investment, initially by setting up "free zone" industrial parks that would allow foreign companies to relocate to Dubai and enjoy 100 percent ownership without need of local business partners. Since then, many other free zones have opened, including entire "villages" for branch campuses of foreign universities and health clinics, and even an international financial center.

In parallel to the free zone strategy, Dubai also committed to building up a luxury international tourist industry. By 2008, with hundreds of hotels, the emirate was hosting over six million tourists a year. And backed by a successful airline, two annual shopping festivals, over forty shopping malls, and a host of international sporting and music events, the number of tourists was predicted to climb to ten million or more by 2012. To attract investment from wealthy individuals, a real estate sector was introduced in the late 1990s. Although it was controversial, given that it was against UAE law for foreigners to own

90 *The Times*, January 5, 2010.

property at that time, Dubai bypassed this complication by initially allowing foreigners to buy renewable leases, and then in 2006 allowed full freehold ownership for foreigners. By the summer of 2008 Dubai had succeeded in diversifying its economy, with the non-oil sectors accounting for more than 95 percent of the Emirate's GDP.

However, as the global credit crunch entered its second year, Dubai's economy was already experiencing difficulty. Foreign investors' interest in real estate was declining markedly and hotel occupancy rates began to falter as tourists turned to cheaper destinations. Most seriously, Dubai's banks and mortgage lenders were struggling to find credit on the international market and it was revealed that state-backed companies had accumulated a debt of more than $80 billion, most of which was due for re-servicing over the next few years. By February 2009, Dubai was effectively bankrupt as it struggled to service even the first of 2009's major debt renewals. Since then, the Emirate has had little option but to seek substantial assistance from Abu Dhabi. At present it is unclear what the full economic and political implications will be with regard to Dubai's position in the UAE, but there are already indications that Abu Dhabi is seeking to underscore, subtly at least, its primacy within the federation.

10

Good, Bad or Both?

The Impact of Oil on the Saudi Political Economy

Steffen Hertog

In the face of significant economic diversification in the Gulf Cooperation Council (GCC), the consensus that oil is bad for development seems to be crumbling—at least when it comes to high-rent countries such as the oil monarchies of the Gulf. But no new paradigm has replaced the "resource curse" school. Based on the Saudi case study, this chapter will argue that it is difficult to systematically assess the impact of oil on development as long as

a) the yardstick of what is good or bad has not been clearly defined, taking into account the appropriate counterfactuals; and,
b) development results are not disaggregated on a sectoral or institution-to-institution basis.

The argument developed here is that compared to where it would arguably be without oil, Saudi Arabia clearly has achieved impressive development results on most run of the mill indicators of economic and institutional maturity. We should not be confused by the fact that it scores worse than non-oil countries with comparable GDP per capita. The more relevant "control group" are developing countries, to the poorer segment of which the kingdom would probably belong if oil had not been found eight decades ago. On most indicators, Saudi Arabia scores better than most members of this group.

Secondly, institutional and developmental results within the kingdom differ drastically depending on which segment of the system one looks at. While in some cases typical "resource curse"-style ailments have undoubtedly set in, other institutions have developed high levels of efficiency thanks to the availability of prudently deployed oil income. Analyzing nationally aggregated results obfuscates more than it reveals about the impact of oil on development. At least under conditions of a politically autonomous state elite, oil income dramatically enlarges the menu of institutional choices. It allows the expansion of patrimonial fiefdoms and of mass patronage at the same time that it enables the elite to create politically protected and well-endowed islands of institutional efficiency.

Adding to my previous work on the Saudi political economy, the chapter will briefly discuss the internal functioning of each of these types of institutions, commenting on recent developments in all of them, with special focus on institutions of mass distribution and their expected long-term trajectory. Against this background, it will then discuss the limits of the "islands of efficiency" model and the apparent path-dependencies that make it harder to shift from a model of enclave development, to one of more diffuse innovation and value generation.

The chapter will end with some remarks putting Saudi Arabia in regional comparative perspective and discussing to what extent it has, against all our expectations, functioned as a "developmental state"—a peculiar type of developmental state, however, whose model of development will exhaust itself in the coming decades unless very painful adjustments are made that would overcome the very segmentation that was the kingdom's original recipe for success.

How bad is bad?

We cannot discuss the impact of oil on a country's development without using some implicit or explicit yardstick. Do we compare a case like Saudi Arabia to developed Organization for Economic Cooperation and Development (OECD) countries, to developing countries or to other rentiers? Depending on which we choose, we will reach quite different results as to how good or bad things are in the kingdom. Many discussions of rentier states, especially qualitative and case study research, seem to implicitly use the developed country yardstick, inevitably arriving at the conclusion that the state of affairs in oil states is awful, as they are a lot less functional—however that is defined—than the implicit control group of comparably rich non-oil countries.

Now of all the possible comparisons, this is arguably the most misleading one to make. To measure the causal impact of a specific variable such as oil income on nation-states over time, we would ideally need a "control group" and a "treatment group": two sets of cases that at the time of treatment (that is, the appearance of oil on the scene) are similar in all respects, except the fact that some are subject to the treatment while others are not.

This limits the utility of a comparison of Saudi Arabia with other oil states, unless we want to find out about the impact of different levels of oil income, an effect that might well be non-linear. More important, it makes a comparison with developed non-oil countries nigh on useless, as these were different in so many other respects at the time of "treatment"—notably, they in most cases were a lot richer, developed and powerful—that we are truly comparing apples and oranges.

The most promising real-world comparison would seem to be with non-oil developing countries; more specifically, countries that were in a similar stage of development to Saudi Arabia at the time of "treatment," so that subsequent differences between cases are more likely to be explained by oil. Given that we will never be able to match real-world cases perfectly and that there are numerous exogenous factors influencing the "post-treatment" development of any country, the comparison will still be quite imperfect. But certainly it will tell us more than a comparison with cases that were never similar to Saudi Arabia in any meaningful respect.

To put it differently, estimating the causal effect of oil relies on assumptions about a counterfactual:[1] what would Saudi Arabia look like today without oil? Answering this question requires heroic assumptions. But we'll get closest to an answer by looking at countries which shared some characteristics with the kingdom in the pre-oil era. We could do this with small-n, matched qualitative comparisons, looking for example at (parts of) Yemen, attempting to "match" Saudi Arabia with a similar case in terms of pre-oil resources and level of development, social structures and culture, geopolitics etc. The obvious conclusion would be that oil has tremendously boosted Saudi development on

---

[1] On counterfactuals in comparative politics see James D. Fearon, "Counterfactuals and Hypothesis Testing in Political Science," *World Politics* Vol. 43, No. 2 (1991), pp. 169–95.

almost any indicator (with the level of democracy as a potential, but important exception).

Such paired comparisons are quite imperfect, however, and the case choice of particularly poor and unstable Yemen could be construed as biased. It might therefore be more useful to compare Saudi Arabia with a broader universe of cases, which are not carefully matched, but where various confounding factors are more likely to "average out" across the group. This group should, however, be similar to the kingdom on the arguably most important control variable: low levels of pre-oil development.

In practical terms, this can be approximated by comparing Saudi Arabia with all current non-oil developing countries, as the vast majority of currently poor countries were poor at the time of oil discovery in Saudi Arabia, and only a handful of countries that were poor back then managed to become rich in the meantime (mostly cases in East Asia whose cultural and institutional endowments arguably were very dissimilar from those of Saudi Arabia).

The following graphs will help us to make all three of the comparisons outlined above. Due to the heroic nature of our counterfactual assumptions we deliberately forego more sophisticated statistical manipulations, instead simply looking at the current bivariate relationship of GDP per capita to a number of development indicators. At the very least, we will show that any Saudi "particularity" is relative to the standard applied. If we put some faith into our counterfactual argument, we will also conclude that oil in most regards was a boon for the kingdom, if less so than other forms of domestically generated income have been in non-oil cases.

The orthodox comparative political science argument about the impact of oil is that it reduces a country's democracy score, whether because those countries are less likely to undergo democratic transitions or because those transitions are more easily reversed.[2] The below graph uses the World Bank Governance Indicator on "Voice and Accountability" as proxy for the level of democracy and meaningful political participation, and plots it against the logged GDP per capita of all countries for which data were available for the year 2005.

We see several things: Saudi Arabia and, to a lesser extent, the other Gulf states score much worse than other countries with comparable incomes. So do less rich non-Gulf rentiers, although the distance from their peers in income appears somewhat less distinct, as the mid-income group is more

---

[2] The first attempt to demonstrate this statistically is Michael Lewin Ross, "Does Oil Hinder Democracy?" *World Politics* Vol. 53, No. 3 (2001): 325–61.

scattered vertically. As important, there appears to be no clear trend among rentiers: richer ones seem neither less nor more democratic than poorer ones, while among non-oil countries (rest of world or "ROW") there is a clear and highly significant relationship between income and the "voice and accountability" score.

Figure 10.1: Voice and Accountability

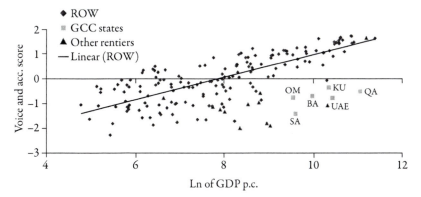

Based on World Bank Governance Indicators, World Bank Development Indicators, IMF data.
* ROW: "rest of world".

On the face of it, if oil has an impact, it does not appear to be particularly strong. More recent fixed effects panel regression tests which focus on changes within countries over time as opposed to cross-sectional differences between them seem to confirm this finding.[3] If we assume that the average oil-rich state would be a lot poorer without oil, this makes sense: imagine horizontally moving the rentier dots in the graph to the left, to where most of them arguably would be without oil, and their y-axis scores will look less unusual. If we moved the Saudi dot to the income level of (largely) non-rentier neighbors like Egypt or Yemen, its low score would appear quite typical or at least would not stand out.

[3] Stephen Haber and Victor Menaldo, "Do Natural Resources Fuel Authoritarianism? A Reappraisal of the Resource Curse," *American Political Science Review* Vol. 105, No. 1 (February 2011), pp. 1–26.

In addition to the well-researched oil-democracy issue, there are a number of other hypotheses on oil that relate to development in a stricter sense. There is a debate about oil and growth,[4] the econometrics of which are however fairly complicated, and a debate about the impact of oil on institutional structures. The latter is more interesting for political scientists and the Saudi case is particularly instructive in this context. In addition to a number of qualitative case studies positing a negative impact of oil on the quality of institutions and the state's regulatory capacity, at least one paper has shown statistically that there is a negative correlation between oil and quality of governance.[5]

The latter inference suffers from the same counterfactual problem as all orthodox arguments about "the impact of oil on XX." The statistical model in the paper by Isham *et al.* (2005) controls for GDP per capita. But of course

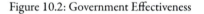

Figure 10.2: Government Effectiveness

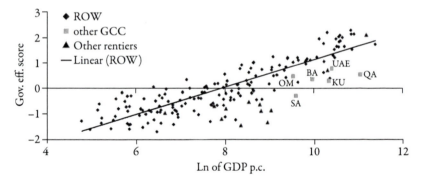

Based on World Bank Governance Indicators, World Bank Development Indicators, IMF data.

---

[4] For one of the earlier statements of the oil-reduces-growth argument, see Jeffrey Sachs and Andrew Warner, "Natural Resources and Economic Development: the Curse of Natural Resources," *European Economic Review* Vol. 45, No. 4–6 (2001), pp. 827–38.

[5] Dirk Vandewalle, *Libya Since Independence: Oil and State Building* (Ithaca, NY: Cornell University Press, 1998); Kiren Aziz Chaudhry, *The Price of Wealth: Economies and Institutions in the Middle East* (Ithaca, NY: Cornell University Press, 1997); Jonathan Isham, Michael Woolcock *et al.*, "The Varieties of Resource Experience: Natural Resource Export Structures and the Political Economy of Growth," *World Bank Economic Review* Vol. 19, No. 2 (2005): 141–74.

Figure 10.3: Regulatory Quality

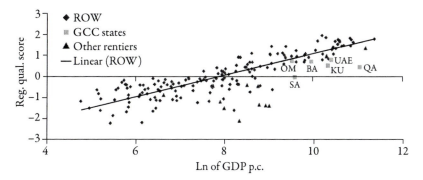

Based on World Bank Governance Indicators, World Bank Development Indicators, IMF data.

Figure 10.4: Rule of Law

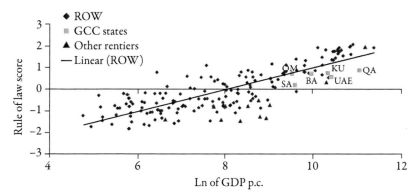

Based on World Bank Governance Indicators, World Bank Development Indicators, IMF data.

GDP per capita in rentier countries is (heavily) influenced by oil income and hence reflects a very different type of economy than that of non-oil states with similar scores. It also tells us nothing about what GDP per capita would look like without oil.

And this time around, the scatterplot evidence is even more problematic for the proponents of resource curse arguments. Consider the graphs below with data on Governance Indicators from the World Bank that relate to the "technocratic" qualities of state institutions. In all of them, rentiers by and

Figure 10.5: Control of Corruption

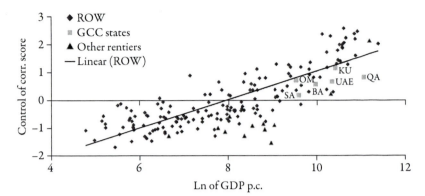

Based on World Bank Governance Indicators, World Bank Development Indicators, IMF data.

large do worse than similarly rich non-rentiers. But the richer rentiers, which are by and large as wealthy as they are because they have higher oil income per capita, are doing visibly better than the poorer rentiers. This seems to suggest that oil income, at least above a certain threshold, is good for institutions—although probably less so than non-oil income.

Looking at the graphs, one is tempted to conclude that small amounts of oil income make institutions worse, while larger ones make them better, leading to a u-shaped relationship. But given the limited number of cases in the rentier universe (and the fact that mid-rentier status is heavily correlated with being located in sub-Saharan Africa, introducing a potential regional bias), this is speculation, at least as long as time series on governance-related indicators are so short that we still need to rely on cross-sectional evidence.

None of this is precise science. But because of the counterfactual problem outlined above, it is so almost by definition, and with the current state of data, no amount of sophisticated statistical technique is capable of avoiding this problem.

Oil is what you make of it: The heterogeneous impact of rents on institutions

Even if we could measure the statistical impact of oil on institutions over time with more confidence, this would beg the question of the causal mechanisms linking oil and institutional outcomes. This is where case studies, whose capacity to measure the "effect size" of the impact of oil in comparative terms is quite limited, can be of great value.

So what does the Saudi case study tell us about the causal linkages between oil and institutional outcomes? Further undermining our confidence in large-n studies of the resource curse, it shows most of all that to the extent that there are systematic causal mechanisms, they can differ dramatically from one institution to the next. National-level aggregate data arguably obscures more than it reveals: there might be "average" effects of oil on state institutions across cases, but they hide a large internal variability.

As I have argued elsewhere, state institutions in Saudi Arabia, although all built with oil money, are heterogeneous.[6] If oil has had any systematic effect, it has been to increase the leeway for elites to embark on institutional experimentation which can go in very different directions in different parts of the state, as budgetary constraints are loosened and institutional and distributional strategies that would usually be rival to each other can be pursued at the same time.

For elites to be able to experiment with institutions or, more broadly, for institutions to be crucially shaped by elite preferences, a regime needs to be fairly autonomous from societal demands when it makes its decisions about the allocation of oil rents. This was the case in Saudi Arabia in the 1940s and 1950s, where patronage was largely localized and individualized and no larger, national groups could stake systematic claims on the new riches. This might seem quite an extraordinary condition, but it was in fact fulfilled by the majority of oil-rich post-colonial countries at the onset of oil: politics was controlled by small elites and societies were fragmented and not systematically mobilized.

A sudden rent inflow under these conditions enlarges the menu of political choices for the leadership, whose members can "have their cake and eat it" by building a heterogeneous state that fulfills several desirable functions at once:

a) *building political coalitions* through distribution of resources to political clients, both individually and through larger-scale bureaucratic employment and provision of subsidized goods and services;
b) *self-enrichment* through both direct appropriation of rents and the building of various types of institutional fiefdoms; and,

---

[6] Steffen Hertog, *Princes, Brokers and Bureaucrats: Oil and the State in Saudi Arabia* (Ithaca, NY: Cornell University Press, 2010).

c) *institution-building* in strategic sectors that are useful for long-term economic development and macro-economic stabilization.

None of the outcomes are automatic: elite preferences and conflicts intervene to select the particular uses to which rents are put. The point is that a significant rent surplus makes all three possible at the same time, as choice constraints are dramatically loosened; and there are good, if non-overlapping, reasons to pursue all three courses. This is indeed what happened in the Saudi case: new surpluses were so large and societal claims on them so small that elite players could expand the state simultaneously in very different directions, building the three different types of institutions mentioned in the introduction: institutions of mass patronage, patrimonial fiefdoms, and islands of institutional efficiency. These different institutions are radically different in their internal functioning and are tied together into a common system only by their shared links to royal patrons.

Compared to non-rentiers, the economic costs of mass patronage and fiefdoms are lower. This is due to the (temporary) availability of unusually large surpluses whose full productive deployment in the domestic economy would be difficult in the short run, but also because the economically detrimental effects of distribution and rent-seeking have little impact on the state's fiscal situation: there is no domestic tax income that would be damaged as a result of corruption, unfair competition and other factors related to fiefdom-building

Figure 10.6: Choices Faced by an Early Rentier Elite.

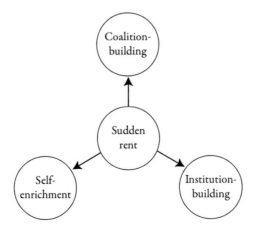

and patronage that might deter business from investing and contributing to the fisc.[7]

The regime elite's early autonomy to shape the institutional landscape tends to be a passing phenomenon: once institutions are built, they tend to create distributional obligations that are hard to reverse in a patronage-based system. At the same time, collective societal challenges that could change the shape of the existing institutional disposition are also rare. Finally, links of patronage in the elite, often reflected in sinecures and institutionalized distribution, tend to be long-term in Saudi Arabia, often spanning several generations.

Mechanisms of recruitment, bureaucratic turf defense, and royal protection for vital state institutions all tend to keep the organizational landscape of Saudi Arabia exceptionally stable. It is only incremental oil income above already committed spending levels that allows for new institutional experiments. Institutional decisions are very "sticky" in the Saudi and GCC context. It is all the more important to analyze which paths institutions are set on at the early stage of state-building, as each type of institution functions according to its own rules and produces very different results for national development.

Islands of efficiency

The most surprising outcome of the enhanced choice set of oil elites in the Saudi case has been the creation of a number of "islands of efficiency"—institutions that, if not world-class, are dramatically better than the rest of the Saudi state and significantly more efficient than the average developing country institution. They are protected from bureaucratic and other forms of predation through royal patronage, run by technocratic confidants of senior princes, and are endowed both with ample resources and a clear mandate to hire competitively, build up lean and efficient structures and fulfill a limited set of tasks in a delimited, high-priority policy area in which other bureaucratic entities are prevented from interfering. Their rapid emergence would have been unthinkable without the deployment of oil rents to buy foreign expertise, build infrastructure and attract the brightest young nationals with competitive salaries. Islands of efficiency are largely shielded from rent-seeking, which is more easily and profitably pursued in other institutions and policy fields.

---

[7] State income remains protected unless corruption and patronage affect the oil upstream sector itself to the extent that its revenue generating capacity is compromised. This has been rare in the GCC context.

The most visible outcome of such institution-building is arguably the national industrial champion Saudi Basic Industries (SABIC), one of the world's largest and most profitable petrochemicals companies, which is still 70 percent state-owned. Saudi Aramco, the national oil company, is an even more important pocket of efficiency. Although its managerial structures were largely inherited from American concessionaire companies, the royal leadership has managed to prudently protect them against royal and bureaucratic predation—a difference from nationalized oil companies in most other OPEC states.[8]

In a recent Ernst & Young poll of citizens in twenty-four different countries, Saudis consistently gave the highest ranks to management and services of their public companies and agreed more than any other nationality that strategic enterprises should be in state hands.[9] This is not the result one would expect on the basis of the received wisdom about the corruption of the public sector in oil-rich states.

There are similar cases of efficient state-created companies in other GCC countries, all structured and politically embedded quite similarly. Although their profitability cannot be easily compared with that of private companies, it stands in stark contrast to loss-making public companies in most of the rest of the developing world.[10]

Similar islands of efficiency exist also outside of the public enterprise sector: strategic agencies such as the Saudi central bank SAMA (Saudi Arabian Monetary Agency), the Royal Commission for the Industrial Cities of Jubail and Yanbu, the Saudi Ports Authority or, more recently, the Capital Market Authority, have a track record of competence and efficient administration that stands out in the Saudi and regional context. In all cases, senior princes have given formal or informal mandates to these institutions to operate outside of the regular bureaucracy, hire separately and deliver results. Unlike the bulk of the state apparatus, they have not been used for mass (and lower salary) patronage employment and are characterized by an ethos of efficiency and relative institutional autonomy. The organizational culture in several of them

---

[8] For details on the two companies, cf. Steffen Hertog, "Petromin: The Slow Death of Statist Oil Development in Saudi Arabia," *Business History* Vol. 50, No. 5 (2008), pp. 645–67.

[9] Ernst & Young, *Government as Best in Class Shareholder*, report in E&Y's "Government and Enterprise" series, October 2010.

[10] For a comparative explanation of SOE efficiency in rentier states, cf. Steffen Hertog, "Defying the Resource Curse: Explaining Successful State-Owned Enterprises in Rentier States," *World Politics* Vol. 62, No. 2 (2010), pp. 261–301.

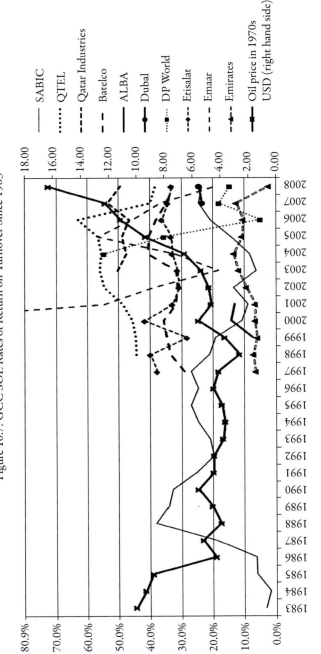

Figure 10.7: GCC SOE Rates of Return on Turnover Since 1983

Sources: Company reports, Markaz Financial Center, Reuters.

defines itself informally, but quite explicitly in contradistinction to the rest of the state apparatus.

The relative autonomy is of course granted by the senior royal leadership and hence can in principle be revoked. In practice, royals have been content to let islands of efficiency operate on a fairly long leash, and their performance and managerial structures have by and large been stable over long periods. The elevated status of the senior management is in the final analysis a result of royal patronage; since at least the 1960s, senior princes have developed a knack at identifying and co-opting technocratic talent. This developmental patronage and productive use of clientelist structures are perhaps equivalent to some of the thick social links that have characterized the South Korean and Taiwanese authoritarian-developmental bureaucracies.[11] But they are completely at odds with conventional ideas of "rentier" patronage.

It seems to be the very top-down nature of politics in Saudi Arabia, a country with a politically demobilized society, that has allowed for such patches of developmental bureaucracy to emerge. By contrast, the legacy of more "modern," mobilizational politics in oil-rich republics like Algeria, Mexico or Venezuela has politicized and retarded a public sector that had become a weapon in class politics, and nowadays is shot through with organized interests. To the extent that bureaucracy and public sector have been used for experiments of social engineering, the initial autonomy of these rentier regimes has declined even more drastically than in the Saudi case, and with less efficient outcomes.[12]

There is a natural affinity between administrative enclaves and enclave industries: an enclave institution like SAMA is best positioned to look after a limited number of large and comparatively well-run banks, while the Royal Commission for Jubail and Yanbu has been successful because it had to deal with only a limited number of larger-scale public and private industries. Even the most efficient enclave institution will not be able to regulate a large number of actors whose level of organizational development is much lower than that of the regulator itself. This is arguably why more diffuse markets in ser-

---

[11] Robert Wade, *Governing the Market: Economic Theory and the Role of Government in East Asian Industrialization* (Princeton, New Jersey: Princeton University Press, 2003); Stephen Haggard, Tun-jen Cheng and David Kang, "Institutions and Growth in Korea and Taiwan: the Bureaucracy," *Journal of Development Studies* Vol. 34, No. 6 (1998), pp. 66–86; Peter Evans, *Embedded Autonomy: States and Industrial Transformation* (Princeton, New Jersey: Princeton University Press, 1995).

[12] cf. Hertog, "Defying the Resource Curse."

vice, retail and light industry are not as well controlled in Saudi Arabia, and why diffuse reforms involving the general regulation of Saudi business remain unstuck in many cases. Smaller institutions and players are also harder to protect from bureaucratic and other predation.

Several of the more recent institutional reforms in Saudi Arabia have followed the established enclave/island model, including the creation of the King Abdullah University of Science and Technology (KAUST) and of the King Abdullah City for Atomic and Renewable Energy (KACARE). Both were entrusted to old technocratic confidants of the royals and both operate in parallel to an existing system of less efficient institutions to which they have little organic linkage.

It appears particularly striking that Saudi Aramco was tasked with building up KAUST as a more efficient (and culturally liberal) alternative to existing Saudi universities. Unless one knows Aramco's own history as a protected island of efficiency, it would be hard to understand why the creation of a new university was entrusted to an oil company. The recent move of Aramco into petrochemical heavy industry can be interpreted similarly. The capital-intensive and concentrated nature of the nuclear industry also seems to make the model of enclave regulation through KACARE a natural fit in the Saudi context, with good chances for success.

Islands of efficiency in the Saudi state are almost by definition separated from their institutional environment through fairly sharp boundaries, to the policing and defense of which they themselves contribute. Their organizational identity is strong, recruitment and promotion are largely in-house, and other bureaucracies are kept at arm's length on all levels of hierarchy.

Despite these structures of insulation, the efficient institutions directly involved in production have especially played a pivotal role in building up the Saudi private sector and its sizeable managerial stratum: not only through infrastructure provision, contracting, and training initiatives, but also through the transfer of skills (and networks) in the shape of public sector managers who move to the private sector to set up their own companies or join existing private groups. Many of the leading players in private heavy industry in Saudi Arabia have experience as public sector managers. In that sense, the enclaves have produced significant spillover effects, as reflected in increasingly large private investments in heavy industry that would have been unthinkable at the time when SABIC was first set up.

To the extent that they are involved in production, Saudi islands of efficiency have benefitted from the huge comparative advantage of cheap energy and feedstock. The big question now is whether they will manage to profitably expand into economic sectors without a strong comparative advantage. To some extent, SABIC is already trying this in its 2007 acquisition of GE Plastics for $11.7 billion. Aramco's gradual move into renewable energy could be another important test case.

The recent travails of Abu Dhabi's Mubadala, an enclave institution with a much shorter track record that has expanded rapidly into real estate as well as various high-tech sectors, demonstrates the perils of moving too quickly into too many new areas. But Mubadala's gung-ho approach is very different from the methodical expansion of Saudi organizations; its experience only underlines the potential virtues of Saudi gradualism.

Royal fiefdoms

Another form of highly protected enclave institution is the royal fiefdom. The most important ones are the Ministry of Defense and Civil Aviation, the Ministry of Interior and the National Guard. Similar to the technocratic islands of efficiency, these operate largely autonomously and were created early on in the state-building process as a result of often contingent processes of elite bargaining. Thanks to the patrons at the top of such institutions, their stability and political inviolability are even higher than those of any technocratic institution, as is reflected not least in the constancy of their budgetary allocations across the decades. They are to some extent run as states within the state, with their own housing, education and medical systems—again a sort of duplication hard to imagine without the temporary availability of huge fiscal surpluses.

The core fiefdoms do of course perform important roles in national security, and certain sections of the Ministry of Interior for example are exceptionally well run. But these institutions are also large-scale resources of patronage for the various princes attached to them and hence are much larger and more bloated than the technocratic islands of efficiency. The Ministry of Interior alone is reported to have half a million individuals on its payroll.[13] Although self-enrichment has without a doubt been in play, what is perceived as corruption often results from pervasive expectations of generosity that lower-level clients harbor vis-à-vis their royal patrons. In that sense, the royal fiefdoms combine functions of patronage, sometimes on a mass scale, with the phenomenon of self-enrichment.

[13] Saudi British Bank, *Giving a Boost*, economic report, February 7, 2008.

Figure 10.8: Protected Zones: The Saudi Security Budget in Comparison.

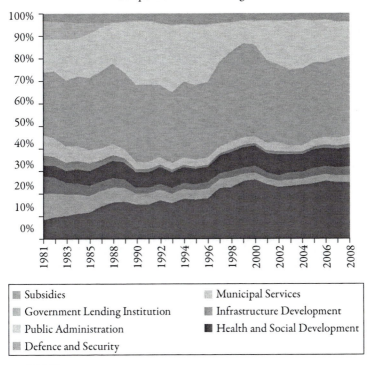

Composition of annual budgets

Source: SAMA.

The departure from the scene of the current generation of royal leaders in the years to come will be a test case for the stickiness of the core institutional arrangements of the Saudi state. The takeover of all core institutions by sons of the current incumbents is very likely, but this does not mean that certain parts of the fiefdoms might not be hived off or downsized. The size and inertia of their core assets are however so great that even a weak heir will dispose of enormous powers of patronage from day one, influencing his role in the royal pecking order.

Institutions of mass distribution

While technocratic islands of efficiency are comparatively free of surplus employment and rent-seeking, the core fiefdoms of the Saudi state provide a significant share of the rentier resource distribution to the Saudi populace at large. But distributional structures go beyond these core institutions: surplus employment also extends to many of the non-royal ministries and agencies, in particular the cabinet-level "line ministries" that do not have the royal charters and autonomy in employment decisions that most islands of efficiency enjoy. Their efficiency therefore is often drastically lower.

Saudi Arabia's rentier status has allowed the creation of large-scale, formalized patronage structures: probably more than half of the economically active Saudi population is employed by the state,[14] compared to about a fifth in

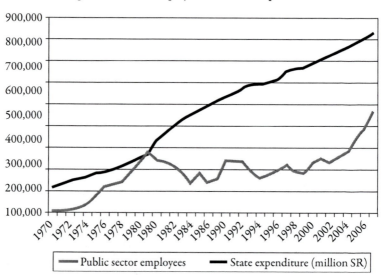

Figure 10.9: State Employment vs. State Expenditure.

Source: SAMA and Ministry of Civil Service.

[14] The precise estimates depend on the sources used, as Ministry of Labor and Central Department of Statistics figures are strongly at variance. The former however appear more reliable, as they are based on the social security registrations of national workers. According to these, only some 700,000 Saudis are employed in the private sector.

Figure 10.10: Public Sector Size vs. Productivity.

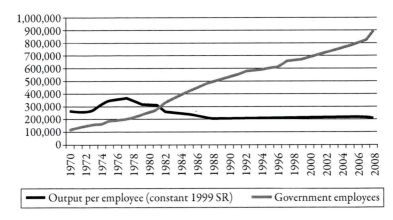

Source: SAMA, Ministry of Civil Service.

Figure 10.11: The Structure of State Spending in Saudi Arabia (Million SR, Current).

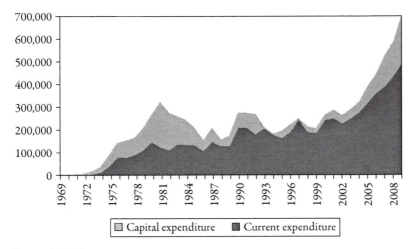

Source: SAMA.

The public sector officially employs about 900,000 individuals, but informal estimates including all security agencies and the religious sector are up to twice as high.

OECD countries and even less in most developing countries. The public sector payroll has been expanding continuously even through the lean years of the 1980s and 1990s when the government ran large deficits. More than that, the share of bureaucrats in the total population has consistently increased despite high population growth. This reflects the difficulty of reversing, or at least a deep unwillingness to reverse distributional obligations.

In the course of the "Saudization" of the bureaucracy since the 1970s, productivity as measured by output per employee has declined significantly; this is another indicator of patronage employment to the detriment of institutional performance.

The "stickiness" of mass distribution is reflected also in broader budget figures: while the government's capital spending declined precipitously in times of fiscal crisis—to the extent that Saudi infrastructure suffered significant damage—there was never a major reversal in current spending, which mostly goes into public employment and free or subsidized public services.

The importance of public employment in the Saudi political economy becomes even more obvious when one takes into account salary levels, which according to late 1990s data were higher in the civil service than in the private sector on all levels of qualification.[15] Since then the gap has further widened: while average public wages have been rising due to a number of increases in recent years, average private sector wages have been falling; Saudis who do not have access to bureaucratic jobs are willing to take up increasingly ill-paid private work.

Figure 10.12: Average Monthly Wage in the Private Sector 2004–2007 (SR).

Years	2004	2005	2006	2007
Saudi	4367	3878	3596	3624
Non-Saudis	1037	1028	1060	1011
Total	1385	1360	1384	1354

Source: Ministry of Labour.

All this is not to say that no one is doing any work in the regular bureaucracy. Due to unequal distribution of resources and over-centralized planning and decision-making, some in fact find themselves overburdened. But there is no doubt that the Saudi bureaucracy at large is a system with enormous slack.

[15] Ishac Diwan and Maurice Girgis, *Labor Force and Development in Saudi Arabia*, World Bank/Ministry of Planning, 2002.

The "lock-in" of large-scale public employment is a long-term fiscal threat and probably the least sustainable aspect of the Kingdom's segmented institutional set-up. Saudi Arabia has recently been expanding its provision of higher education dramatically, with the number of new entrants to the system increasing from about 100,000 in 2000 to about 240,000 in 2010 (SAMA data). This strategy of "parking" young Saudis in universities has temporarily alleviated the employment problem created by the demographic momentum of a very young population. But it is likely to exacerbate it in the mid-term, as it leads to an escalation of socio-economic expectations with no concomitant increase in job opportunities.

Increasing socio-economic pressures will lead to a gradual Saudization of the private labor market, as pauperized Saudis will be willing to compete with expatriates at ever lower wages. But this will be a disruptive process that will fundamentally challenge the Al Saud's image as benevolent patriarchs.

In an ideal world, the regime would trim down the size of the public service and create a proper social security and unemployment insurance system or a minimum "citizens' income" for all Saudis based on a share of oil rents. That way, rentier distribution would be possible without distorting labor market incentives and undermining the quality of the administration. But the Kingdom has travelled too far down the path of mass patronage employment for this change in tack to be possible without hurting large vested interests in a way that seems inconceivable in a system historically based on the gradual accrual of entitlements.

In contrast to a social security system, the provision of public jobs creates the illusion of reversible, discretionary patronage. Even if existing employment levels are "locked in," one might argue that there is no automatic expansion of state employment through population growth, as there can be under a social security system. Patronage *qua* discretionary employment hence appears fiscally more prudent, if much less equitable, than broader distribution based on citizenship. The expansion of public employment has been quasi-automatic in the past, however, and for reasons mentioned above, pressures to expand the payroll are likely to become, if anything, more severe.

The larger and more expectant a society is, the harder it is to run an economy on an enclave basis. The fiscal and institutional cost of mass patronage will grow, potentially reducing resources for enclave development. And even if that does not happen, enclaves will be unable to contribute to national employment on the scale required in the Saudi case. Saudi Arabia might have the most impressive institutional enclaves in the GCC, but due to its population size the model is also under the strongest pressure in regional comparison.

The recent public debate about the price of electricity, water and gasoline in Saudi Arabia demonstrates that there is some awareness of the increasing burden that mass patronage is putting on the state. While public employment remains a political no-go area, a debate about the pricing of subsidized utility services such as electricity is now possible.[16]

The historical record is not encouraging, however: there is a long tradition of deferring and reversing increases of utility and public service prices. Price reductions happen almost every time the regime feels under political pressure. A recent revision of electricity tariffs increased prices for industrial consumers, who constitute 20 percent of total demand. Residential customers, however, whose consumption amounts to 53 percent of the total and who benefit from particularly low prices, were spared any tariff adjustment.[17] King Abdullah reduced already low gasoline prices further in 2006, arguably reacting to political pressures created by boom-induced consumer price inflation.

While surplus production capacity in oil and gas made the provision of cheap electricity, desalinated water and gasoline affordable in the era of low oil prices in the 1980s and 1990s, the opportunity costs of domestic consumption have increased dramatically: spare capacity is lower than during most of the two previous decades, oil can be sold internationally at much higher prices, and Saudi Arabia is now incapable of producing enough gas to fire its power stations, forcing it to burn diesel or internationally purchased fuel oil. Capacity expansions in gas production and electricity plants are expensive and barely keep up with rapidly rising demand.

Traditionally reticent institutions like Aramco are getting more vocal in the debate about energy pricing, reflecting the looming threat that the distributional system poses for their sustenance in the long run. Aramco representatives have publicly warned about a "business as usual" scenario in which the equivalent of six million barrels of oil per day would be consumed domestically by 2030, strongly reducing the amount of energy available for export and hence impacting the fiscal balance as well as Aramco's own cash flow.[18]

There is a long-term danger that the efficient enclaves in the Saudi system could be eaten up by the distributional needs of a growing society of clients.

[16] "Saudi Arabia May Raise Electricity Price," *Bloomberg*, October 5, 2010.

[17] For consumption statistics, see Japan International Cooperation Agency, *The Master Plan Study for Energy Conservation in the Power Sector in the Kingdom of Saudi Arabia*, draft final report, 2008.

[18] "Saudi Mulls Renewables Targets," *The National*, May 20, 2010.

The combination of mass patronage with an extensive landscape of royal fiefdoms puts a great onus on the Saudi budget. While the creation of parallel institutions and entitlements in boom times has helped to stabilize the Saudi system and allowed a unique combination of patronage and development, the rent-enabled institutional redundancy is costly in the long run and makes systemic adjustments politically difficult and hard to coordinate.

The recent subsidy debate is the first sign of a conflict between previously separated spheres. Saudi fiscal reserves are still huge—equivalent to more than two full annual budgets—but the cost of mass patronage, through both employment and through cheap domestic provision of energy and other services, is growing.

There could be technocratic solutions to reduce over-consumption of public services without giving up on the state's distributional commitments. These include a system of steeper stacked electricity and water tariffs in which larger residential consumer pay considerably higher marginal prices, or a system of consumption accounts in which consumers receive an annual allocation of free utility services, where over-consumption is penalized with high tariffs and under-consumption is rewarded with cash payouts. But even these appear politically too touchy to be implemented any time soon.

The private sector in the segmented system

To what extent can the private sector relieve the state, taking over the provision of public services and creating non-patronage employment? Saudi business now plays a much more substantial role in the national economy than in the 1970s. Its share in GDP has remained substantial throughout the second oil boom and, more importantly, it caters to a much larger private demand, with state contracts comparatively less important. Its share in capital formation has increased drastically after the state stopped spending on infrastructure in the 1980s (although much of this is real estate investment).

Despite a return to high state spending in the 2000s, the short-term fiscal policy elasticity of business growth is much reduced compared to the 1970s and 1980s, meaning that fiscal policy shocks have a smaller impact on the private sector growth trajectory.[19]

---

[19] This is the result of both time series regressions and cointegration tests on the relationship of state spending and private sector activity in various sectors. Short-term spending elasticity of business activity is much larger in the pre-1985 than the post-1985 period.

Figure 10.13: Composition of Saudi GDP (current prices).

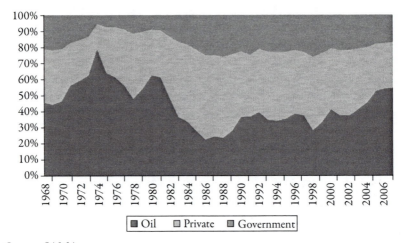

Source: SAMA.

So far, however, this has not translated into large-scale employment opportunities for Saudis. This has much to do with an open-doors labor import policy that forces nationals to compete with easily exploited workers from low-wage countries. It also has to do with the governance of the private sector itself.

Saudi business itself is to some extent segmented: it contains some enclaves of excellence such as the agro-industrial concern SAVOLA, the Abdullatif Jameel Group with its comprehensive community programs, and a number of professionally run banks (not, incidentally, regulated by SAMA). All these groups are governed professionally and pursue a human resources policy that is sophisticated enough to offer attractive salaries and career options to young, motivated Saudis.

Most of the Kingdom's businesses, however, are still run along patriarchal lines, not dissimilar to some of the royal fiefdoms in the state apparatus:[20] informal at the core, highly centralized, opaque and unaccountable, they offer limited scope for career development of non-family employees. They lack the managerial sophistication to create and utilize higher-quality human resources

---

[20] The issues of cohesion and succession faced by larger family businesses are strikingly similar to those of the Al Saud ruling family at large.

and—as a difference from state institutions—they mainly employ low-cost foreign labor.

Corporate governance in the Saudi private sector is slowly improving in the wake of the financial crisis, as banks demand clearer business plans and accounts from their clients. The process is slow and uneven, however, and could lead to a bifurcation of the business sector into a smaller group of professionally run, externally financed and internationally competitive players, and a larger section of slower-growing, more traditional groups.

Governance lacunae are particularly acute among small and medium enterprises (SME), which tend to operate on low margin, low-tech business models. A significant share of SMEs are "*tasattur*" businesses—companies formally owned by a national but in fact financed and run by a foreigner. Here, as in public employment, nationals draw on their privileges as rentier citizens to earn income that is not necessarily commensurate with work effort. Such opportunities reduce incentives for productive activities and further distort labor markets. The share of foreign employees is particularly high—estimated at up to 98 percent—among SMEs which tend to pay bad wages and often have no human resources policy to speak of.

Although the evolutionary trajectory of business since the 1970s has been more promising than that of the state, it is not yet capable of reducing the distributional burden on the latter. The situation could be improved through reforms of the labor market that would increase the price of foreign workers to bring it closer to that of Saudi labor. Even then, however, the governance of many private groups would need to see significant improvement before they could become competitive employers of nationals. Collectively, business has considerable lobbying power, but it lacks a comprehensive policy agenda that could allow it to negotiate a grand bargain with the regime in which labor market nationalization could be exchanged for regulatory reforms or accountability mechanisms.

Can the Saudi system evolve beyond segmentation?

The segmented Saudi system with its stark combination of deep inefficiencies and high-performance institutions has been remarkably stable over time: islands of efficiency, just like patrimonial fiefdoms and structures of mass patronage, have tended to persist over decades. But given the high fiscal costs of institutional redundancy, can the Saudi system ever evolve into something else?

There has been an undoubted positive impact of the Kingdom's islands of efficiency on the economy and the private sector at large. Skills acquired by managers in state-owned enterprises have been transferred to the private sector and, together with the requisite administrative networks, have made the fortunes of many business families in sectors that private investment had previously not dared to venture into. Such skills transfer and demonstration effects will exhaust themselves with the increasing maturity of the private sector, however. More generally, positive spillover effects have arguably also been accompanied by sorting mechanisms which have reinforced the path-dependent divisions between the better-run parts of the Saudi system and their environment.

As long as Aramco, SABIC etc. are available to take care of core development tasks, and function as recruiters of a large share of top Saudi talent, this is likely to make it harder to improve other institutions which have to make do with worse human resources and of which the leadership has lower performance expectations to start with. That Aramco has been tasked with creating Saudi Arabia's flagship university reflects the failure of the existing educational bureaucracy and the tendency to delegate high-priority tasks to bodies outside of the regular administration—a strategy that only reinforces existing cleavages. And KAUST, a very selective university with a small share of nationals among its student body, will mostly add to the numbers of the small technocratic elite in Saudi Arabia, many of whom will again serve extra-governmental entities like SABIC or Aramco. KAUST might create healthy competition with the established universities, but perhaps it also relieves pressure on the rest of the system by creating yet another sector-specific pressure valve without reforming the system itself.

The under-performance of significant parts of the Saudi system feeds the need for islands of efficiency; conversely, the presence of these islands lowers the reform pressure on the overall system. These islands are incapable of sufficient job creation, however, not least as they focus on large, capital-intensive projects, which are easy to administer in an enclave fashion. This means that they cannot relieve the growing distributional burden on the state.

The natural defense reflexes of islands of efficiency in terms of information policy, recruitment and inter-agency politics also wall them off against other institutions, making learning and adaptation harder and reducing their influence over their environment. The hierarchical hub and spoke system of institutions around the royal elite makes reform coalitions hard to construct, as in the final analysis each institution is on its own, owing its existence to royal patronage.

A fundamental shift in labor market incentives would be necessary for higher-quality administrative structures to spread more widely through the Saudi system. This however would call into question large-scale entitlements that have proved impossible to remove in the past. For the time being, private wages are too low to attract high-calibre Saudis into the private sector in significant numbers; corporate structures remain predicated on low-cost, low-quality labor. When the government attempted in the mid-2000s to reduce the supply of foreign labor and thereby increase wages, Saudi business fought the reduction of visa numbers tooth and nail—and successfully.

At the same time, bureaucratic wages in regular ministries remain comparatively high, further undermining incentives for Saudis to seek private employment (only a fairly small group of elite graduates has sufficient incentives to seek even better-paid employment with islands of efficiency like SABIC or Aramco). A reform of bureaucratic employment is however hard to imagine and, different from most other economic reforms, is not even seriously considered in Riyadh. Yet, mass employment in the bureaucracy both undermines the quality of the bureaucracy and reduces interest in productive employment or education that is relevant to the private labor market. A move to a more neutral distributional system would be possible in principle, but very hard in practice given the size of unequal and distortionary entitlements that have been historically locked in.

Conclusion

It is difficult and in many ways futile to generalize about "the Saudi state" or the impact that oil has had on it. A discussion of different indicators of development shows that Saudi Arabia scores better on most of them than it arguably would have done if oil had not been found—refuting cruder versions of the "resource curse" hypothesis. This generic finding however leaves the most interesting aspects of the Saudi rentier state unexplained: although all of it has historically been financed by oil income, different parts of the state apparatus function very differently and serve radically different purposes. Levels of institutional performance in the Saudi state vary widely, and I have argued that to some extent the good performance of some parts—including Aramco, the nation's revenue generator—makes the bad performance and redundancy of others possible.

To some extent, Saudi Arabia displays features of the classical "developmental state": a combination of deep state intervention with a pro-capitalist orientation, active formal and informal state guidance of business and an important role of the public sector, a Weberian bureaucracy in important lead agencies, export orientation and rapid, successful industrialization.[21] Differing from East Asian developmental states, however, the Saudi state combines these features with the parallel existence of large, wasteful fiefdoms and mass distributional arrangements. The latter would be unthinkable in a developmental state whose resource are derived through domestic resource extraction, and in which tough decisions on fiscal priorities have to be made in the course of state-building. Related to the availability of external resources is the fact that development in Saudi Arabia also does not involve the bulk of the populace, which has been deeply implicated in development in East Asia through "forced savings" or at least an unusually large industrial work effort.

The unusual segregation of the Saudi system has been exceptionally stable: most institutions and the attendant clientelist links in the segmented Saudi system have been very "sticky"; systemic reforms are difficult and an ad hoc approach of adding new organizations to solve new problems is preferred. In a system dominated by vertical links of communication and authority, organizations often do not communicate with each other except through their royal patrons. This setup protects islands of efficiency, but also unproductive structures.

In other developmental states, a maturing business class has increasingly assumed policy leadership over the decades; this has not been the case in Saudi Arabia so far. Perhaps this is just a question of time, but for the time being Saudi business is part of the segmented clientelist system rather than a force that could transcend it. The Saudi private sector, brought into being through mechanisms of rent recycling, is itself very heterogeneous, if less dramatically so than the state. It contains a number of islands of efficiency and regional corporate leaders, but also a large number of low-margin, low-innovation operations that continue to depend on cheap imported labor.

Saudi business is not yet ready to alleviate the fiscal pressures that the fragmented patronage structures of the state create, whether through paying taxes or through providing employment at reasonable wages for nationals. It lacks

---

[21] Evans, *Embedded Autonomy*; Atul Kohli. *State-Directed Development: Political Power and Industrialization in the Global Periphery* (Cambridge: Cambridge University Press, 2004); Robert Wade, *Governing the Market: Economic Theory and the Role of Government in East Asian Industrialization* (Princeton, New Jersey: Princeton University Press, 2003).

a coherent policy vision, and its lobbying is mostly reactive. Business development has been more dynamic over time than the development of the state, however, and while the state has mostly changed through addition of new institutions, many businesses have matured internally over the decades.[22]

Saudi Arabia is not the only segmented system in the GCC: Bahrain, the United Arab Emirates (UAE) and Qatar also have redundant and fragmented state apparatuses with administrative bodies of often dramatically variegated quality, created rapidly and in a top-down fashion through discretionary rent allocation by a fairly autonomous elite. Oil has been used for radically different purposes, increasing the heterogeneity of the state rather than having a uniform effect on institutions. In the UAE and Qatar, royal fiefdoms and mass patronage employment coexist with technocratic islands of excellence. In Bahrain, a whole parallel government of "ad-hocracies" has been created during the last decade in order to circumvent the opaque and slow-moving regular state apparatus. Led by the Crown Prince, it appears that this development can again be explained only with the (renewed) availability of oil surpluses.[23]

Due to its population size, Saudi Arabia is probably the GCC country in which the segmented state will be put to the most severe test in the coming decades; an economy of 30 million cannot forever be run through enclave structures. A reform of supply and pricing structures on the labor market is the core prerequisite to reducing the costs of bureaucratic structures of mass patronage and, through incentivizing development of local human resources, spreading good management beyond the country's islands of efficiency. But in the GCC, only Bahrain has taken meaningful first steps in this direction.

A truly competitive labor market would require the separation of public employment and public patronage. The political inevitability of mass distribution in Saudi Arabia is beyond doubt; the challenge is to re-engineer this distribution in a less distortionary and more equitable way. Steps towards this goal could contribute much to overcoming a segmentation of administrative and economic spheres, which served a valuable developmental purpose for decades, but now seems to be reaching the limit of its capacity.

---

[22] Giacomo Luciani, "Saudi Arabian Business: From Private Sector to National Bourgeoisie," in Paul Aarts and Gerd Nonneman (eds), *Saudi Arabia in the Balance: Political Economy, Society, Foreign Affairs* (London: Hurst, 2005).

[23] Hasan al-Hasan, *Labour Market Politics in Bahrain*, working paper, JISR project (Dubai: Gulf Research Center, 2010).

11

The Political Economy of Rentierism in Iran

Massoud Karshenas and Ziba Moshaver

The concept of the rentier state was first introduced by Hussein Mahdavi in his seminal study of the patterns and problems of economic development in the Middle Eastern economies, with Iran as its special case study.[1] As an economist Mahdavi's concern was mainly to highlight the structural regularities that characterize the economies of rentier states. The concept of the rentier state, and the important regularities that Mahdavi identified as likely outcomes in rentier economies, have become subjects of a voluminous literature in the four decades since the publication of his paper. This literature can be divided into two different strands. The first one is the large number of economic models put forward to reproduce the type of outcomes similar to structural traits observed in Mahdavi's paper. The second strand has focused on the concept of rentier state itself and the political economy underpinnings of rentierism.

The first strand of literature is best exemplified by the so-called Dutch Disease models, constructed under convenient assumptions to reproduce various

---

[1] Hussein Mahdavi, "Patterns and Problems of Economic Development in Rentier States: The Case of Iran," in M.A. Cook, *Studies in Economic Development of the Middle East: From the Rise of Islam to the Present Day* (Oxford: Oxford University Press, 1970), pp. 428–67.

251

aspects of structural features of rentier economies: features such as overdevelopment of the services sectors, exchange rate overvaluation and crowding out of the traded goods sectors, even unemployed labor in the face of rising incomes.[2] These features of rentier economies were already identified as real possibilities in Mahdavi's study in the context of the Iranian economy over the 1954–65 period. Indeed, Mahdavi's insights go beyond the issues discussed by the Dutch Disease literature, covering areas such as taxation, income distribution, and the impact of volatility of rentier income on growth which have only recently become the focus of the economics literature on oil economies.[3]

The abstract economic models of rentier economies which developed during the 1970s and after were based on restrictive assumptions and took the interventions of the state as given or, at best, as control variables in scenario analysis. The second strand of literature which developed in the wake of Mahdavi's study was, on the other hand, mainly concerned with explaining the behavior of the rentier state itself. As discussed in Kamrava's chapter in this volume, this type of literature went through an early phase, where rentier income played a dominant and determining role in the formation and functioning of the state, to a later and more mature phase, where context specificity and path dependence mattered equally if not more.[4] This approach is not far from the original approach Mahdavi adopted, where interaction between rentier income and underlying socio-political and organizational structures is seen to lead to development outcomes in a country specific context.

In this chapter we follow the same approach by focusing on context specificity and path dependence as critical aspects in analyzing the impact of oil on the Iranian state and economy. The main difference between our approach and Mahdavi's is that due to the availability of data and information over a much longer period of time, we are able to take a long-term view of the interactions between rentier income and evolution of the state in Iran in different historical epochs.

---

[2] See W.M. Corden, "Booming Sector and Dutch Disease Economics: Survey and Consolidation," *Oxford Economic Papers* Vol. 36 (November 1984), pp. 359–80; W.M. Corden and J.P. Neary, "Booming Sector and Deindustrialization in a Small Open Economy," *Economic Journal* Vol. 92, pp. 825–48.

[3] See for example F. Van Der Ploeg and S. Poelhekke, "Volatility and the Natural Resource Curse," *Oxford Economic Papers* No. 61 (2009) pp. 727–60.

[4] See G. Luciani, *The Arab State* (London: Routledge, 1990); G. Luciani, "Resources, Revenues and Authoritarianism in the Arab World: Beyond the Rentier State?" in R.B. Brynen, Korany and P. Noble (eds), *Political Liberalization and Democratization in the Arab World* (Boulder: Lynne Rienner, 1995), pp. 211–28.

To do this we focus on the interaction between rentier income and state formation and the resulting development outcomes, by taking a historical view of the Iranian political economy from the discovery and first export of oil in the early twentieth century up to the present. The next section broadly examines this relationship during the Pahlavi era, up to the 1979 revolution. This section forms the background within which the more detailed study of state structures in the post-1979 era is conducted in subsequent sections.

The chapter then examines the period after the 1979 Revolution, the impact of oil revenues in the shaping and subsequent development of new Islamic state. It is argued that during this phase, too, the impact of oil revenues varied depending on state structures, political priorities and, more important, factional interests of the Islamic Republic and its leadership or what we refer to as the "core state."

The chapter also compares two phases of management of oil revenues in the pre- and post-revolution periods in order to highlight the key political economy underpinnings of the impact of oil. It shows that despite the centrality of oil rents in the political economy of the two regimes the development outcomes are radically different and they face different sustainability problems.

Oil and the development of the Iranian state prior to the 1979 Revolution

This section covers the period between the 1920s and 1979, beginning with the emergence of the modern Iranian state system under the Pahlavi dynasty, and coinciding with the discovery and export of oil early in the twentieth century. During this period oil and state did not interact in a lineal fashion and three distinct phases are recognizable. Each phase has its own specific characteristics with regard to both the role of the state and the influence of oil in the political economy of the country.

The emergence of the modern Iranian state

The main characteristic of this early period up to the 1950s was the relatively small size of oil revenues, which nevertheless were instrumental in the creation of modern state institutions and centralization of state power, especially during the 1920s and 30s under Reza Shah. Oil revenues were used primarily to finance newly constructed state institutions including the military, considered crucial for the unification of the country and territorial defense. Measures were taken by the state to rationalize and expand central administration to help consolidate the military-bureaucratic state structures. This modern state was to take away the political power of a conservative coalition of landlords and traditional aristocracy, supported by factions of the clergy opposed to the modernization project.

During the latter half of the 1920s finances of the state were reorganized and effective measures were taken to regulate the civil service by establishing educational standards, introducing life tenure, and providing a regular scale of meritocratic promotion and salaries. The same bureaucratic criteria were applied to the judicial and education systems. A comprehensive civil code and penal and commercial codes were devised which gradually transformed judicial practices from the prerogatives of the clergy, conducted according to their personal interpretation of *Shari'a*. Bureaucratization of administration of law was completed by the 1936 legislation, introducing special examinations and university degrees for presiding over courts.

Rationalization of the state administration was accompanied by functional and structural differentiation of the state and specialized ministerial branches which could play a more direct and active role in the economy. In 1928, the National Bank (Bank Melli) was established by the state, which took over the government's accounts as well as the monopoly right of bank note issue from the British-owned Imperial Bank of Persia.

The formation of this centralized and unified bureaucratic machinery, considerably aided by the availability of oil revenues in a predominantly pre-capitalist economy and amidst a diversity of socio-political structures, also enhanced the ability of the state to intervene in the economy. The economy as a whole was not directly impacted by oil revenues and oil did not substantially contribute to domestic capital formation. Government investment in infrastructure and industry in this period was financed by taxes on trade and profits of state monopolies.[5]

This pattern changed in the mid-1950s. After the Second World War nationalist sentiments against foreign intervention and concessionary privileges of oil companies, British Petroleum in particular, led to nationalization of Iranian oil by the elected National Front government under Prime Minister Mossadegh. Although this attempt was defeated by a Western-instigated coup in 1953, a new agreement on 50–50 percent profit sharing led to a considerable increase in Iran's oil revenues. This increase in oil revenues marked the begin-

---

[5] See Chapter 3 in M. Karshenas, *Oil, State and Industrialization in Iran* (Cambridge: Cambridge University Press, 1990).

ning of a new era in the role of oil in the political economy of modern Iran. To begin with, the share of oil revenues in total government revenue increased to over 50 percent by the end of the 1950s and to over 75 percent in the mid-1970s (Figure 11.1). This growth in oil income gave a boost to economic growth in general, and also introduced a qualitative change in the role of oil in the political economy of the country as compared to the pre-1950s period.

Figure 11.1: Oil Revenues as Percent of Total Government Revenues, 1925–1975.

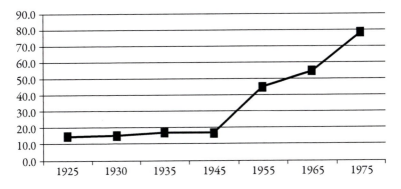

The most important characteristic of this period of sustained growth in oil revenue was a parallel growth in the size and functions of state institutions and the bureaucracy. The economic system during this phase, the 1960s and 1970s, could be characterized as a mixed market economy similar to many other developing countries at the time. The state made a policy-choice in favor of investment in infrastructure and industries complementary to the private sector, within the framework of five year development plans. Government planning encouraged private sector activities and was instrumental to the growth of a thriving private sector. Through focused credit subsidies and technical assistance provided by development banks, a strong import substitution industrialization strategy followed suit. This way the state became instrumental in creating a new class of private industrialists with many new industries and technologies in close collaboration with foreign capital.

The other area where the state extended its reach during this period was in the agricultural sector and among the rural populations. The land reform program in the 1963—coupled later with other initiatives together known as the White Revolution—undermined the power of the absentee landowners, opening the agricultural sector to commercial farming and increased labor mobility. The White Revolution went beyond radical land distribution to encompass other social changes including a universal literacy program, extension of voting right to women, reform of family laws and so on. These reforms evidently required expansion of the state bureaucracy, connecting various social strata more tightly with the state system and central government. Through these ties, the state hoped to raise support among the country's rural population and neutralize the appeal of radical opposition groups.

This period of relatively balanced growth during the 1960s and 1970s was interrupted with the oil boom of 1972–74. The boom led to an overheated economy characterized by wasteful and ambitious investments, bureaucratic and administrative expansion, and high defense and security expenditures. These expansionist policies were in part to compensate for the government's inability to deliver what was promised by the White Revolution, and were further encouraged by the increasingly autocratic nature of the Shah's rule. During this phase, the state also turned its attention to the urban population and middle classes to increase its support base. Creating employment opportunities by enlarging the state bureaucracy was among policies to help this process. In this context, the Shah initiated formation of the political party, Rastakiz, in 1975 in order to open the political space. This party was to encompass different political tendencies and participation in the political processes of urban middle class and state bureaucracy.

The mismanagement of increased oil revenues by the autocratic and expansionist state created imbalances leading to the recession that began as early as 1976. This was followed by serious cracks in the system from 1977 with a mass-based social uprising challenging and, finally, ending the monarchy in 1979-revolution.

Whether the Shah and the autocratic political and economic order he had developed over time could have accommodated the post-boom realities and initiated the required reforms remains unknown. But what is certain is that his highly expanded state bureaucracy and development plans based on high oil revenues could not be sustained with the bust in oil demand and prices. By 1979 his state had lost even the support of the sections of the society that had most benefitted in the expansionary years. In similar situations, such as earlier in South Korea or in Turkey in the 1980s, the state leadership allowed greater technocratic intervention and gave a greater role and independence to the new industrial elites. Whether the Shah could do the same by opening up to these forces and, if so, whether the system could successfully pass this period of lowered financial resources was never tested.

THE POLITICAL ECONOMY OF RENTIERISM IN IRAN

Oil and the development of the post-1979 Islamic state

The early years of the post revolutionary decade were dominated by what could be called the invention of a theocratic state under the guidance of the clergy, as envisioned by Ayatollah Khomeini's notion of Velayat-e-Faghih.[6] In competing with other contestants for state power, the clergy devised institutions and practices that have remained in place ever since, and have further grown in size and political power. Oil revenues played an important role in this process, as will be discussed below.

The evolution of the theocratic state was also influenced by the exigencies of the war of 1980–88, an unfavorable international context, and changing geostrategic circumstances. Radicalization of Iran's foreign policy, especially after the American hostage crisis and the international embargo that followed, was also important in changing Iran's status from a friend and supporter of the West in the Middle East to a foe hostile to the Western-dominated regional order.

State institutions and state power in the Islamic Republic

The Constitution of the Islamic Republic laid the foundation for a dual state where the official state structures, namely the elected parliament and the executive, live side by side with an unofficial network of institutions controlled by the clergy and headed by the supreme leader. We refer to the latter as the unofficial core state. The unofficial core state controls important state apparatuses such as the judiciary and the security forces. Furthermore, through its institutions such as the Guardian Council, it screens candidates for parliamentary and presidential elections, has veto power over legislation passed by the parliament, and exerts considerable influence over the day to day affairs of the official government.

Chart 11.1 provides a schematic view of government institutions of the Islamic Republic, classified according to elected and non-elected groupings. The main difference between these two components of the state is not, however, only the fact that one is elected and the other is not. Another key difference is that the official state institutions are designed to work within a framework of bureaucratic rules and regulation and codified laws, while the

---

[6] See Z. Moshaver, "Revolution, Theocratic Leadership and Iran's Foreign Policy: Implications for Iran-EU Relations" in Gerd Nonneman (ed.), *Analysing Middle East Foreign Policy* (London: Routledge, 2005).

unofficial core state mainly operates as a network of individuals and interest groups wielding power through informal and sometimes interpersonal relations, and their actions are not governed by transparent and bureaucratic rules and regulations. This has had immense repercussions, particularly with respect to state-economy interactions and the role of oil resources in the political economy of post-revolutionary Iran.

Chart 11.1: State Structures of the Islamic Republic.

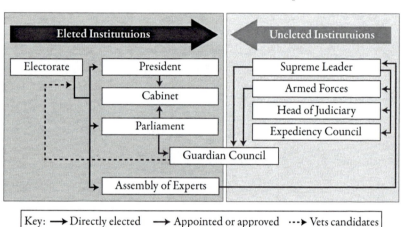

Key: ⟶ Directly elected ⟶ Appointed or approved ···▶ Vets candidates

Source: BBC, 2010.

The state and the economy in the Islamic Republic

The new Islamic state embarked upon extensive nationalization of almost all of the modern large-scale enterprises in industry and services, including the banks. A large part of the nationalized assets were transferred to semi-official charity institutions *(bonyads)*, which have constituted an important part of the resources controlled by the core state. Despite the fact that *bonyads* control a major part of the corporate sector of the economy, their legal and official status is such that they are neither part of the private sector nor part of the official public sector. This is integral to the peculiar dual state structures of the Islamic Republic.

The Constitution of the Islamic Republic gives the state, both official and un-official, considerable power over economic resources and gives the private sector a subordinate role. Article 44 of the Constitution reads:

The economy of the Islamic Republic of Iran is to consist of three sectors: state, cooperative, and private, and is to be based on systematic and sound planning. The state sector is to include all large-scale and mother industries, foreign trade, major minerals, banking, insurance, power generation, dams and large-scale irrigation networks, radio and television, post, telegraph and telephone services, aviation, shipping, roads, railroads and the like; all these will be publicly owned and administered by the State. *The cooperative sector is to include cooperative companies and enterprises concerned with production and distribution, in urban and rural areas, in accordance with Islamic criteria.* The private sector consists of those activities concerned with agriculture, animal husbandry, industry, trade, and services that supplement the economic activities of the state and cooperative sectors. (emphasis added)

Over time, however, it has been the semi-official institutions of the core state, namely the *bonyad*s, that have grown considerably by accumulating more and more assets. They operate under the auspices of the office of the supreme leader, not the official government. They are governed neither by the laws governing public enterprise sector, nor by those of the private sector (for example, these institutions do not pay taxes and their accounts are not public). Operating under the auspices of the supreme leader, these *bonyad*s evade regular parliamentary oversight. They also evade all forms of supervision, accountability and independent financial audit. They are scrutinized neither by the government nor by shareholders. These semi-private semi-official foundations become meaningful in the context of Article 44 of the Constitution above as being "in accordance with the Islamic criteria," and fit well with the characterization of the "cooperative" sector in the Constitution.

The expanded economic position of the core state has not been confined to the accumulation of assets within the institutions under its direct control such as the *bonyad*s and the Revolutionary Guards, which over time have accumulated substantial economic assets. But it has also worked through these institutions having access to and benefitting from indirect interventions in government regulation of the foreign exchange markets, interest rates and allocation of bank credits, as well as rationing and direct price controls of a large section of product markets.

Attempts at reforming the system

The period following the consolidation of the Islamic state and the end of the war in 1988 is referred to as reconstruction phase when the state tried to adopt more pragmatic and rational policies. It began with the partial liberalization and economic reform attempts after the war, combined with a large reconstruction and investment program by the government. Economic planning which had been abandoned during the war years was reinstated with the first five year plan of the Islamic Republic under President Rafsanjani. Privatization of state enterprises was put on the agenda, and government ministries were ordered to prepare a list of public enterprises for privatization. The upshot of the economic reform program was the unification of the exchange rate in March 1993.

But this reform period was short-lived. The unbridled credit expansion and unsustainable foreign borrowing led to the abandonment of much of the reform program. Since the major part of Iran's foreign debt in 1993 was in short-term commercial credit, and because of economic sanctions, the government found it difficult to reschedule these debts, and trade and foreign exchange restrictions were reintroduced. By December 1993, foreign exchange unification was effectively abandoned. The expansion of bank credit and unsustainable foreign borrowing forced the government to end the reform program. The rest of the 1990s was a period of economic retrenchment and repayment of the considerable foreign debt accumulated during the boom of the early 1990s.

The failure of the economic reform program during the first five-year plan highlighted the tensions within the Islamic Republic's political economy, which also dominated the fate of subsequent reform attempts. In all of the subsequent five year plans (the fourth five-year plan ended in 2010) various elements of the reform program of the first plan period have been reiterated, and in some periods serious attempts at reform with limited success have been made. Two areas of relative success have been the unification of the exchange rate and the setting up of an oil stabilization fund (OSF) in 2000 to smooth out the effect of oil revenue fluctuations on government expenditures. The need for the oil stabilization fund was driven home by the painful experience of boom and bust of the early 1990s, and the extreme vulnerability of the regime given its international isolation. The more conservative fiscal stance of the government as compared to the early 1990s, combined with a sustained increase in oil prices, created the conditions for the relative success of the Central Bank in supporting a unified exchange rate since 2000.

At a more basic level, however, there has been very little reform in the fundamentals of the economic system that emerged during the first decade of the revolution. If anything, there has been a considerable shift of economic power from the official elected government—the "legal rational" arm of the state— toward the less transparent and more murky and informal core state, and the independent private sector has become increasingly marginalized, as originally envisioned by the Constitution of the Islamic Republic. Since the early 1990s, privatization of government enterprises has been going on with fits and starts. During the third five year plan, under President Khatami, the process intensified as an ambitious program of privatization was ratified, despite opposition from sections of the core state. The privatized government enterprises, however, have been by and large either taken over by the semi-public *bonyad*s or sold via public offering on the Tehran stock exchange with the majority shares controlled by government owned banks or other public or semi-public institutions.

Since the privatization program sat uneasily with Article 44 of the Constitution, around which forces opposed to privatization congregated, in 2004 the Expediency Council announced a reinterpretation of Article 44 with far-reaching effects. This has been reinforced by a new executive order by the Supreme Leader in 2006 with a strict deadline for divestment of government enterprises by the end of the fifth development plan (2014). According to the new interpretation, all government enterprises, including heavy chemicals and petrochemicals, telecommunications, electricity generation, all the downstream activities in oil and gas, mining, banking and insurance, etc. are to be privatized. Government ownership will be limited to a few strategic activities such upstream oil and gas, some banks and a few companies in the utilities and transportation sectors. The majority of the shares of privatized companies are to be sold to non-government foundations at 50 percent discount, to be managed on behalf of the poor.[7] This was the culmination of a process that has been taking place on a more informal basis since the beginning of the privatization process in the late 1980s.

The dual state and the distortion of private-public boundaries

One of the intriguing phenomena related to officially published statistics under the Islamic Republic is the ambiguity in the definition of private and public investment. There seems to be a considerable discrepancy in the available information on what constitutes private or public investment in the official data. According to the Central Bank statistics, the share of private investment in the economy has grown rapidly since the early 1990s, reaching double that of the public investment. On the other hand, according to the Central Statistical Office data the ratio of private to public investment has

---

[7] International Monetary Fund (IMF), "Islamic Republic of Iran: 2006 Article IV Consultation," IMF Report 07/100 (Washington, DC: IMF, March 2007).

remained stable in the same period and is much lower than the ratios indicated by the Central Bank data (see Figure 11.2).

What lies behind this apparent discrepancy between official statistics is the role of parallel or semi-official institutions active in Iranian economy. Investment expenditures by the quasi-state institutions are often treated as private investment even though for all practical purposes these investments are directly or indirectly controlled by the core state, albeit in a haphazard and uncoordinated manner. To be treated as public investment, the budget of semi-public foundations should be presented to the parliament as a supplement to the government budget with their credit position with the banking system separated from the accounts of the private sector proper. But this is rarely done. There is a serious lack of information regarding the functions and performance of these organizations. Their accounts are not publicly disclosed and, in the absence of credible data, it is almost impossible to evaluate the costs and benefits of their various programs.

Shortage of credible and independently verifiable data on these organizations precludes an objective assessment of their programs. During the 1990s Iran's Revolutionary Guards also emerged as a significant economic player. Like the *bonyad*s, the Revolutionary Guards enjoy an extra-legal status that affords them indemnity from public scrutiny as well as taxes. This new mili-

Figure 11.2: Ratio of Private to Public Investment according to the Central Bank and CSO Statistics.

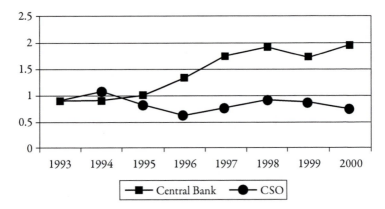

Source: Central Statistical Office (CSO), National Accounts of Iran, and Bank Markazi Iran, National Accounts Statistics.

tary-business complex controlled by the Guards has considerable economic and financial muscle. Enjoying strong ties with the core clerical state, *bonyad*s and the Revolutionary Guards have both thrived under patronage of the core state. Their growing control of the market and their preferential access to state favors prevent the emergence of a truly private sector. They undermine competition and distort private incentives for wealth generation. Economic activities of these quasi-state actors may hold the key to explaining the notoriously low efficiency of investment in Iran. The commercial functions of these foundations, though said to be formally separate, are not compatible with aims of economic efficiency and commercial profitability. As noted in the previous sections, these parallel institutions have been important obstacles to economic reform, as they represent powerful political and economic constituencies of the Islamic Republic.

The presence and power of these foundations provide an interesting example of the workings of Iran's distinct political economy. They are a product of the country's dualistic power structure and a manifestation of the financial influence that Iran's unelected core state enjoys. The *bonyad*s and Revolutionary Guards, including the Basij (paramilitary), serve as convenient conduits for distributing state favors and public employment to ideological supporters of the regime. In this milieu, these institutions help consolidate and maintain the political authority of the ruling elite. They have become important tools for socio-economic mobility of the lower and middle classes who had previously supported the revolutionary regime.[8] As noted in the previous section, the dominant role of *bonyad*s has not been challenged by the privatization process. In some instances, they have in fact been beneficiaries of that process, as shares of national companies undergoing privatization have also been sold to *bonyad*s and Revolutionary Guards.

Management of oil rents and economic growth: Comparing the pre- and post-Revolution periods

In this section we compare two phases with regard to management of oil revenues in Iran in order to highlight some of the political economy underpinnings of the impact of oil, often neglected in the literature which is overly concerned with theories or models believed to be generally applicable to all

---

[8] Ali A. Saeidi, "The Accountability of Para-Governmental Organizations (bonyads): The Case of Iranian Foundations," *Iranian Studies* Vol. 37, No. 3 (September 2004), p. 480.

oil economies. To do so we identify two similar periods of the economic history of Iran since the late 1950s. The periodization in previous sections distinguished between the pre-revolution period of the 1960s and 1970s, the decade of revolution and war from the late 1970s to the late 1980s, and the period since the Iran-Iraq war, from 1989 onwards. The growth cycles of the Iranian economy during these distinct periods are shown in figure 11.3. Prior to the 1960s reliable statistics on macroeconomic variables, which can be used for our study, did not exist.

The period prior to the 1979 Revolution is divided into two sub-periods in Figure 3. One is the long period of sustained economic growth during the 1960s up to the oil price boom of 1972–74. During this period GDP growth in Iran was amongst the highest achieved by any country at that time on a sustained basis. Economic growth was particularly spectacular between 1963 and 1971 after the economy emerged from the economic stabilization program and political upheavals of the early 1960s. The second sub-period in this phase coincides with the oil price hike of 1972–74, and the mismanagement of the hefty oil revenues by the government. This led to an overheated economy followed by a recession as early as 1976. This also ushered in the end of the long constant trend of growing oil export volumes that had started in the mid-1950s. Iranian oil production reached its peak in 1976.

The next main phase is the period of revolution and war from the late 1970s to the late 1980s. Oil exports declined drastically and the economy

Figure 11.3: GDP Growth Cycles, 1960–2007.

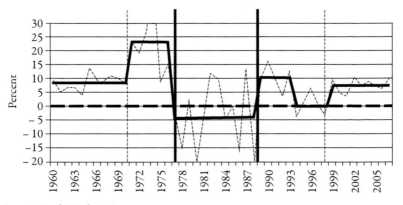

Source: Bank Markazi Iran.
Note: Solid line refers to average of annual growth rates.

followed a sharp declining trend. By 1988 real per capita national income had declined to 50 percent of its peak in 1976. As discussed above, the political structures and many of the current economic institutions of the Islamic Republic took shape in that period.

The phase of revolution and war years is of interest due to the institutional changes it brought about, which distinguish the post-Revolution growth experience from the pre-Revolution years. This was followed by the boom and bust of the first and the second planning period of the Islamic Republic during the 1990s.

The two boom and bust sub-phases of 1972–79 and 1989–98 have similar lessons in the sense that they represent periods of macroeconomic mismanagement, unbridled credit expansion, and short-term inflationary growth in an overheated economy, followed by a long period of stagnation. The two interesting sub-periods which we shall concentrate on here, however, are the 1963–71 and 1998–2007 periods where the economy experienced long periods of sustained growth.

As can be seen from figure 11.4, the trends in oil-GDP ratio in these two sub-periods show remarkable similarities. In both cases oil-GDP ratio increased from about 10 percent to over 25 percent. An important difference between the two periods with regards to oil revenue growth is that during the first sub-period oil revenues grew by and large as a result of the expansion of production and exports, while during the recent sub-period it has taken the form of oil price increases. This is important in that it highlights the lack of investment in the oil industry in the recent period, and indicates an inherent

Figure 11.4: Oil Value Added as Percentage of GNP, 1962–2007.

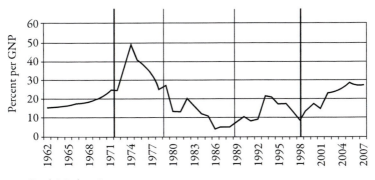

Source: Bank Markazi Iran.

problem in the long-term sustainability of the recent bout of oil revenue growth. The differences in the growth experiences in these two sub-periods, as we shall demonstrate, show the critical effect of political economy factors in economic growth, even in the same country and with relatively similar magnitude and growth rate of rentier income, as is the case here.

Political economy of 'unsustainable' growth in the two periods

An important phenomenon highlighted by the pattern of the Iranian economy's growth cycles is the close association between economic growth and the growth of oil revenues. Periods of sustained growth in oil revenues coincide with overall economic growth, and periods of stagnation in oil revenues invariably lead to a collapse of economic growth. More important aspects of development, however, pertain to the type of growth during long episodes of oil revenue increase, which nevertheless comes to an end with the reversal of fortunes in the oil sector. A comparison of the two growth phases of 1962–71 and 1998–2007 in Iran can highlight some of the underlying political economy and institutional reasons for this phenomenon, and help focus on the sustainability of the current growth episode.

Table 11.1 shows some of the key macroeconomic and growth indicators for the two periods. As can be seen, GDP and investment growth rates during the latter period are well below the first period of 1962–71. This may come as a surprise, as average investment rates during the 1998–2007 period, at 28 percent, were higher than investment rates of 25.6 percent in the earlier period. The dynamics and productivity of investment in the two periods, however, were very different.

While investment during the 1960s period accelerated and investment rate increased from 20 percent of GDP to over 30 percent along with the growth of productive capacity of the economy, investment rates in 1998 started at relatively high rates of close to 30 percent and fluctuated within the range of 25 to 30 percent (figure 11.5). The fact that relatively higher investment rates during the 1998–2007 period translated to much lower GDP growth rates in that period, attests to the extremely low efficiency of investment in the post-Revolution period. This is clearly reflected in the glaring rise of incremental capital output ratio in this period. Incremental capital output ratio increased from 2.4 during 1962–71 to the incredibly high rate of 6.1 in 1998–2007 (see Table 11.1).

This further calls into question the efficiency of investments in the recent period, particularly since the economy has benefitted from a much better edu-

Table 11.1: Macroeconomic Indicators, 1962–71 and 1998–2007.

GDP growth	10.5	5.4
Investment growth	14.0	7.8
Investment rate (I/GDP)	25.6	28.0
Saving rate	24.9	37.6
Incremental captial/output ration $\Sigma(I)/\Delta Y$	2.4	6.1
Inflation	2.0	13.5
Annual growth rates by sector		
Non-oil GDP	8.7	5.8
Agriculture	4.3	4.4
Oil and gas	12.9	2.2
Industries and mines	12.2	8.8
Mining	12.8	11.6
Manufacturing	11.4	9.7
Electricity, gas and water	22.8	7.6
Construction	12.9	5.6
Services	9.7	4.9

Source: Bank Markazi Iran.
Notes: Growth rates are trend extimates.

cated labor force by comparison with the 1960s. Investment rates are also well below the potential that is suggested by the relatively high savings rates (see figure 11.6).[9] Furthermore, investments rates are well below the potential that is offered by the growth and improved quality of the labor force. Unemployment among the young and educated is 24.7 percent and has been on the rise.[10]

The nature of the investment process is the key to understanding some of the central paradoxes of the Iranian economy: high unemployment combined with excess savings and its high and accelerating inflation. Apart from its direct public investment, the government attempts to control private and other non-public investment through the allocation of cheap credit by the

[9] Since Iranian national accounts statistics are measured on production and expenditure, they do not report the income side. Hence, statistics for national savings should be treated with care. The high savings rates in this period, however, are not entirely unexpected, due to the rapid population transition that Iran has experienced since the 1990s. A young and rapidly growing labor force, combined with rapidly declining birth rates and dependency rates, are no doubt important determinants of the rising savings rates.
[10] Bank Markazi Iran, *Annual Review*, 2009/10, p. 12.

Figures 11.5 and 11.6.

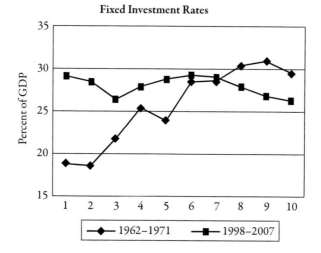

Fixed Investment Rates

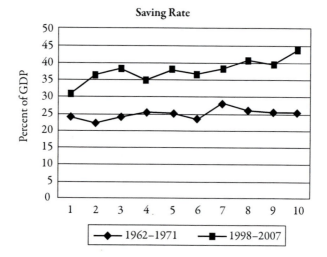

Saving Rate

Source: Bank Markazi Iran.

banking system and the government's provision of other subsidies and forms of protection in product markets.

The apparent lack of efficiency of allocation and use of resources during the 1998–2007 period is closely connected with the politico-economic institutions of the Islamic Republic. As discussed in the previous section, the dominance of economic entities with close political ties to the core unofficial state, and in a position to receive protection and subsidies due to their political ties, lies at the root of this phenomenon. The marginalization of the private sector and lack of market competition means that the semi-official economic entities can remain profitable and even thrive without the need to attain the necessary technical efficiency and without technological upgrading.

Another important factor, closely connected with the nature of the political economy of the Islamic Republic, is the persistence of huge price subsidies, particularly energy subsidies, provided by the state. Some of the glaring price distortions resulting from the system of multiple exchange rates which plagued the economy for much of the life of the Islamic Republic appear to have been remedied since the exchange rate unification of 2002. Nevertheless, with huge subsidies for strategic products such as energy and basic foods, price distortions still remain important impediments to allocative and production efficiency of the system. The huge energy subsidies have inevitably led to the use of inappropriate technologies, and have created the appearance of profitability in activities which remain non-competitive by international standards.

Political economy of oil rents and government budget

The most direct channel of influence of oil on the domestic economy is through the central government budget. The undeveloped fiscal machinery of the Islamic Republic stands out by the very low and declining share of taxes in GDP. The share of government taxes in GDP, which was more than 8 percent during the oil boom years of the mid-1970s, fell to 5 percent in the mid-1990s and has remained at similar rates since. A large part of the existing taxes takes the form of import taxes, which further enhances the dependence of the government on oil revenues. Another indicator of the deficiency of the taxation system in Iran is the low levels of corporate tax take, and particularly its declining trend over time. Taxes on corporations were over 3 percent of GDP in the mid-1970s, but have fallen just over 2 percent in the current period. With the growth of the corporate sector and the rapid decline in the share of agriculture in GDP, one would expect a rising share of corporate taxes in GDP. As pointed out before, however, the major part of the corporate sector in the Iranian economy consists of foundations (*bonyads*) which remain exempt from government taxation. Since 2008 the government has attempted to reform the tax system by introducing a 3 percent value added tax, but this has been resisted by protest marches and closure of the bazaars in some major cities.

Another notable aspect of the dependence of government budget on oil revenues relates to the speed with which unexpected increases in oil revenues are translated into government expenditures. Despite the existence of long-term expenditure plans within the five year development planning framework by the government, during both the pre- and post-Revolution periods, increases in government revenues over and above those budgeted within the plan framework were immediately translated into increased government expenditures. Prominent examples of this were the boom and bust episodes of the 1970s and the early 1990s.

In 2000, the Oil Stabilization Fund (OSF) was set up in order to smooth out the effect of unexpected oil price fluctuations. Withdrawals from the OSF by the government for general budgetary purposes have to be ratified by the parliament and fifty percent of the fund's balances are to be set aside for foreign exchange loans to the private sector via commercial banks for investment in priority sectors. However, over 80 percent of the OSF's funds since its creation has been transferred to the central government budget. The withdrawals by central government in 2006 alone were $17.8 billion, which was equivalent to the entire assets of the OSF at the end of 2006. The withdrawals from the OSF by the government increased to $22.1 billion in 2008. Considering that oil revenue increases over this period have been entirely due to oil price increases rather than expansion of output and export quantities, this high degree of reliance on OSF funds, apart from leading to short-term inflationary pressures, is a recipe for fiscal crises and more serious instability in the medium and long run.

The apparently similar responses of the pre- and post-Revolution governments to unexpected oil revenue increases during the oil price booms may convey the impression that the underlying political economy forces influencing the expenditure of oil rents have remained the same. This is far from the truth. The government prior to the 1979 Revolution was a highly centralized and unified technocratic entity which had a relatively high degree of autonomy from underlying societal forces. Many of the economic problems during that era were associated with the top-down planning characteristic of this configuration of state power. This was also responsible for the overheated economy that developed during the 1973–74 oil boom, as the technocrats did not have the power to stand against the grandiose dreams of the Shah when he ordered a quadrupling of the dimensions of the fifth development plan. The political economy of the Islamic Republic, however, is very different. The duality of power within the state, the control of enormous economic assets by the core clerical state, and the need of the clerical state to reward its supporters through employment creation and charitable transfers introduce critical differences in the resource allocation mechanisms between the two regimes. Important aspects of this are reflected in government expenditure patterns.

An important change in the structure of the budget during the post-Revolution period is the decline in the share of government development expenditures and the relatively large increases in the share of current expenditures. In particular, from the mid-1990s the share of current spending has been increasing, and what is even more remarkable is that with the start of the oil price boom, since 1999, the share of development spending has remained low, at around 20 percent of the total compared to close to 40 percent in the 1960s. This may be to some extent due to the new interpretation of Article 44 of the Constitution, which inhibits the official government from engaging in investment in industrial and commercial activities. However, investment in infrastructural activities such as electricity generation has also remained low.

An important reason for the increase in the share of current expenditures in total government expenditures appears to be the political pressures to create public employment and maintain extensive public subsidies. Food subsidies for example have increased from about 1.4 percent of GDP in 2000 to about 3 percent in 2007, during a period when total government development spending has not been more than 5 percent of GDP on average. Implicit subsidies arising from the pricing of energy and other public utility services have been an even more significant drain on government revenues. For example, according to the IMF estimates, implicit subsidies in the oil and gas sector were about 20 percent of GDP in 2007.

Since 2008 the government has embarked upon what appears to be a serious attempt to address the issue of subsidies. In January 2011 the parliament approved a law on the replacement of price subsidies by direct cash transfers to households. The thorny issue related to the main component of subsidies— energy subsidies—is however related to energy consumption by the productive sector of the economy. This entails serious industrial and technological restructuring, which are long-term issues and do not appear to have been adequately addressed in the new law. Without efforts to address such long-term structural elements of the reform, the fate of these reforms is likely to be similar to that of the reform attempts in the early 1990s.

The increase in the share of current government expenditures under these conditions has not necessarily meant improvement in the quality of public services provided. On the contrary, the quality of public sector health and educational services appears to have been deteriorating, as those who can afford it appear to be resorting increasingly to private health and educational services. Figure 11.7 shows how public spending per student has been declining as a share of per capita GDP during the post-Revolution period.

Conclusion

In this study we have examined the evolution of rentierism in Iran by focusing on the interactions between oil income and the development of the state in a historical perspective. Our analysis is based on the view that the concept of the rentier state in general and abstract terms is not adequate to explain the complex processes and outcomes in the development of oil economies such as Iran. As we have argued, these developments are to a large extent context specific and path-dependent. Viewed in a dynamic context, however, the role of oil income in the formation of state structures and the outcome of state interventions also becomes prominent. These complex interactions were analyzed by highlighting the nature and development of the rentier state during various phases within two distinct eras, namely the Pahlavi era and the post-revolutionary Islamic state.

In the first phase of the Pahlavi era, the inter-war period, oil revenues were relatively low and the economy was too archaic for oil to have a direct impact on economic development. Nevertheless the role of oil income was critical as it facilitated the creation of the modern state and emergence of centralized state institutions. This was itself a precondition for modern economic development and improved bargaining power vis-à-vis the oil companies and higher oil revenues in subsequent periods.

One of the prominent aspects of the development of the modern state system pertained to the oil sector itself and its relation to the budgetary processes of the state. Modernization of the state during the 1920s led to the emergence of more transparent formal budgetary processes and the separation of the government budget from the personal prerogative of the sovereign. As a result, oil revenues accrue to the government through the national banking system and are reflected accurately within the public sector accounts. This

Figure 11.7: Public Expenditure per Student, 1980–2007 (% of GDP per Capita).

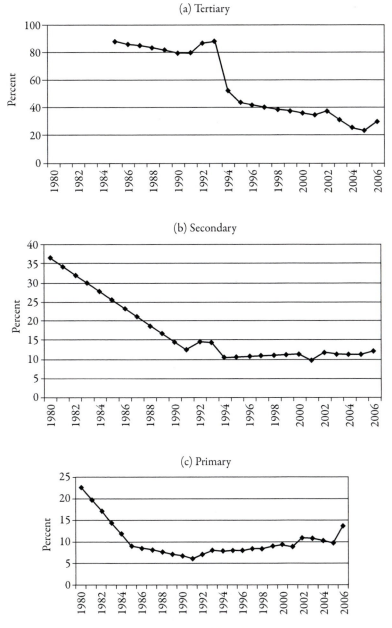

(a) Tertiary

(b) Secondary

(c) Primary

Source: World Development Indicators, World Bank, April 2010.

marks an important difference with some other oil rich countries in the region where oil revenues are still mainly controlled by the sovereign who allocates a part to the government budget.

The building of centralized state institutions helped by oil revenues in this period also contributed to the strengthening of Reza Shah's authoritarian tendencies. However, with the Allied occupation of the country during the Second World War, and Reza Shah's fall in 1941, a new era of open politics and increased parliamentary activism began. This period is marked by participation of different political groupings and tendencies, especially the emergence and consolidation of a liberal democratic centrist party, the National Front. This resulted in coming to power of the first democratically elected government in Iran under the premiership of Dr Muhammad Mussadegh, and the subsequent oil company nationalization.

This democratic experience was aborted by a combination of a prolonged economic boycott and, finally, the US-initiated military coup in 1953. The post-1950s period witnessed a considerable rise in oil revenues of the government and ushered in a period of sustained growth of oil exports up to the mid-1970s. The economic system during this phase was that of a mixed market economy within the framework of five year development plans. Government planning encouraged private sector activities and was important for the growth of a thriving private sector, and became instrumental in creating a new class of private industrialists. Other important measures were the land reform program of the 1960s, coupled with other important reforms which constituted the so-called White Revolution. These reforms evidently required expansion of the state bureaucracy and connected various social strata more tightly with the state system and central government.

This period of relatively balanced growth during the 1960s and 1970s, which was made possible by giving a greater degree of autonomy to the technocratic elements within the state, was interrupted with the oil boom of 1972–74. The oil boom once again increased the autocratic nature of the Shah's rule, whose growing interferences led to an overheated economy characterized by wasteful and ambitious investments, bureaucratic and administrative expansion, and high defense and security expenditures.

With the end of the oil boom era, from the mid-1970s, the economy entered a recessionary phase with growing economic imbalances giving further impetus to social tensions. Whether the Shah and the autocratic political and economic order could manage the necessary reforms, as was done for example in South Korea and Turkey in similar situations, could not be tested as the 1979 revolutionary upheavals changed the course of history and ushered in a new phase of rentierism in Iran.

The emergence of the Islamic Republic after the 1979 Revolution brought about a radical transformation of the political economy of oil and development in Iran. The Constitution of the Islamic Republic laid the foundation for a dual state whereby the official state structures, namely the elected parliament and the executive, live side by side with an unofficial network of institutions controlled by the clergy and headed by the supreme leader. We have referred to the latter as the unofficial "core state." The core state controls important state apparatuses, such as the judiciary and the security forces. Furthermore, through its institutions such as the Guardian Council, it screens candidates for parliamentary and presidential elections, has veto power over legislation passed by the parliament, and exerts considerable influence over the day to day affairs of the elected official government.

The official state institutions are designed to work within a framework of bureaucratic rules and laws ratified and upheld by elected representatives. The unelected core state, on the other hand, operates mainly as a network of individuals and interest groups wielding power through informal and sometimes interpersonal relations, and their actions are not governed by transparent and bureaucratic rules and regulations. As argued, the events immediately following the Revolution, as well as the war years of the 1980s, played an important role in the formation of this dual state. This duality has had immense repercussions, particularly with respect to state-economy interactions, and the role of oil resources in the political economy of post-revolutionary Iran. This pertains both to the nature of new economic institutions which have emerged under the Islamic Republic, such as the *bonyad*s (foundations), and to the dynamics of economic change and the evolution of these institutions. For example, as discussed, concepts such as privatization, and the very notion of private/public distinction, take different meanings within this configuration of state power. The fate of the various attempts at economic reform since the 1990s has also been very much shaped and undermined by the interplay of forces within this dual state configuration.

An important aspect of economic change since the 1990s has been a considerable shift of economic power from the official elected government—the "legal rational" arm of the state—toward the less transparent and more murky and informal core state, with the independent private sector becoming increasingly marginalized. The expanded economic position of the core state has not been confined to the accumulation of assets within the institutions under its direct control, such as the *bonyad*s and the Revolutionary Guards. It has also worked through indirect interventions and government regulation of the foreign exchange markets, interest rates and allocation of bank credits, as well as rationing and direct price controls of a large section of product markets. As demonstrated, the result has been a glaring rise in allocative and productive inefficiencies in the system, and increased dependence of the economy on oil revenues.

Some of the glaring price distortions resulting from the system of multiple exchange rates which plagued the economy for much of the life of the Islamic Republic appear to have been remedied since the exchange rate unification of 2002. Nevertheless, with huge subsidies for strategic products such as energy and basic foods, price distortions still remain important impediments to allocative and production efficiency of the system. The huge energy subsidies have inevitably led to the use of inappropriate technologies, and have created the appearance of profitability in activities that remain non-competitive by international standards.

The glaring production inefficiencies observed in the economic system under the Islamic Republic once more raise the question of whether the system has the flexibility necessary to conduct the required reforms.

Index